BUYER'S REMORSE

How Obama Let Progressives Down

BILL PRESS

Threshold Editions

NEW YORK   LONDON   TORONTO
SYDNEY   NEW DELHI

Threshold Editions
An Imprint of Simon & Schuster, Inc.
1230 Avenue of the Americas
New York, NY 10020

The cartoon on page 7 appears Courtesy of the Artist and Susan Conway Gallery, Santa Fe, NM

First Threshold Editions paperback edition October 2016

THRESHOLD EDITIONS and colophon are trademarks
of Simon & Schuster, Inc.

For information about special discounts for bulk purchases, please contact Simon & Schuster Special Sales at 1-866-506-1949 or business@simonandschuster.com.

The Simon & Schuster Speakers Bureau can bring authors to your live event. For more information or to book an event, contact the Simon & Schuster Speakers Bureau at 1-866-248-3049 or visit our website at www.simonspeakers.com.

Interior design by Paul J. Dippolito

Manufactured in the United States of America

10 9 8 7 6 5 4 3 2 1

Library of Congress Cataloging-in-Publication Data is available.

ISBN 978-1-4767-9261-3
ISBN 978-1-4767-9289-7 (pbk)
ISBN 978-1-4767-9262-0 (ebook)

To my colleagues in the White House Correspondents Association, who excel in their dual responsibility of holding the president's feet to the fire and telling the American people the truth

CONTENTS

CONTENTS

INTRODUCTION

I speak as a proud liberal.

I speak as a strong supporter of President Obama.

I also speak as a liberal Democrat disappointed in his presidency, because he let progressives down so badly.

Indeed, you could sum up this book in one sentence: On too many issues, once he got to the White House, President Obama abandoned his campaign promises and disappointed the people who worked so hard to elect him.

At this point in the twilight of the Obama administration, looking at the differences between what was promised and what was delivered, more and more progressives want to know:

We voted for hope and change, Mr. President, but what did we get?

Sure, we got a better economy than Bush left us with, but we also have stagnant wages, a struggling middle class, rising income inequality, and a diminished social safety net.

Sure, we got "health insurance reform," but without single-payer and with a monopoly for private insurance companies.

Sure, the Iraq and Afghanistan wars were ended, but now we're still in Afghanistan and back in Iraq and Syria, fighting ISIS.

Sure, we decimated al Qaeda's leadership, but now we've got killer drones raining death from the sky without due process, and the NSA spying on all our phone calls and emails.

And that's just the beginning.

Throughout this book, we'll go over the countless ways Obama fell short of what he could have accomplished. Time and again, he abandoned the progressive beliefs he'd promised to uphold, on issues across

1

the board, from the economy to the environment, from immigration reform to gun control—yes, even on health care.

Ironically, from a progressive point of view, Obama's best years may be his last two years. It was almost as if the burden of elections had weighed him down. Once the midterm elections of 2014 were behind him and he was freed from the obligation to campaign for himself or anybody else ever again, Obama suddenly got tougher and began to flex his political muscles at last, using the power of the executive order to take bolder action on immigration reform and climate change.

But by then, it was too little, too late on most fronts. For the most part, Obama's efforts were limited to actions he could take using executive powers alone. On Capitol Hill, Republicans, who now controlled both houses of Congress, were often able to block him and did.

That in itself was a painful reminder of all he might have accomplished, but did not, during his first two years in office, when Democrats were in charge of both House and Senate.

The Promise

What makes our disappointment in Obama so hard to take is: It wasn't supposed to be this way. For passion and excitement, American politics had seldom seen a phenomenon like the Obama campaign of 2008.

For a dyed-in-the-wool liberal like me, that campaign was especially exciting. It was something I'd been waiting my whole political life for. I got my start in Democratic politics in San Francisco—by volunteering for Eugene McCarthy for president in 1968. I went on to run local and statewide campaigns. I worked for Governor Jerry Brown for four years. I led a statewide initiative campaign and ran for statewide office in California. I served three years as chair of the California Democratic Party.

And since 1980, I've been a liberal commentator and talk show host on radio and television. In Los Angeles, on KABC-TV and KCOP-TV, and KABC Radio and KFI Radio. For six years, I was the liberal cohost of CNN's *Crossfire*. I also cohosted *The Spin Room* with Tucker Carlson on CNN, and *Buchanan and Press* with Pat Buchanan on MSNBC. Since 2005, I've been host of *The Bill Press Show*, broadcast on radio stations nationwide and simulcast, first on Current TV and now on Free Speech TV. And since 2009, I've been a member of the White House Correspondents' Association and attend daily press briefings at the White House.

I'll proudly match my progressive credentials against those of anybody in the media. I've been promoting and defending liberal ideals on radio and television for thirty years. And I've defended Obama, too. My last book, *The Obama Hate Machine*, outlined the relentless, racist, over-the-top (and often Koch-funded) personal attacks by the right against the president.

So, when it comes to fighting for liberals, I feel like I'm the real deal. And in 2008 I thought President Obama was the real deal: the truly progressive president we've been waiting and working for all our lives.

And I wasn't the only one. Even celebrities—otherwise cool, rational people who live and breathe this kind of hype every day—suddenly caught a public case of "Obamamania." Those gushing over Barack Obama included:

- Halle Berry: "I'll do whatever he says to do. I'll collect paper cups off the ground to make his pathway clear."
- George Clooney: "He walks into a room and you want to follow him somewhere, anywhere."
- Congressman Elijah Cummings: "This is not a campaign for president of the United States, this is a movement to change the world."
- Caroline Kennedy: "I have never had a president who inspired me the way people tell me that my father inspired them."
- Toni Morrison: "Of one thing I am certain: this opportunity for a national evolution (even revolution) will not come again soon, and I am convinced you are the person to capture it."
- Oprah Winfrey: "For the first time I'm stepping out of my pew because I've been inspired. I've been inspired to believe that a new vision is possible for this country."[1]

The 2008 campaign was one of the most brilliant and strategically executed political campaigns ever. It ran an aggressive, daily, and flawless
message operation. It outfoxed and outmaneuvered the fabled Clinton political machine in an extended and hard-fought primary season.
And its goal of electing a smart, young newcomer to Washington—and
the promise of electing the nation's first black president—inspired millions of Americans who'd never before taken any interest in politics to
get involved: making phone calls, walking precincts, talking to their
friends and family, and turning them out to vote.

Voter turnout, in fact, was the greatest demonstration of Obama's
unique appeal. Over 130 million Americans, or 64 percent of the electorate, cast their ballots on November 6, 2008. Those numbers were
swelled by a surge in young and minority voters, the vast majority
of whom came out to vote for Obama. He won 66 percent of voters
ages eighteen to twenty-nine, 66 percent of Latinos, and 95 percent of
African-Americans.[2]

The most important element in Obama's success may have been
first-time voters. He turned them on like no other presidential candidate has ever done. Out of 131,406,895 ballots counted, 15,112,000 be-
longed to Americans who were voting for the very first time—and 68.7
percent of them gave Obama their votes, adding up to a million votes
more than his ultimate margin over John McCain. It's no exaggeration
to say that the Americans whom Barack Obama inspired to go out and
vote for the first time in their lives elected him the forty-fourth president of the United States.[3]

Nobody felt that excitement more than liberals like me, who saw
in Barack Obama the kindred progressive spirit we'd long been yearning for. In a sense, we agreed with John McCain when he acidly called
Obama "The One." There was something "messianic" about the candidate. In our eyes and dreams, Barack Obama—the "skinny kid with the
big ears and funny name," as he described himself—was, indeed, "The
One," the one who'd bury the failed policies of George Bush and Dick
Cheney, fix the broken politics of Washington, and move the country
in a dramatically new and different direction. He promised no less.[4]

Even the media got caught up in the giddiness of the moment. People made fun of MSNBC's Chris Matthews when he told then–*NBC Nightly News* host Brian Williams he "felt this thrill going up my leg" whenever he heard Obama speak during the 2008 campaign. But what liberal didn't experience that same feeling? It *was* thrilling to hear Obama vow, after winning the South Carolina primary, that he would carry across the country his message "that out of many we are one, that while we breathe we will hope, and where we are met with cynicism and doubt and fear and those who tell us that we can't, we will respond with that timeless creed that sums up the spirit of the American people in three simple words: Yes, we can."[5]

We were even more convinced we were part of something new and different when Obama clinched the Democratic nomination in June, after a long and intense primary battle against Hillary Clinton, who'd been the overwhelming favorite until just a few weeks before the Iowa caucuses. That night he told a crowd of supporters in St. Paul, Minnesota: "We will be able to look back and tell our children that this was the moment when we began to provide care for the sick and good jobs to the jobless; this was the moment when the rise of the oceans began to slow and our planet began to heal; this was the moment when we ended a war and secured our nation and restored our image as the last, best hope on earth."[6]

Five months later, on election night, November 6, anchoring a nationwide broadcast in front of a live audience in San Francisco, I wept openly when Obama and his family walked out onstage at Chicago's Grant Park to declare victory: "If there is anyone out there who still doubts that America is a place where all things are possible, who still wonders if the dream of our founders is alive in our time, who still questions the power of our democracy, tonight is your answer."[7]

The Disappointment

The promise was so great. The hope was so real. But it didn't take long after Obama made it to the White House for that bubble to burst. And it happened so fast.

Of course, you expect the love affair with any president to cool down by the end of a presidency. He or she (someday!) is bound to let you down, sooner or later. What stunned Obama's liberal supporters, however, was how soon and how often he disappointed them—and how quickly he chose to compromise with conservative forces, rather than stand up to them. Congressman John Conyers learned that early on.

Conyers did not intend to get in trouble when he agreed to appear as a guest on my radio show in early December 2009. Nor did I intend to get the senior Democrat from Michigan, one of the most liberal members of Congress, and a forty-nine-year veteran of the House, in trouble when I booked him. But that's what happened.

Near the end of our interview, I asked Conyers whether, as a liberal, he was happy with President Barack Obama's first year in office. After a long, pregnant pause, Conyers replied: "Now, why did you ask me that?" Another pause. Then: "Frankly, I'm getting tired of saving Obama's can in the White House." He went on to accuse Obama and then–chief of staff Rahm Emanuel of "bowing down to nutty right-wing" health-care proposals in a desperate attempt to win passage of the Affordable Care Act, and complained about liberals in the House being forced to hold their nose and vote for a health-care bill that no longer contained a "robust public option."[8]

Conyers's blast at Obama made the front page of *The Hill* newspaper the following morning. Two days later, he was back on the front page—as the recipient of an angry phone call from the president himself, who told Conyers he was not pleased that the senior African-American congressman was out on the radio "demeaning" him. It wasn't personal, Conyers assured the president, just an "honest difference of opinion on the issues."[9]

Like any good foot soldier, Conyers then walked back his criticism somewhat. But too late. He'd already spoken aloud what many liberals were already feeling even this early in the Obama presidency: disappointment with Obama's caution in the top job, and frustration at his apparent reluctance to seize the reins of presidential power and run with them.

Even by December 2009, all too many progressives had come to the same grim conclusion as Conyers: Barack Obama the president wasn't at all what we had come to expect, or been promised, by Barack Obama the candidate.

That doesn't mean liberals were sorry they voted for Obama. They certainly didn't regret not voting for John McCain or Mitt Romney. They just felt let down. On so many issues, progressives began wondering: What happened to "Change We Can Believe In"? What happened to "the Fierce Urgency of Now"? Or, as John McCain's vice-presidential candidate, Sarah Palin, once teased Democrats: "How's that hopey, changey stuff working out?"[10]

By that time, too, the media had begun to reflect the disillusionment among many Democrats. On February 24, 2009, only thirty-five days after Obama's inauguration, Pulitzer Prize–winning political cartoonist Pat Oliphant depicted the new president as a cold, distant, aloof, and inscrutable Easter Island statue, who avoided any direct answers to pleas from supporters about what he was going to do about the nation's many problems, now that he was in office. In a September

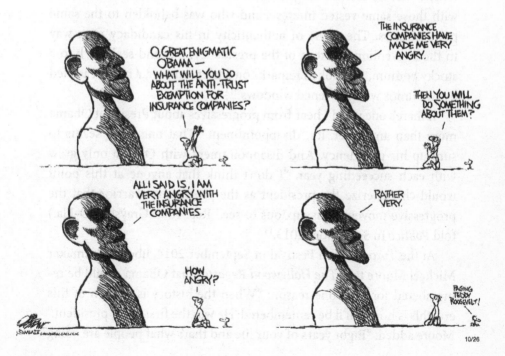

2014 interview for *The Atlantic*, political reporter Les Daly asked Oliphant if he felt "extraordinarily incisive and prescient" in being the first to note a character flaw in Obama that everybody was talking about six years later. "I'll take that," the Australian-born cartoonist responded. "I just had this feeling about him, that maybe he thought he shouldn't be there. We were looking for and imbued him with qualities which he never had and still doesn't have, inflated expectations."[11]

Eight months later, October 26, 2009, Oliphant depicted Obama back on Easter Island, refusing to say what he'd do about tax breaks for big insurance companies. Oliphant closed by having his signature character Punk plead: "Paging Teddy Roosevelt!"[12]

In his book *Revival*, which charts Obama's rough-and-tumble efforts to build support for health-care legislation, author Richard Wolffe notes that by the time Obama signed the Affordable Care Act in March 2010, it looked like Washington had changed him more than he had changed Washington. "He campaigned as an outsider who could battle the nation's vested interests and the tired old political class," Wolffe writes. "Yet he seemed to govern as an insider who would cut deals with those same vested interests and who was beholden to the same political class. The sense of authenticity in his candidacy gave way to the conventional tokens of the presidency: a round seal stuck to a stocky podium, precooked remarks on a teleprompter, a motorcade led by two limos with darkened windows."[13]

If there's one word I hear from progressives about President Obama more than any other, it's "disappointment." That one word seems to sum up his presidency. And disappointment with Obama only grew with each succeeding year. "I don't think that anyone at this point would characterize the president as the progressive warrior that the progressive movement is anxious to see," Rep. Alan Grayson (D-Fla.) told *Politico* in September 2013.[14]

At the Toronto Film Festival in September 2014, liberal filmmaker Michael Moore told *The Hollywood Reporter* that Obama would be remembered for only one reason: "When the history is written of this era, this is how you'll be remembered: He was the first black president." Moore added: "Eight years of your life and that's what people are going to remember. Boy, I got a feeling, knowing you, that—you'd probably wish you were remembered for a few other things, a few other things you could've done."[15]

Grayson and Moore had company. Asked about his views on Obama five years into his presidency, left-leaning actor and advocate Matt Damon told *BET* in August 2013, "he broke up with me. There are a lot of things I really question, you know: The legality of the drone strikes, and these NSA revelations . . . you know, Jimmy Carter came out and said we don't live in a democracy. That's a little intense when an ex-president says that. So you know, he's got some explaining to do, particularly for a constitutional law professor."[16]

A year later, professor and prominent liberal intellectual Cornel West was even more dismissive. "The thing is, he posed as a progressive and turned out to be counterfeit," West told Thomas Frank in August 2014. "We ended up with a Wall Street presidency, a drone presidency, a national security presidency. The torturers go free. The Wall Street executives go free . . . he acted as if he was both a progressive and as if he was concerned about the issues of serious injustice and inequality and it turned out that he's just another neoliberal centrist with a smile and with a nice rhetorical flair."[17]

One of the harshest criticisms of Obama from the left came from former Ohio congressman Dennis Kucinich, who ran against him in 2008 for the Democratic nomination. In a 2013 interview with *Politico*'s Edward-Isaac Dovere, Kucinich accused Obama of poisoning the liberal movement by seeming to support it, while actually betraying it. As long as Obama was widely and wrongly perceived as our most "liberal" president, Kucinich argues, he prevented any real liberal agenda from taking hold.[18]

In May 2015, *Esquire* magazine interviewed artist Shepard Fairey, who created the iconic "Hope" poster that became Obama's political calling card in 2008. When asked if he thought Obama had lived up to his promise in that campaign, Fairey replied, "Not even close. Obama has had a really tough time, but there have been a lot of things that he's compromised on that I never would have expected. I mean, drones and domestic spying are the last things I would have thought [he'd support.]"[19]

You could almost feel the air leaking out of a balloon. It reminded me of the euphoria I first experienced among young people in San Francisco in 1967, true believers in the revolutionary, transformative nature of the countercultural movement of the mid-sixties—and the huge letdown we experienced watching it all fall apart with the blowup of the Vietnam War, the violence in Chicago's Grant Park, the election of Richard Nixon, and the triumph of the establishment.

At that time, nobody described the transition from hope to disappointment better than Hunter Thompson, in his classic book *Fear and Loathing in Las Vegas*. "There was a fantastic universal sense that whatever we were doing was right, that we were winning," Thompson recalled. "And that, I think, was the handle—that sense of inevitable victory over the forces of old and evil. Not in any mean or military sense; we didn't need that. Our energy would simply prevail. We had all the momentum; we were riding the crest of a high and beautiful wave. So now, less than five years later, you can go up on a steep hill in Las Vegas and look west, and with the right kind of eyes you can almost see the high-water mark—that place where the wave finally broke and rolled back."[20]

Flash forward to the early days of the Obama presidency. As disappointment started to set in, and some progressives dared express it openly, Obama's team openly ridiculed his critics. In the first year of the administration, former White House press secretary Robert Gibbs bristled at criticism from people he called the "professional left" over Obama's compromises on health-care legislation: "I hear these people saying he's like George Bush. Those people ought to be drug tested. . . . They will be satisfied when we have Canadian health care and we've eliminated the Pentagon. That's not reality. They wouldn't be satisfied if Dennis Kucinich was president." For all his tantrum, however, Gibbs was kinder than former chief of staff Rahm Emanuel, who lashed out at Obama's critics on the left as "fucking retarded."[21]

Today, as the Obama presidency winds down, progressives find themselves especially disillusioned, frustrated that the change they worked so hard for, believed in, and were promised was never delivered. At least not on the scale they needed or expected. As the economist John Maynard Keynes once said of Woodrow Wilson, another progressive president who promised to change the world, after the Treaty at Versailles in 1919: "The disillusion was so complete that some of those who had trusted most hardly dare speak of it."[22]

The Reality

So, what happened?

Part of the answer may lie in Gibbs's rant, which, however mean-spirited, did contain a kernel of truth. Let's be honest: Liberals, as a group, are never satisfied. And, again, I say this as a proud liberal myself. There's a good reason why politicians often find liberals a thorn in their side: Because sometimes, it's true, in our heart of hearts we let the great become the enemy of the good, and get too easily dismayed by half-measures. Even if politicians finally get something right, we'll complain about why it took so long.

At the same time, however, most liberals are also pragmatic realists. We understand the political process. We know we're never going to get 100 percent of what we want on any issue. And we accept that—but here's the key—as long as you fight like hell for that 100 percent before you compromise for much, much less. Which is what, too often, on too many issues, President Obama has failed to do.

It's also possible—in fact, it's altogether likely—that we fundamentally misread Barack Obama. Maybe we made the same mistake with him we had once made with Bill Clinton. In a kind of national political Rorschach test, American progressives across the board projected onto Obama their own liberal beliefs and dreams. African-Americans were proud of one of their own. Latinos saw the promise of a minority brother on immigration reform. Women respected a man raised by a single mother and unusually sensitive to women's issues. Young people gravitated to Obama's laid-back cool, and his openness on issues like his early drug use. And limousine liberals welcomed the black man who was more comfortable on the Upper East Side than in the housing projects.

Obama appeared to be all things to all people. But, as Vermont's congressman Peter Welch observed, perhaps no human being could meet those outlandish expectations: "The president was the embodiment of the dreams and aspirations of a better country and better future. To some extent the person that he's not is a person that he ultimately could never be."[23]

A closer look at Obama's past voting record, however, might have warned us that he was really no liberal at all. As senator, for example, Obama enraged liberals by endorsing—right after winning the Democratic nomination—legislation granting immunity to telecommunications companies that cooperated with the Bush administration in wiretapping American citizens without prior approval of the FISA Court, legislation he had vowed to oppose as candidate. He also shocked progressives by applauding a Supreme Court decision that knocked down Washington, D.C.'s ban on handguns.[24]

Of course, Obama's right-wing critics, whom I branded—correctly—in an earlier book as the "Obama Hate Machine," have always painted his politics as on the extreme left. It's politically convenient for them to do so. But they're totally wrong, and they know it. The reason Obama is widely perceived to be so liberal is that the Republican Party has moved so far to the extreme right that Richard Nixon and Ronald Reagan look lefty by comparison. Obama's no socialist or communist. Not even close. But he's no liberal, either. At best, he's a bona fide centrist, or centrist-left.

Still, the misperception of Obama as "Mr. Liberal" wasn't entirely our fault, either. In many ways, we were deliberately misled by the candidate himself.

Candidate Obama certainly had a knack for making us believe he was on our side. After all, this was the man who, at an anti–Iraq War rally in Chicago in September 2002, had called George Bush's war in Iraq "a dumb war" and "a rash war" at a time when Democrats in Washington were tripping over themselves to vote for it. That speech alone may have elected Obama, but it also blinded us to the fact that Obama was not as progressive as we might think on other issues. Even on Iraq, we never would have believed that he'd wind up sending American troops, even as only advisers, back into that snake pit before the end of his presidency.[25]

To take another example, consider candidate Obama's much-heralded speech on civil liberties and the war on terror in August 2007: "I will provide our intelligence and law-enforcement agencies with the tools they need to track and take out the terrorists without undermining our Constitution and our freedom," he said then. "We will again set an example for the world that the law is not subject to the whims of stubborn rulers, and that justice is not arbitrary. . . . This administration acts like violating civil liberties is the way to enhance our security. It is not. There are no short-cuts to protecting America." Tell that to Edward Snowden, James Risen, Chelsea Manning, and the prisoners still locked up at Guantanamo seven years later, with no hope of trial.[26]

Yes, progressives are big dreamers, and perhaps we projected too much onto Barack Obama in 2007 and 2008. But in the end, progressives' disappointment in President Obama stems from something a lot more substantive than that. It's based on a grim, simple truth: On too many issues, he let us down. He simply failed to lead.

As will be seen in the chapters that follow, time and time again, when bold leadership was needed, he either refused to fight for what he wanted, gave up too early, compromised too soon, or too quickly settled for half a loaf. Too often, when action was needed, he hit the pause button. When decisions were due, he dithered.

To some extent, that is Obama's personality. That's why he's called "No Drama Obama." He's a professor of constitutional law, and likes to deliberate. Granted, after eight years of George Bush's "shoot first, ask questions later" style of governing, it was refreshing to have a president who didn't rush into matters, especially foreign wars, without knowing the facts. Still, there's a big difference between deliberate decision-making and no decision-making. Too often, Obama adopted a laissez-faire style of governing that made him look weak. *New York Times* columnist Maureen Dowd lamented that America had drifted from "mindless certainty" under George W. Bush to "mindful uncertainty" under Barack Obama.[27]

One big surprise was that Obama, who is so gifted at making

speeches, and drew such huge, enthusiastic crowds during his campaign, put those talents to so little use once in the White House. Many times, when Obama was stonewalled by congressional Republicans on items high on his agenda—the public option, gun safety, an increase in the minimum wage, immigration reform—we in the White House press corps expected him to take off around the country and rally public support in order to put pressure on Congress. But it seldom happened. Instead, most of the time, he'd make one strong statement in the Rose Garden or Briefing Room, or give one rousing speech in front of a friendly audience, then move on to other matters and let others worry about the follow-through.

Vermont senator and 2016 presidential candidate Bernie Sanders, among many others, faults Obama for not using the unique opportunities of the presidency to stoke public outrage. For example, he told *Meet the Press*: "I think he should've gone to the people in a more aggressive way" and rallied supporters of an increase in the minimum wage to descend on Washington in protest.[28]

In her monumental work *The Bully Pulpit*, documenting the presidencies of Teddy Roosevelt and William Howard Taft, historian Doris Kearns Goodwin sums up the secret of TR's success: "The essence of Roosevelt's leadership . . . lay in his enterprising use of the 'bully pulpit,' a phrase he himself coined to describe the national platform the presidency provides to shape public sentiment and mobilize action."[29]

The bully pulpit's still there. Obama, however, seldom used it, and his success rate suffered because of that. Despite having such a great orator in the White House, psychology professor Drew Westen wrote in 2010: "I don't honestly know what this president believes. But I believe if he doesn't figure it out soon, start enunciating it, and start fighting for it, he's not only going to give American families hungry for security a series of half-loaves where they could have had full ones, but he's going to set back the Democratic Party and the progressive movement by decades."[30]

There's one other key factor: President Obama's stubborn failure to build personal relationships with Democrats in Congress. For the most part, he simply ignored or snubbed them. He seldom reached out, except to ask for a key vote. And he simply refused to do the kind of schmoozing that, while somewhat phony, means so much to ego-driven politicians. Cocktail parties, exclusive dinners in the private quarters, or movie nights with members of Congress, the calling cards of the Clinton presidency, practically disappeared in the Obama White House. It became hard for members of Congress not to conclude that Obama didn't like them and didn't enjoy hanging out with them.

"For him, eating his spinach is schmoozing with elected officials," Senator Claire McCaskill told the *New York Times*. "This is not something that he loves. He wasn't that kind of senator." West Virginia's Joe Manchin, a key bridge-builder between Senate Democrats and Republicans, described his relationship with the president as "fairly nonexistent." And Connecticut senator Richard Blumenthal says he can count "on both hands" the number of times he's been invited to the White House for any event, large or small, since he took office in 2011.[31]

If Obama doesn't like hanging out with Congress, he sure doesn't want to play golf with them, either. A round of golf is President Obama's favorite form of relaxation, which he engages in as often as possible. But he clearly doesn't want to waste any time on the course doing what most businessmen or politicians do: chatting up friends and building relationships. He'd rather play golf with White House aides or old friends than members of Congress. As of November 3, 2015, Obama had played 260 rounds of golf as president, according to Mark Knoller, the White House correspondent for CBS Radio. Only on five of them did he invite any member of Congress. Only once did he invite Speaker John Boehner.[32]

That fifth round was on July 19, 2015, just days after announcement of a successful Iran nuclear deal, when Obama invited three Democratic members of Congress—John Yarmuth of Kentucky, Joe Courtney of Connecticut, and Ed Perlmutter of Colorado—to join him for a round of golf at Andrews Air Force Base, the first time Obama had played with a full congressional foursome. At our White House briefing the next day, Press Secretary Josh Earnest insisted this was just fulfillment of a promise made long ago to play golf with the four, and had nothing to do with the president's "full-court press" on the Iran agreement.[33]

Two days later, Yarmuth told me on my radio/TV show that the president never discussed Iran during the four hours on the golf course. But, as he was climbing into his SUV for the return to the White House, Obama told them: "Don't be surprised if I call on you soon to talk about the Iran nuclear deal." All three Democrats ended up supporting it.

That still remains the one and only time Obama arranged an outing with congressional members only. Having a drink, watching a movie, playing a round of golf together may be the old kind of politics, but it was politics that Democrats like Lyndon Johnson and Bill Clinton excelled at. And as both would tell you, staying aloof from Congress is not a recipe for legislative victory.

Ironically, while avoiding contact with Democrats, Obama spent an inordinate amount of time meeting with House Republicans, especially in his first term—and none of those meetings produced any positive results. After several one-on-one private meetings with John Boehner, for example, the president and the Speaker announced they'd agreed on a "grand bargain"—a balanced mix of spending cuts and new outlays for the next year's budget. But no sooner had Boehner returned to the Hill than Majority Leader Eric Cantor and Tea Party Republicans pulled the rug out from under him, rejecting the grand bargain outright.[34]

Still, Obama continued meeting with Boehner and others, determined to achieve his goal of becoming the "postpartisan" president he'd rhapsodized about during his campaign. He didn't seem to realize that, with this gang of Republicans, that dream was impossible. They rejected the very notion of compromise. Their goal was to prevent Obama from succeeding at anything. Whatever he was for, no matter how reasonable, they were against—even if they'd supported it before, under George W. Bush. Everybody in America seemed to understand that except Obama himself.

The Republicans' anti-Obama agenda was made most pointedly by Senate Republican Leader Mitch McConnell in an interview with the *National Journal*'s Major Garrett in October 2010. It was all very straightforward, he admitted. The number-one legislative goal of Republicans was "for President Obama to be a one-term president." Knowing that, many Democrats openly questioned why Obama was wasting so much time meeting with Republican leaders. "He just can't sit in a room and negotiate with people who refuse to negotiate," fumed Senator Bernie Sanders.[35]

Sanders spoke for many progressives. I got nervous, sitting in the White House briefing room, every time I heard Obama brag about how far he was willing to go in compromising with Republicans. He told reporters from AP in August 2012 that if Republicans were willing, "I'm prepared to make a whole range of compromises" that would irritate his party. That same month the *New York Times* reported: "He particularly believes that Democrats do not receive enough credit for their willingness to accept cuts in Medicare and Social Security." The essence of the president's so-called grand bargain, in fact, was that Republicans would agree to tax increases on the very wealthy if Democrats would agree to cuts in benefits for the elderly, including cuts to Social Security brought about by "chained CPI"—a different way of calculating cost-of-living adjustments that would result in lower monthly benefits.[36]

"Stop this train," I was tempted to shout out loud, "I want to get off." We didn't elect Obama to be the "compromiser-in-chief," cutting programs like Medicare and Social Security that Democrats had fought so hard for and that millions of Americans depended on.

And yet, as *Washington Post* columnist E. J. Dionne put it in 2010, Obama seemed addicted to making "preemptive concessions . . . [he] seems to have decided that showing how conciliatory he can be is more important than making clear where he stands . . . he will soon have to decide whether he wants to be a negotiator or a leader." As it was, Obama's conciliatory strategy—which Drew Westen called "the politics of the lowest common denominator"—was a failure. It "is always a losing politics," Westen points out. "It sends a meta-message that you're weak—nothing more, nothing less. . . . And in fact it is weak."[37]

Obama's indifference toward Congress and the gritty business of politics manifested itself in other ways as well. The last thing he wanted to do was get down and dirty in congressional battles, not even for his own legislation or nominees. Senate Majority Leader Harry Reid told the *New York Times* of an Oval Office meeting on Iraq in late June 2014 with the four congressional leaders: Reid, Senate Republican Leader Mitch McConnell, Speaker John Boehner, and House Democratic Leader Nancy Pelosi. After Obama had briefed them on Iraq, Reid told the president he had one other important matter to discuss: the fact that Senate Republicans continued to block confirmation of dozens of Obama's qualified nominees for ambassador.

Reid fully expected the president to join in and put some Oval Office pressure on McConnell. After all, the president had given several speeches urging Republicans to confirm his ambassadorial appointments. Instead, Obama coolly dismissed the whole idea and cut off any further discussion with a curt: "Harry, you and Mitch work it out."[38]

It was hardly the first time Democrats in Congress had looked for leadership from the White House and didn't get it.

The Counterargument

The most important lesson I learned on the debate team at Salesianum High School in Wilmington, Delaware—one that served me well for years on *Crossfire*, *Buchanan and Press*, *The Spin Room*, and *The Bill Press Show*—was how to anticipate and respond to arguments from the other side. Whatever the topic—the death penalty, nuclear disarmament, or homelessness—we spent as much time anticipating opposition arguments as we did preparing our own case.

That means I'm ready for all the howls of protest I know I'll hear from many of my liberal, Democratic friends once they discover that I've dared write a book critical of Barack Obama. Just watch. Their complaints will be some combination of these five:

- At least Obama was better than Mitt Romney or George W. Bush.
- How dare you criticize a fellow Democrat?
- How can you ignore all the good things President Obama has accomplished?

- You're overlooking racism. Obama has faced unprecedented obstructions only because he's black.
- Don't blame him, blame Republicans in Congress for refusing to cooperate with him.

Okay, let's deal with those criticisms one at a time, starting with the silliest of all.

Better Than Bush or Romney

Yes, of course, Barack Obama's a far better president than George W. Bush was or Mitt Romney would have been. But—do we really want to set the bar that low? Any number of Democrats—Hillary Clinton, Bernie Sanders, Nancy Pelosi, Joe Biden, John Kerry, Jerry Brown, Chris Dodd, or Dennis Kucinich—would have been better than Bush or Romney.

But we elected Barack Obama, instead. Why? Not just because he'd be better than Bush. But because we believed we could count on him— certainly over Mitt Romney, and even over Hillary Clinton—to fight for and deliver the progressive agenda.

Maybe our expectations were too high, but we voted for Barack Obama because we expected him to be the progressive champion we'd been yearning for, for years. To the extent he fell short, there's nothing disloyal or disrespectful about expressing our disappointment.

Criticizing a Fellow Democrat

There are some Democrats who believe you should never publicly criticize another Democrat. No personal attacks, but no public disagreements on policy, either. Politics is a blood sport, so party loyalty above all.

Yes, I know that school of Democrats exists. I just don't belong to it, and wouldn't want to join. I've been a Democrat all my life. But I've never been a blind party loyalist. Yes, I usually vote the party label, but I've also voted for a few Republicans in my life. And when evaluating presidents and political leaders, I look at the public policies they put forward, not just the D or the R behind their names.

Early in my television career, I blasted President Reagan on everything from Star Wars, to Iran-Contra, to the War on Drugs. But I also supported his actions on immigration and nuclear disarmament.

Later, at CNN, I roasted George W. Bush on countless issues: tax cuts for the rich, stem cells, the unmasking of Valerie Plame, the Iraq War. But I also supported him on immigration reform and his initial invasion of Afghanistan to overturn the Taliban.

It should go without saying that I would apply that same "play it as it lays" philosophy to Democratic presidents. I was one of the first TV commentators to criticize Clinton for his new Pentagon policy of "Don't Ask, Don't Tell." I also didn't hesitate to condemn Clinton for signing the Defense of Marriage Act. But when the Monica Lewinsky scandal broke, as cohost of CNN's *Crossfire*, I defended Bill Clinton from day one. Not because his personal behavior was acceptable, but because whatever happened between him and Lewinsky, two consenting adults, was not an impeachable offense.

On television, on radio, in print, and in this book, I have applied that same "speak truth to power" approach to President Obama. Most of the time, over the last seven years, I've been in his corner. But when he's fallen short and failed to deliver—or, worse yet, when I believe he's gone in the wrong direction—I won't hesitate to say so.

In my view, the willingness to criticize our own is one thing that distinguishes conservatives from liberals. Generally speaking, conservatives, usually hierarchical and authoritarian in temperament, will always coddle their own. That's where what's often known as Reagan's "eleventh commandment" comes from—"Thou shalt not speak ill of other Republicans." But liberals should either support or criticize their own, depending on where they stand on any given issue. That's the liberal tradition I proudly embrace: to seek and speak the truth, even if it's rough on a fellow Democrat.

Obama's Good Record

I'm the first to admit there's a lot in Barack Obama's record that progressives can rejoice about. And I'd be wrong, and this book would be incomplete, if I did not recognize those achievements.

I certainly believe in giving credit where credit is due. So let's acknowledge the progressive honor roll Obama has racked up. On that list, I would include, in no particular order:

The Supreme Court: Given the openings provided by the resignations of Justices David Souter and John Paul Stevens, President Obama made two outstanding appointments to the Supreme Court: Sonia Sotomayor in 2009 and Elena Kagan in 2010. Together with Justice Ruth Bader Ginsburg, they make a powerful and long-overdue female bloc of votes, easily intellectually outpacing conservative justices Antonin Scalia, Clarence Thomas, and Samuel Alito.

Gay rights: While it may have taken far longer than it should for him to come around, Barack Obama's still the most gay-friendly president America has ever seen. Flat out. Nobody else comes close. That's partly a reflection of his times. But it's also a tribute to his growth. In the area of gay rights, Obama will be celebrated for four major accomplishments: ending "Don't Ask, Don't Tell"; overturning the Defense of Marriage Act; naming hundreds of LGBT Americans to key positions in his administration; and helping make same-sex marriage the law of the land.

Criminal justice reform: Legislation to reform federal sentencing guidelines—which are racially biased and result in a disproportionate number of young African-American males in prison for nonviolent crimes—had bounced around Congress since the mid-1990s with no results. That finally began to change under President Obama. He signed the Fair Sentencing Act, which reduced the disparity between the penalties for crack and powder cocaine and eliminated the five-year mandatory minimum sentence for crack possession. He supported legislation in Congress to reduce sentences for those already serving time for nonviolent drug offenses and allow well-behaved prisoners to earn shorter sentences. And, as of October 2015, without waiting for Congress to act, he had commuted sentences of eighty-nine inmates in federal prison for nonviolent crime—a drop in the bucket, but still more

commutations than granted by Presidents Ronald Reagan, George
H. W. Bush, Bill Clinton, and George W. Bush combined.[39]

The economy: There are still fundamental weaknesses in the economy,
as President Obama is the first to admit and as we lay out in Chapter
One. But Obama can still point to success on several fronts. He brought
the economy back from the brink of disaster. As of November 2015, the
Obama administration could boast of sixty-eight straight months of
private sector job growth and more than 13.5 million new jobs created.
He rescued the auto industry. Corporate profits are at a record high,
and, despite some shakiness in the summer of 2015, the stock market
has more than doubled since January 2009. Unfortunately, that rising
tide did not lift all boats. While the wealthiest Americans fared very
well, the poor got poorer, and middle-class Americans were stuck in
neutral: Employee compensation sank to the lowest level in sixty-five
years, and wages grew at the slowest rate since the 1960s.[40]

Health care: We will discuss the disappointing aspects of Obamacare
in Chapter Two: the lack of a public option; the fact that it still leaves 30
million Americans without health insurance and requires every American who doesn't receive health insurance with their job to buy a policy
from a private insurance company. But, on the plus side, it must be said
that President Obama brought the nation closer to the goal of universal
health care than any president before him. As of September 2015, 9.9
million Americans had purchased health insurance under Obamacare
and a total of 17.6 million were covered, including those on Medicaid,
young people on their parents' plan, and those who had signed up for
their own plan.[41]

Foreign policy: On the world stage, like every president before him,
Barack Obama has been a prisoner of events outside his control. Still,
despite the problems we'll talk about in Chapter Four, he can chalk up
some significant foreign policy successes. As promised, he ended the
wars in Iraq and Afghanistan—only, of course, to engage in another
undeclared war in Iraq and Syria. He reversed fifty-five years of failed

policy and restored relations with Cuba. And he led world powers in negotiating a historic deal preventing Iran from developing a nuclear weapon.

Because He's Black

The excuse for Obama's shortcomings I hear most often is: Of course, Republicans won't cooperate with him. It's racist. It's all because he's black. Now, that's a very convenient excuse. But I don't buy it. Are there some people who hate Obama only because of the color of his skin? Absolutely. Nobody can deny racism still exists in this country. Yet in 2008, despite the lingering stench of racism, we Americans elected our first African-American president, and we re-elected him in 2012. And Barack Obama stepped in as leader of the free world with all the power, and all the opportunities, every president enjoys, regardless of the color of his skin. Where he failed to exercise that power in support of strong progressive policies, the fault lies with him, not his racist critics.

It's too simplistic to blame all of Barack Obama's shortcomings or failures as president on the fact that he's faced significant opposition because of his race. Republicans in the House did not refuse to pass an immigration reform bill because President Obama's an African-American. They refused because they believe too many Latinos will become citizens and vote for Democrats. And it's not because he's an African-American that President Obama was not tougher on Wall Street, abandoned the public plan option, or expanded the use of killer drones. Those were decisions he made as president. He could just as easily have decided the opposite.

Blame Those Damned Republicans

If only those pesky Republicans didn't control the House of Representatives for the middle four years of his presidency, and both the House and Senate for the final two. That's the "fantasyland" excuse for Barack Obama. So neat—and so wrong. Of course, Obama faced stubborn opposition from Mitch McConnell and John Boehner from day one. But other Democratic presidents had been forced to deal with a Republican-led Congress. Bill Clinton actually accomplished more under a Republican House than he had in his first two years when Democrats were in charge.

Obama's problem is that, too often, in dealing with his Republican opposition, he was either too quick to compromise or unwilling to twist arms and knock heads together. At other times, he just didn't seem willing to fight for what he believed in. He'd watch from the sidelines, refusing to get down and dirty. Or he'd throw in the towel before stepping into the ring. Combine that reluctance with the fact that he also didn't cultivate many close allies among his fellow Democrats, and you have the perfect formula for a flawed record.

End of the Road

So here we stand now, reaching the end of the Obama administration with a great deal of disappointment. As excited as we progressives were at the beginning of his presidency, we can't hide our frustration that, on so many issues, Barack Obama refused to exercise the full powers of his office on behalf of the causes we believed in.

So much of the idealism and energy we felt in the beginning has disappeared. Washington is still broken, and people are more disaffected than ever. The income gap between rich and poor is wider. Forty-five million Americans still live in poverty. America's public infrastructure is crumbling. Despite increasing and incontrovertible evidence of climate change, little action's been taken. The surveillance state is even bigger, more powerful, and more intrusive. Guantanamo Bay is still open for business. We ended one war in Iraq—only to enter another war in Iraq, three years later, against ISIS.[42]

And, most disappointing of all, Obama turned out to be a cautious, hesitant, almost timid chief executive, not the dynamic, bold, fearless leader we were all counting on.

As progressive blogger David Dayen wrote in 2010, "Nobody had a bigger challenge coming into office than Barack Obama but nobody had a bigger opportunity. And liberals like myself are generally peeved that the opportunity has been squandered. Yes, squandered: I know I'm supposed to talk about all the accomplishments and victories and how things would have been much worse if, say, McCain-Palin won. That's a given and it's not good enough."[43]

Again, Obama's failure to deliver can't be blamed entirely on Republicans in Congress—nor on George W. Bush, economic hard times, or public malaise. The burden rests squarely on his shoulders. We gave him the job he wanted. We trusted him to take full advantage of the powers of the presidency to move this country in the bold, new direction he promised. The sad fact is, he didn't.

And I say this regretfully. Not as an Obama critic, but as an Obama fan and supporter. Unfortunately, like so many others, a disappointed Obama fan and supporter.

Today, when many Democrats think of Obama, they feel a bad case of buyer's remorse. Not buyer's remorse as in "I'm sorry I ever bought this car." But buyer's remorse as in "Man, I sank a lot of money in this car, and it sure hasn't run as well as I expected."

In short, Obama squandered the once-in-a-generation groundswell of support he enjoyed and the clear mandate for change he brought with him to the White House. So many of the new people he brought into the system in 2008 have given up on politics, disappointed once more. The transformative new era of leadership Obama promised never happened. His presidency looms as a huge opportunity wasted.

Eight years ago, we chanted: "Yes, we can." Today, on too many issues, we lament: "Yes, we could have—but we didn't."

As the poet John Greenleaf Whittier put it in 1856, "Of all sad words of tongue or pen, the saddest are these: It might have been!"[44]

ONE

Budget Battles and the Obama Economy

We start here because that's where President Obama starts.

In any speech about his record as president, or in response to any question about his economic policies, Obama invariably starts off with some version of: "First, we saved the country from a Second Great Depression."[1]

And, in a sense, that's true. No president since Franklin Roosevelt had entered the Oval Office facing such economic disaster. Thanks to endemic foul play and often outright criminal behavior by leaders of financial institutions, brought on by a relaxing of controls on Wall Street that started under Bill Clinton and continued under George W. Bush, Obama inherited an economy in free fall.

In January 2009, he discovered things were far, far worse than most economists or the Bush administration were willing to admit when the bottom fell out in September 2008. Almost overnight, the GDP contracted by 5.1 percent, making the Great Recession the worst financial crisis since the Great Depression. According to the Department of Labor, 8.7 million jobs were lost from February 2008 through February 2010, and unemployment rose from 4.7 percent in November 2007 to a peak of 10 percent in October 2009.[2]

Acting quickly, Obama did manage to stanch the bleeding, avoid the "double-dip" recession many feared, and slowly put the economy back on the path to recovery. (European countries were less lucky. Addicted to austerity measures that further contracted the economy,

England and the Eurozone experienced a double recession, and only narrowly avoided a "triple-dip.")[3] But, as would prove true of his handling of other challenges during his presidency, Obama's response to the fiscal crisis was too tentative and too timid. In the end, his actions fell far short of what was needed and not only stunted and delayed the recovery but, in some areas, made matters worse.

As a result, today, seven years later, we are still not completely out of the hole. While financial markets have soared, the overall economy remains sluggish. Progress, while steady, has been slow. The income gap is wider than ever before. Wages are stagnant, and have been for over a decade. Forty-five million Americans are still stuck below the poverty line. As of this writing, job growth still hasn't recovered to pre-recession levels: We are still 3 million jobs short of where we need to be. Some 8.5 million Americans are out of work. And consumer confidence remains low. Obama will leave office without bringing the country back to full economic recovery. In fact, under his watch, inequality grew even worse.[4]

Cast of Characters

On these economic matters, there's little doubt where Obama first went wrong. It all began with the people he appointed to his team of economic advisers.

Trying to pull the country back from the economic brink, of course, was not how Barack Obama wanted to begin his presidency. He had other priorities in mind: health care; climate change; ending the wars in Iraq and Afghanistan; changing the poisonous atmosphere in Washington; and introducing a new era of postpartisan governance. But events forced his hand. With the entire economy about to go belly-up, Obama had no choice but to make that his first priority.

To do so, he needed a lot of help. After all, he wasn't a businessman, manager, or economist. He had no experience in finance or Wall Street. He needed to recruit his own band of experts. That was not surprising. What was surprising was that, instead of reaching out to new people—

fresh faces like him, who represented a clean break from the failed economic policies of the recent past—Obama surrounded himself with a couple of big Wall Street insiders and a gaggle of leftover Clinton and Bush administration officials. In other words, many of the very people whose reckless policies had caused this gigantic mess in the first place. And who now spent more time arguing among themselves than devising a solid recovery plan for the Obama administration.

Leading the team was former Clinton Treasury secretary Larry Summers, whose specialty seems to be pissing people off. Everything about Summers should mark him as the last person on earth Barack Obama would agree to be in the same room with, let alone make his chief financial adviser. At Treasury during the Clinton years, he helped trigger the 2008 recession by advocating repeal of the Glass-Steagall Act, the New Deal–era legislation that had put up a wall between commercial and investment banks to prevent reckless speculation. He also blocked efforts by the much-more-prescient Brooksley Born, head of the Commodity Futures Trading Commission, to regulate derivatives, the financial instruments that did so much damage in 2008.[5]

He spent his next five years as president of Harvard, before being forced to resign after making disparaging remarks about women and African-Americans, while losing Harvard about $1.8 billion through risky investments. Summers then moved to Wall Street, where he made millions as partner in a hedge fund, advising major financial institutions including Goldman Sachs, JPMorgan Chase, Citigroup, Merrill Lynch, and Lehman Brothers—the very firms he was expected to crack down on later. But didn't.[6]

Given that checkered past, you'd think Larry Summers would be persona non grata around the Obama White House. Instead, he emerged as Obama's first choice for Treasury secretary, and probably would have landed the job were it not for Hillary Clinton. Once she emerged as the leading candidate for secretary of state, Obama's advisers decided it wouldn't look good to have two top Clintonites in the cabinet. So Summers was named chairman of the president's internal, powerful National Economic Council, instead.[7]

Note: Whatever magic Summers worked on Obama did not dissipate even after two contentious years as chair of the NEC. In mid-2013, Obama stunned the financial world by openly floating the name of Summers as a leading candidate to replace Ben Bernanke as chairman of the Federal Reserve. A vocal outcry from progressives, the media, and veteran Fed-watchers finally forced him to throw Summers overboard and nominate Janet Yellen.[8]

Obama's number-two choice as Treasury secretary was Tim Geithner, another Clinton alumnus and Wall Street insider—and another big mistake. During the Clinton administration, Geithner had worked briefly at Treasury under Summers and Secretary Robert Rubin (the two guys we have to thank for financial deregulation) before becoming head of the New York Federal Reserve. In his book *Revival*, Richard Wolffe reports that another reason Geithner became Treasury secretary was that he told Obama that was the only job he'd leave the New York Reserve for—whereas Summers, desperate to redeem himself after his humiliating departure from Harvard, was willing to take anything.[9]

Still, Geithner was a strange choice. At the New York Fed, he had worked closely with Treasury Secretary Hank Paulson on two major decisions in the early crisis period: letting Lehman Brothers collapse, yet bailing out the giant insurance company AIG. Major AIG shareholder Hank Greenberg alleges that Geithner, Hank Paulson, and Fed chair Ben Bernanke actually acted illegally by deciding to "rescue" AIG, while in effect funneling whatever financial resources the company still held to big banks. In June 2015, federal judge Thomas Wheeler agreed with Greenberg that the Fed had exceeded its legal authority, arguing that "there is nothing in the Federal Reserve Act or in any federal statute that would permit a Federal Reserve Bank to take over a private corporation and run its business as if the Government were the owner." In addition, Judge Wheeler concluded that "the Government treated AIG much more harshly than other institutions in need of financial assistance" and that this treatment "was misguided and had no legitimate purpose." As of this writing, the case is under appeal.[10]

In any event, at Treasury, Geithner was expected to coddle his former Wall Street drinking buddies. Which he did, and then some.

And Geithner wasn't a one-off. Late in his term, Obama tried to smuggle Antonio Weiss, another Wall Street insider, into his administration. A senior investment banker at Lazard, Weiss was nominated as undersecretary of Treasury for domestic finance, but he was shot down by Senators Elizabeth Warren and Bernie Sanders, who claimed he didn't have enough regulatory experience and was too close to the financial industry. In January 2015, realizing he could never win Senate confirmation, Weiss withdrew his name from consideration and accepted a position as counselor to Geithner's successor, Treasury Secretary Jack Lew.[11]

Back to 2009. Three more Clinton White House survivors also made the president's economic team: Gene Sperling, Bruce Reed, and the aforementioned Jack Lew. Having once helped Bill Clinton reach a historic budget compromise in 1997 with Newt Gingrich, this trio of Clintonites believed they could pull the same rabbit out of the hat with John Boehner, and convinced Barack Obama to try, time and again. As we will soon see, that was a nonstarter. Republicans in Congress were now much more extreme than before. So extreme, in fact, that Speaker Boehner was unable to deliver his own caucus for any deal he might want to make with the president. But that didn't stop the White House from trying. And trying. And trying.[12]

One addition to the gaggle of leftover hard-liners was Peter Orszag, who left his job as head of the Congressional Budget Office to become Obama's first director of the Office of Management and Budget. He quickly gained a reputation as the administration's chief deficit hawk. He even looked the part. And he gets credit or blame for convincing Obama to accept cuts in Social Security benefits and extension of the Bush tax cuts as part of a compromise with congressional Republicans.[13]

Rounding out the team were two new faces who brought a more practical and progressive approach to economic policy, and who often disagreed with Summers and Geithner. Austan Goolsbee, chief economic adviser of the Obama presidential campaign, moved into the White House as one of three members of the Council of Economic Advisers. And Christina Romer, economist from UC Berkeley and expert on the Great Depression, was appointed chair of the Council of Economic Advisers. She, especially, clashed with Summers, as we will see in a moment.[14]

What was Obama thinking? Take the most serious crisis facing a new administration and put a motley collection of economists who don't like or trust each other in charge—and what can you expect? The result was what Wolffe calls "the most dysfunctional group of the president's advisers." Senator Elizabeth Warren summed it up best, when she told *Salon* magazine: "He picked his economic team and when the going got tough, his economic team picked Wall Street. That's right. They protected Wall Street. Not families who were losing their homes. Not people who lost their jobs. Not young people who were struggling to get an education. And it happened over and over and over."[15]

First Round: The Stimulus

Obama not only inherited a state of economic disaster from George W. Bush. He was also saddled with a major element of Bush's unfinished economic agenda: the $700 billion Troubled Asset Relief Program, passed by Congress and signed into law by Bush in October 2008. As sold to Congress, the purpose of TARP was to protect the economy from total collapse by bailing out Wall Street firms and buying substantial shares of their equity and troubled assets.

Bush Treasury secretary Hank Paulson (and later Larry Summers) touted TARP as a clever, but expensive, way to save the financial industry and make a handsome profit for taxpayers at the same time. By January 2009, 61 percent of Americans opposed TARP, viewing it as nothing more than a plan to reward Wall Street firms with bailouts and bonuses in return for criminal behavior. Despite serious questions about how the money was distributed, who benefited from it, what lies were told to secure its passage, and the fact that its end result could only mean that banks would be bigger than ever, Obama, who had voted for TARP as a senator, decided not to interfere with the program—either because he felt the horse was already out of the barn, or because he didn't dare take on the big dogs of Wall Street so early in his presidency.[16]

Instead, he decided to focus on the rest of the economy. His answer: the American Recovery and Reinvestment Act of 2009, or "Stimulus," which he signed into law on February 17, 2009—a $787 billion program to create jobs and spur new investment, which passed the Senate with only three Republican votes.

Pumping $787 billion into the economy? Sounds like a lot of money, and it is. But that stimulus was actually much smaller than many leading economists—including Martin Feldstein (previously the chair of Ronald Reagan's Council of Economic Advisers), the White House's own Christina Romer, and the Nobel Prize–winning Paul Krugman—recommended at the time. In fact, debate over the size of the stimulus represented the first real test of Obama's economic team—and in many ways revealed a weakness in governance that would mar his entire presidency.[17]

At his first meeting with his entire team of economic advisers in Chicago on December 16, 2008, President-elect Obama was handed a fifty-seven-page memo that described the serious fiscal crisis the nation faced and laid out two proposals for dealing with it: a $600 billion stimulus, or a $850 billion stimulus. However, as reported by both Ryan Lizza for the *New Yorker* and Noam Scheiber for the *New Republic*, by that time Obama was already shooting too low. He was working from options representing less than half of what Christina Romer had originally recommended as necessary.[18]

In the first draft of her memo to Obama, Romer proposed setting their sights high: "An ambitious goal," she wrote, "would be to eliminate the output gap by 2011-Q1 [the first quarter of 2011], returning the economy to full employment by that date." Getting there, she noted, would take a bold plan of action: "To achieve that magnitude of effective stimulus using a feasible combination of spending, taxes, and transfers to states and localities would require a package costing about $1.8 trillion over two years."[19]

But Obama never saw those words. Putting political considerations above economic necessity, on the unproven theory that not even Democrats in Congress would vote for a stimulus so big, Summers rejected Romer's $1.8 trillion target as impractical and bound to face certain defeat in Congress. In a second draft Romer pared the proposed stimulus down to $1.2 trillion, which Summers also dismissed as "nonplanetary." In the end, Romer reluctantly offered Obama only the two options noted above: $600 billion or $850 billion. Obama settled for $787 billion.

This was still $1 trillion short of what was needed, according to her estimate and those of many others, to jumpstart the American economy in this time of crisis, and it represented both an economic and political failure of leadership. Economically speaking, stimulus spending is based on the well-proven idea that the government must be the spender of last resort when the rest of the economy is in dire straits—the deeper the crisis, the greater the need for "countercyclical spending." Besides, as any progressive or businesswoman worth his or her salt can tell you, money invested now in priorities like infrastructure, education, and energy efficiency will pay back massive dividends down the road.

As for the politics—and this would also be a common failing of this administration—neither Obama nor Summers seemed to understand the simplest fundamentals of haggling. When working toward a compromise, you *start* with a very big number so you *end* somewhere close to where you want to be. You don't make your final compromise the opening position. In this case, Obama and Summers bartered themselves down to an inefficient stimulus, right out of the box.

While she never complained about it publicly, that lesson was not lost on Christina Romer, especially when leading economists later criticized the stimulus as too small. Larry Mishel of the Economic Policy Institute, for example, estimated that a larger stimulus would have created an additional 5 million new jobs, which would have made a big difference for those workers and, through the multiplier effect, for the entire economy.[20]

Not only that, Romer knew Larry Summers was wrong on the politics of the issue. Obama could have easily won the necessary three Republican votes for a stimulus package twice as big. Or, at the very least, bargained down to a much higher number than what was eventually passed. It wasn't the size of the stimulus most Senate Republicans voted against. It was the fact that, unlike TARP, the stimulus was a Barack Obama program—and they didn't want him to succeed at anything, not even saving the nation from economic collapse.

Before long, the White House was on the defensive for not proposing an even bigger stimulus. Already on February 4, 2009, Martin Wolf, chief economics commentator for the *Financial Times*, had written: "Instead of an overwhelming fiscal stimulus, what is emerging is too small, too wasteful and too ill-focused." Obama had proven himself to be "too cautious in fearful times," Wolf complained, and predicted the result would be a sluggish recovery marked by a lengthy period of weak growth and high joblessness. Which proved to be spot-on.[21]

The debate led to one tense moment reported by Noam Scheiber for the *New Republic*. As part of preparations for her appearance on one of the Sunday morning talk shows, Christina Romer was hammered with questions by top political adviser David Axelrod. Here's one question you're bound to get, said Axelrod: "Was the stimulus big enough?" "And here's what I'm going to say on national television," Romer shot back: "Abso-fucking-lutely-not." According to Scheiber, Axelrod was not amused. Romer never said it. Publicly, that is.[22]

But its insufficient size wasn't the only problem with the stimulus. Two other factors also set it up for failure: Half of it was devoted to tax cuts. And there was no follow-up.

In an early indication of how he would deal with Congress on other major issues, and how naïve he was about the hostility of House and Senate Republicans, Obama decided to craft the stimulus in such a way that it should have been guaranteed to win Republican votes. Remember, to placate the opposition, his team had already cut the stimulus from $1.8 trillion to $787 billion. Now he decided to sweeten the pot even further. His theory: Since Republicans like tax cuts, let's give them tax cuts. And he did.

Progressives often likened this constant tendency of Obama to try to appease the unappeasable to Charlie Brown's experience with a football in the old *Peanuts* cartoon strip. Time and time again, Lucy would convince Charlie to kick the ball while she held it. And, every time, she'd pull it away at the last second and Charlie would fall on his back. So, too, with Obama, who never seemed to understand, until far too late, that he was trying to strike a bargain that could never be struck. Republicans held the football.

In any event, as part of the American Recovery and Reinvestment Act, $116 billion went directly to American families in the form of tax cuts: up to $400 a year for individuals and $800 a year for married couples. The way it was designed, nobody actually got a check from the federal government—unlike rebate checks sent out by the Bush administration in 2008. Instead, under the Obama plan, less money was withheld from monthly paychecks, giving the average family an extra $65 a month.[23]

Great idea. In theory. But there were three real-world problems with the Obama tax cuts. First, that was a whopping $116 billion that did not go into job creation, the most pressing need of the moment— and the primary purpose of the stimulus.

Second, the tax cuts did not serve their main purpose. They did not win Obama any extra Republican votes. Republicans still attacked the stimulus as too much big government. For Obama, it was another preemptive compromise made for nothing.

Third, and perhaps most important from a political perspective, because of the stealthy way in which they were distributed, most Americans never even realized they got a tax cut under the stimulus. At the time, I remember appearing as a guest on the Ronn Owens show on KGO-AM in San Francisco. Ronn's one of the best, and most well-informed, talk show hosts in the business. But when I mentioned that 95 percent of America's working families had already received a tax cut under President Obama, he didn't believe it.

When I backed it up with evidence, telling him about the "Making Work Pay" tax credit included in the stimulus, he asked: "Why didn't I know about this?" Good question. For Obama, the sad fact was that nobody knew about it because, again, of the way it was distributed— and because the administration itself kept it such a secret. In a September 2010 *New York Times/CBS News* poll, fewer than one in ten respondents knew the Obama administration had lowered taxes for most Americans. Half of those polled said they thought their taxes had stayed the same. A third of Americans thought that their taxes had actually gone up.[24]

For Obama and Democrats, this was the proverbial tax cut that fell in the forest. Nobody heard it. Consequently, it never gave them the boost they were counting on in the 2010 midterm elections.

Despite its weaknesses, a half-baked $787 billion stimulus plan might still have worked—had it been followed by a second or third stimulus, which Christina Romer and many other leading economists were calling for. That never happened. As reported by Noam Scheiber in the *New Republic*, when Romer proposed a second stimulus to President Obama, he shot it down with the observation: "The American people don't think it worked, so I can't do it."[25]

Curiously enough, Romer had an ally at this point in Larry Summers, who joined her call for sticking it to Republicans with a defiant, follow-up stimulus. But the two of them were outmaneuvered by OMB director and deficit hawk Peter Orszag, who insisted that any new stimulus be combined with deficit reduction. Enough with spending, said Orszag, let's start cutting. Obama agreed. And that, of course, led to another disaster.[26]

In October 2012, Christina Romer, then back at UC Berkeley, finally broke her silence about the stimulus in an article for the *New York Times*. The stimulus was too small, she wrote, and relied too heavily on tax cuts. She also regretted the program did not include any direct funds for public employment, like FDR's Works Progress Administration (WPA). And, with so little money going to job creation, she noted, even after passage of the ARRA, the economy still lost an additional 9 million jobs.[27]

Before moving on, it's important to pause and reflect on what we learned from President Obama's first crucial public policy test. We saw here a pattern of governing—marred by a series of missteps, a weakness in decision-making, and a failure of leadership—that would be repeated throughout his presidency, in dealing with everything from health care to bombing raids in Syria.

On the stimulus package, instead of meeting the fiscal crisis of 2009 head-on and taking full advantage of his decisive victory in November 2008, President Obama:

- Settled for half a loaf, before even fighting for a whole loaf,
- Offered major compromises to Republicans, without getting anything in return,
- Didn't sell the benefits of his program to the American people, and
- Failed to follow through.

It's not how FDR would have handled it. Historians say that much of the success of the New Deal lay not so much in the programs themselves as in the fact that FDR did such a good job of selling them to the American people. In his fireside chats, he assured Americans that he would fight a weak economy with the same strength he'd muster to fight a foreign foe. And the American people thereby gained confidence in FDR's ability to get the economy back on track. Even though the Depression didn't end until World War II—thanks to the massive stimulus afforded by war production—the American people knew the president was working hard, every single day, to turn things around.

President Obama, for his part, started out with an inferior product, and then never made the sale. At this first moment of crisis, Obama and his economic team failed the test. They proposed a stimulus that was too small, even according to some of their own advisers. They relied too heavily on tax cuts, all to appease Republicans, who attacked the stimulus regardless. And they failed to keep momentum going with a second or third stimulus.

To be fair, even the smaller stimulus did a lot of good. The nonpartisan Congressional Budget Office determined that it saved the economy from sinking into a full-on depression; created or saved an average 1.6 million jobs over the span of four years; raised economic output by 2 to 3 percent from 2009 to 2011; and kept the unemployment rate from soaring to 12 percent.[28]

At the same time, it fell way short of expectations. It didn't go nearly far enough, and it ended too soon. The country needed more, but

Obama wasn't willing to go there. And his failure to do so had major consequences. A bolder approach to the stimulus would have rewritten the entire story of the Obama presidency for the better. But as it happened, in the words of Robert Penn Warren in *All the King's Men*, "the crystal was in the steel at the point of fracture." This original failure would redound through the rest of Obama's tenure in office.[29]

Instead of moving forward with more stimulus spending, Obama did a total 180. He became a zealous deficit hawk. It was almost as if he'd changed political parties, shedding his Democratic suit for a Republican sackcloth—and made cutting the deficit, not creating jobs, his number-one priority.

With that new focus, Obama's worst tendencies came to the fore. He became compromiser-in-chief. He embarked on a series of capitulations, each one more damaging than the last, resulting in one disaster after another, which had the cumulative effect of slowing the recovery, seriously eroding the social compact, and leaving the economy sluggish and uncertain.

Obama the Deficit Hawk

So, with the stimulus winding down, and the economy still on life support, Obama's economic team suddenly shifted gears in the second half of 2010: from using the power and resources of the federal government to stimulate the economy to shrinking the size of the federal government in order to encourage private investment.

Across the board, economists today consider that move a serious mistake with even graver consequences. As Paul Krugman wrote in the October 23, 2014, edition of the *New York Review of Books*, "the stimulus could easily have been bigger and gone on longer. What we got instead, however, was a wrongheaded obsession with deficits and unprecedented fiscal austerity which greatly deepened and extended the slump."[30]

To make things even worse, this was all eminently predictable. In 1937, believing the economy was showing signs of health again at

last, Franklin Roosevelt also made the decision to pare back government spending. The result was the "Roosevelt Recession" of 1937–38.
The economy subsequently stalled out once more, and did not return
to health until the massive federal investments that accompanied the
World War II production effort. Unfortunately, Barack Obama was not
looking to learn from the FDR model. Overnight, he threw FDR under
the bus and embraced the rhetoric of Ronald Reagan. He abandoned
job creation and adopted deficit reduction.

The rhetoric, but not the reality. For decades, ever since Reagan,
deficit reduction or balancing the budget had been the mantra of the
Republican Party. Of course, as the numbers show, while Republicans
talked a good game about balancing the budget, they never actually
did anything about it. Take Reagan, for starters. While giving lip service to a "Balanced Budget Amendment," he actually racked up the
biggest federal deficits of any president in history, only to be surpassed
by George W. Bush, who mushroomed the deficit by sponsoring two
rounds of tax cuts for the wealthiest of Americans, and then starting
two wars and expanding Medicare to include prescription drugs (without letting Medicare negotiate their price). And he didn't raise revenue
to pay for any of it. He just charged everything to the federal credit
card, like Reagan before him.[31]

To the dismay of progressives, even before Republicans took over
the House in 2010, Barack Obama began to embrace their narrow-
minded "let's cut spending" agenda—at the very time when, according
to the proven rules of Keynesian economics, the federal government
should have been spending more, not less, in order to kick-start the
economy.

This obviously upset Democratic leaders in Congress. For them,
even conceding the Republicans' argument that debt was the most
important issue facing the nation was pure nonsense. After all, Republicans themselves had created the deficit problem with Bush's
trillion-dollar tax cuts for the rich and two disastrous wars. Now they
were attempting to use the very debt they had rolled up as an excuse to
cut long-standing social programs for the poor and middle class. Congressional Democrats didn't want to let them get away with it. In fact,

they hoped to turn it around and use Republican efforts to cut Medicare and Social Security as campaign fodder for Democratic candidates in the 2010 midterm elections.

But Obama simply ignored their concerns. Determined to be the nation's first "postpartisan president," he dove into deficit-cutting full-bore, and spent much of the next two years in countless, pointless meetings with Speaker John Boehner and other Republican leaders, trying to negotiate a "balanced" budget deal consisting of both new spending cuts and new revenue.

Time and time again—Charlie Brown and the football!—Obama's attempts to reach any reasonable compromise were rejected by the GOP. Meanwhile, by embracing the Republican game plan and abandoning federal government intervention in favor of the Republicans' deficit-cutting agenda, Obama left the economy sputtering. He also opened the door to three potential economic disasters in a row: the wildly overrated Simpson-Bowles plan; the so-called grand bargain with Speaker John Boehner; and the dreaded Sequester, still in place.

It was a change in direction that several key administration players, including Jared Bernstein, soon came to regret. Bernstein was Vice President Joe Biden's chief economic adviser at the time. Looking back in February 2014, he told the *New York Times*: "A deeper understanding of the economic damage should have prevented the precipitous pivot away from stimulus toward deficit reduction." Obama's team got two things wrong, according to Bernstein. They got the politics wrong, coming to believe that "the public disliked the growing deficit a lot more than they liked the stimulus." And they got the economics wrong, fearing that "debt markets would respond to the deficit by pushing up interest rates."[32]

I watched Obama pivot toward deficit reduction close-up while attending his administration's daily press briefings, in my role as a member of the White House press corps. Covering the White House in those days was like taking a graduate course in belt-tightening. I can't tell you how many times during that period I heard President Obama, in the Briefing Room or East Room, lecture the nation on how the government had to cut back on spending in hard times, just as families did.

In his interview with the *Times*, Bernstein shattered that myth once and for all: "By the way, in those days I learned the power of the single worst analogy I know: 'Just as families have to tighten their belts in tough times, so does the government.' It's not just that this is wrong; it's that it's backward. When families are tightening, government (including the Federal Reserve) must loosen, and vice versa. But the phrase, uttered by no less than the president himself at times, makes so much folksy sense that it, too, infected the policy and precipitated the pivot."[33]

Bernstein, of course, was speaking with the benefit of hindsight. Other economists, such as Nobel Prize winner Paul Krugman, didn't wait that long to blast Obama's sudden debt obsession. In his weekly radio address on July 2, 2011, President Obama sounded the familiar family-must-cut-back theme: "Government has to start living within its means, just like families do. We have to cut the spending we can't afford so we can put the economy on sounder footing, and give our businesses the confidence they need to grow and create jobs."[34]

That very same day, Krugman put out a blog post ridiculing the president as "Barack Herbert Hoover Obama." Noting that Obama had evoked "the false government-family equivalence, the myth of expansionary austerity, and the confidence fairy, all in just two sentences," Krugman warned: "This is truly a tragedy: the great progressive hope is falling all over himself to endorse right-wing economic fallacies."[35]

It makes you wonder: Why wasn't Paul Krugman in the White House as Barack Obama's chief economic adviser, instead of Larry Summers, Peter Orszag, or Timothy Geithner?

Simpson-Bowles: Two Unwise Men

In Washington, D.C., a terrible idea often goes around the Beltway several times before the right policy can get its boots on. And so government outlays under the stimulus were barely under way before Obama's economic team in the White House, plus many Republicans and conservative Democrats in Congress, got cold feet on spending and caught the deficit-cutting fever.

Wanting to do something to look busy, but knowing they could never craft a viable deficit plan on their own, a bipartisan group of senators came up with the classic, time-honored government response: create a commission. In this case, the National Commission on Fiscal Responsibility and Reform, now known forever as the Simpson-Bowles Commission, after its two designated chairmen, former senator Alan Simpson, Wyoming Republican, and former White House chief of staff Erskine Bowles, North Carolina Democrat.

Under the original bill, members of the commission were charged with recommending how to keep government running at a reasonable level while resolving the problem of the national debt. But with this unique twist: The legislation also required that all recommendations of the commission receive an up-or-down vote in Congress, with no amendments allowed. Afraid of this potential Frankenstein's monster—a commission whose suggestions must be accepted and voted on as is—six Republican senators who had sponsored the bill changed their minds and voted against it, and it went down 53–46.

Enter President Obama. By now, he'd decided to lead, not just join, the deficit-cutting parade. And here was his opportunity. In January 2010, he created the same Simpson-Bowles Commission by executive order, named its eighteen members, and charged it with determining "policies to improve the fiscal situation in the medium term and to achieve fiscal sustainability over the long run."[36]

On the economy, filling his team with ex-Clintonites was Obama's first big mistake. Putting forth a half-baked stimulus was the second. Shifting priorities from growing the economy to cutting the deficit was number three. And naming the Simpson-Bowles Commission was big mistake number four. He brought that Frankenstein's monster to life. And now, in the name of "fiscal responsibility," Obama had tied himself, at least indirectly, to efforts to gut every middle-class social insurance program that Democrats had fought for over the last eighty years, which he had promised to protect.

Eleven months later, in December 2010, the commission completed its final report. Only eleven out of eighteen commission members voted for it, three shy of the fourteen votes required. So the report was never officially adopted. But it took on a life of its own after it was released as a draft by Messrs. Simpson and Bowles, who spent the next two years trumpeting its recommendations nationwide and basking in the glory of their new reputation, in *Politico*'s words, as the "wise men of Washington."[37]

Simpson-Bowles, the creation of that erstwhile progressive hope Barack Obama—even though he never officially endorsed it—was the repudiation of everything Democrats stood for. It threw away the baby with the bathwater. In order to reduce the deficit, they proposed, among other draconian measures: eliminating almost all tax deductions, including those for home mortgage loans and employer health-care plans; slashing military pensions and student loan subsidies; cutting Medicare and Social Security benefits; raising the retirement age from sixty-five to sixty-nine; and mandating a 15 percent increase in gas taxes. And yet, they somehow still found room to cut the top federal income tax rate to 24 percent, and the top corporate rate from 35 to 26 percent.[38]

Notice how a commission ostensibly designed to increase federal revenue to close the deficit nonetheless chose to advocate lower tax rates on corporations and the super-wealthy. Some might say the fix was in.

Nonetheless, editorial writers, most of whom probably never read the report itself, were rhapsodic in praising the bipartisanship, balance, and fairness of Simpson-Bowles. Even the supposedly liberal *New York Times* praised the plan for doing "what any successful deficit reduction plan must do: It puts everything on the table, including tax reform to raise revenue and cuts in spending on health care and defense. It even dares to mention the need to find significant savings in Social Security, Medicare and other mandatory programs." Simpson and Bowles were almost universally praised for putting forth a plan based on "shared sacrifice."[39]

Nonsense. Just like the economic policies of George Bush and Dick Cheney, the Simpson-Bowles plan heavily rewarded those at the very top of the ladder, while cutting what little benefits are still enjoyed by those at the bottom. More than two-thirds of its proposed savings came from cutting domestic spending, not getting rid of tax loopholes. Remarkably, repealing the Bush tax cuts for the top 2 percent of Americans, which cost $4 trillion over a decade, did not even make the list of cuts. Nor did the report include a widely recommended new tax on financial transactions. But it did call for major cuts to Social Security, which is solvent for at least the next twenty-five years and which does not contribute to the deficit at all.[40]

And remember, because he had created the commission, its report was considered Barack Obama's own.

Progressives went ballistic over Simpson-Bowles. Dean Baker, codirector of the Center for Economic and Policy Research, argued that the commission's entire focus on deficit reduction was wrong, since our economic woes were the result, not of a looming deficit, but of an $8 trillion crash in financial markets—with the resulting loss of personal savings and millions of jobs. Robert Kuttner, economic columnist and coeditor of the *American Prospect*, agreed. The most dire problem facing the country was not what the deficit might be in 2020 or 2030, he argued. "For most people, the crisis right now is lost income, lost jobs, lost homes." This should have been self-evident, not just to progressives, but to everyone.[41]

For Paul Krugman, Simpson-Bowles was simply "terrible." It missed the target in several ways, he wrote. "It mucks around with taxes, but is obsessed with lowering marginal rates despite a complete absence of evidence that this is important. It offers nothing on Medicare that isn't already in the Affordable Care Act. And it raises the Social Security retirement age because life expectancy has risen, completely ignoring the fact that life expectancy has only gone up for the well-off and well-educated, while stagnating or even declining among the people who need the program most."[42]

Writing in the *New York Observer*, journalist Kevin Baker summed it up best and most colorfully. He called Simpson-Bowles "a prescription for hunting every last remaining vestige of the middle class in this country and beating it to death with a stick."[43]

Fortunately, despite the Beltway ballyhoo behind it, Simpson-Bowles mercifully did not go anywhere in the end. It was never endorsed by President Obama, Senate Majority Leader Reid, or Speaker Boehner. It never became law. And Republicans—loath to increase revenues in any way, shape, or form—soon fell in behind the spending-cuts-only plan of Congressman Paul Ryan instead. But it still had a significant impact. It shaped the economic debate for well over a year, and helped prevent the spending needed to get the economy really moving again. Only when the "Occupy" protests broke out in the fall of 2011 did the spell it held over Washington seem to waver. Until then, it helped Obama and others shift the focus of discussion from job creation to deficit reduction. And it served as the template for negotiations between President Obama and John Boehner over what became known as the "Grand Bargain."[44]

Embracing Republican Ideas

On November 2, 2010, Obama suffered an enormous political setback. Republicans won sixty-three seats in the midterm elections and easily took back leadership of the House of Representatives, which they had lost to the Democrats four years earlier. But even before John Boehner was sworn in as new Speaker of the House, Obama decided to offer up some more preemptive compromises—as if to prove he was a bigger deficit hawk than Republicans were. He called for a three-year freeze on domestic discretionary spending, claimed he'd saved $20 billion by eliminating unnecessary programs, and identified another $150 billion in savings from correcting improper payments in programs like Medicare, Medicaid, unemployment, and the Earned Income Tax Credit.[45]

Obama also signed an executive order slapping a two-year freeze on wages for civilian federal workers. That move angered labor leaders, who pointed out that the $5 billion Obama would save by cutting federal employee wages wouldn't even make a dent in a deficit that had exceeded $1 trillion for the last two years. "Sticking it to a V.A. nurse and a Social Security worker is not the way to go," fumed John Gage, then-president of the American Federation of Government Employees.

But Obama, while praising federal employees as "patriots who love their country," still insisted that they had to tighten their belts, just like everyone else.[46]

Which might have made a little more sense, if not for what occurred shortly thereafter. In December 2010, Obama stunned Democrats by signing the Tax Relief, Unemployment Insurance Reauthorization and Job Creation Act—which extended the Bush tax cuts for the wealthiest of Americans for another two years. That move didn't save money. It cost $60 billion a year. Obama, in effect, was saying that everybody had to tighten their belts—except millionaires and billionaires.[47]

Ending the Bush tax cuts had been one of the major promises of candidate Barack Obama. Just two days before Election Day 2008, campaigning in Colorado, Obama blasted the Bush-McCain idea that "we should give more and more to millionaires and billionaires and hope that it trickles down on everybody else." Yet now, less than two years into his presidency, Obama had unilaterally agreed to preserve the tax cuts. Again, at a cost of $60 billion a year.[48]

So why'd he do it? Only because Obama wanted to show that he was willing to do anything—even violate one of his most sacred campaign promises—in order to make a deal with the new Republican leadership in Congress. Which he then spent years trying to do.

The Grand Bargain

Nothing illustrates Obama's shortcomings as president more than the time he spent, and wasted, trying to strike a deal with John Boehner on a compromise budget plan. Not only did he swallow the ridiculous Republican agenda of debt reduction über alles hook, line, and sinker, he tried to make a deal behind the backs of Democrats in Congress. And he did so with a Speaker of the House who could not even control his own caucus.

From beginning to end, efforts to reach the so-called grand bargain was a comedy of errors.

As Matt Bai later reported in the *New York Times Magazine*, Obama began formal negotiations with Speaker Boehner and Majority Leader Eric Cantor in the spring of 2011, in plenty of time to strike a deal before the August deadline for raising the debt ceiling by another $2.4 trillion.[49]

Every time it came up for a vote in Congress, raising the debt ceiling used to prompt the same old Kabuki dance. Members of both parties made angry speeches and put out press releases denouncing reckless federal spending and vowing never to raise the debt ceiling again, but then they held their noses and voted for it, anyway, just so the United States could pay its bills. At least, most of them did. One notable exception was Senator Barack Obama, who voted against raising the debt ceiling in March 2006.

The debt ceiling had been raised seven times under President George W. Bush, each time by a bipartisan vote with no strings attached. But now, for this first debt ceiling vote under President Barack Obama, House Republicans added a demand: They'd vote against any increase in the debt ceiling unless an equal amount of spending cuts was included in the deal. In effect, they announced they were going to hold the nation's credit rating—and by extension the entire American economy—hostage unless Obama acceded to their demands.[50]

And so, negotiations began, and soon fell apart. Obama agreed to $2 trillion in cuts, but insisted on adding new revenue from closing certain tax loopholes. Cantor, speaking for Tea Party members of the House, flatly rejected any new revenue from taxes, even by closing loopholes. Talks between the two sides broke down in June.[51]

But that was just Round One. Without telling Cantor or Democratic leaders of Congress, Obama and Boehner had begun their own round of budget negotiations in secret meetings held at the White House and during one round of golf and drinks at Andrews Air Force Base. Both men agreed to think big and were determined to shape a deal that included fundamental "reforms" to both social insurance programs like Social Security and the tax code. Unlike Cantor, Boehner even agreed to raising $800 billion in new revenue by eliminating tax loopholes and subsidies for some special interests.[52]

On the surface, it looked as if a historic deal—the "grand bargain"—

was in the works. There was only one problem: Boehner couldn't deliver the votes in his own caucus without Eric Cantor's blessing—and Cantor, upset at being cut out of the one-on-one talks, once again rejected any new revenue from closing tax loopholes, which he considered the same as raising taxes. On July 9, believing he had a deal, President Obama went off to Camp David for the weekend—only to receive a phone call from John Boehner that evening telling him the grand bargain was dead.[53]

Except it wasn't. Players simply moved on to Round Three. Five days later, July 14, Boehner called the president and suggested they try again, this time meeting with Chief of Staff Bill Daley and Treasury Secretary Tim Geithner, instead of Budget Director Jack Lew and Legislative Affairs Director Rob Nabors. Boehner and Daley met the next day and agreed on a general set of principles. On Sunday, July 17, Boehner, Cantor, Daley, and Geithner met at the White House. Obama joined them after church. Within a couple of hours, they actually shook hands on a deal, with Boehner and Cantor agreeing to $800 billion in new revenues from closing tax loopholes, and Obama accepting $450 billion in cuts to Medicaid and Medicare. The president also agreed to a new and much more narrow way of calculating Social Security benefits based on inflation called "Chained CPI," which was anathema to progressives since it was tantamount to a $200 billion annual cut in Social Security benefits.[54]

They all left the White House that Sunday thinking they had a deal. All they had to do was sell it to their counterparts in Congress. But such was not to be—this comedy was just beginning. While Obama and Boehner were cooking up a deal, a bipartisan group of six senators was working on their own plan, which they now threw into the mix, catching Obama and Boehner off guard.

The "Gang of Six" was made up of Democrats Dick Durbin, Mark Warner, and Kent Conrad and Republicans Tom Coburn, Saxby Chambliss, and Mike Crapo. Their proposal was much more ambitious than what Obama and Boehner had tentatively settled on: $3.7 billion in spending cuts, and a whopping $2 trillion in new revenue, much more than the $800 billion Boehner had agreed to with Obama.

The mere existence of another budget plan was confusing enough. But then Obama made things even worse by immediately endorsing the Gang of Six plan as the kind of "balanced approach," a mix of spending cuts and new revenue, he'd been seeking for months. For Obama and his economic team—who just wanted a compromise with someone, anyone—endorsing the Gang of Six plan was a serious miscalculation: All it did was put Obama's weight behind a proposal that had no chance of passing the Senate, while pissing off Boehner in the process. The Speaker, indeed, felt betrayed, and told the White House all bets were off. Whereupon Obama invited Boehner to a two-hour, one-on-one Oval Office meeting on July 20 to, once again, try to hammer out their differences.[55]

But by this time it was impossible to put Humpty-Dumpty back together again. Boehner left the White House, telling Obama he wanted to sleep on the latest proposal. He never got a chance. Cantor killed the deal as soon as Boehner briefed him on it. And Boehner knew that, without Cantor's support, he could never round up enough votes in his caucus.

The next morning, President Obama called Boehner to check in, and ended up leaving a private message on his cell phone. He sensed he might be in trouble when, hours later, Boehner still had not returned his call. He learned it was all over when Boehner held a news conference that afternoon, accusing the president of negotiating in bad faith. The grand bargain was finally, mercifully, dead.[56]

As it turned out, Obama and his team of deficit hawks may have been the only Democrats in Washington disappointed by the collapse of the grand bargain. As more details leaked out about how far Obama was willing to compromise, more and more outrage was heard from progressives. Political analyst Ezra Klein, then still with the *Washington Post*, reported that Obama had offered to raise the eligibility age for Medicare from 65 to 67, in addition to adopting the "Chained CPI" Social Security cut. Senior advocacy groups calculated that, because of Chained CPI, a 75-year-old would lose $650 a year in benefits on average, an 85-year-old $1,150, and a 95-year-old $1,600 a year. All of this while the wealthiest of Americans continued to enjoy their Bush-given and Obama-extended tax breaks.[57]

Rather than being angry with him for killing the deal, Klein observed, "liberals should be sending Eric Cantor a fruit basket." After all, he "saved them from a deal they'd hate."[58]

Investigative reporter Bob Woodward, who excels in developing the best network of sources in any administration, actually obtained a copy of the memo President Obama sent to Speaker Boehner outlining his proposed $4 trillion grand bargain. As Woodward described it on *Meet the Press*: "It shows a willingness to cut all kinds of things, like TRICARE, which is the sacred health insurance program for the military, for military retirees; to cut Social Security; to cut Medicare. And there are some lines in there about, 'We want to get tax rates down, not only for individuals but for businesses.' So Obama and the White House were willing to go quite far."[59]

Much too far, in fact, for liberal economist James K. Galbraith, writing for the *Next New Deal* blog, who blamed Obama for selling out his own party: "What do we have, from a President who claims to be a member of the Democratic Party? First, there is the claim that we face a fiscal crisis, which is a big untruth. Second, a concession in principle that we should deal with that crisis by enacting massive cuts in public services on one hand and in vital social insurance programs on the other. This is an arbitrary cruelty."[60]

Despite having been stabbed in the back by both Boehner and Cantor several times, Obama still clung to his dream of a balanced and bipartisan budget plan. It was almost as if he were trying to channel Richard Nixon. Just as only Republican Nixon could go to China, only Democratic Obama seemed ready to dare to slash Social Security and Medicare, the two greatest Democratic achievements of the twentieth century and the bedrock social insurance institutions of modern life. In desperation, he next turned to Congress with a Faustian pact: You come up with a deficit solution in five months—or else. Whereupon Congress did what everybody in Washington said was impossible and everyone else knew to be inevitable: They ended up settling—for "else."

The Sequester

While Obama and Boehner were going through their fruitless, months-long attempt to strike a grand bargain, the clock was still ticking on raising the debt ceiling before the August 2011 deadline.

Both sides were locked in. Democrats simply wanted to raise the debt ceiling with no drama, as both parties had always done in the past. Republicans continued to insist on dollar-for-dollar cuts in spending. If we're going to have spending cuts, Democrats countered, then we also need to close some special-interest tax loopholes. No, that's the same as raising taxes, complained Republicans, which we will never agree to.

You can see why the media started calling this a disaster in the making. And it proved to be just that.

On August 2, President Obama, ever willing to compromise, responded to the crisis by signing the Budget Control Act of 2011. Actually, he didn't just compromise. He gave away the store. While the legislation did, in fact, immediately raise the debt ceiling by $400 billion, with another $500 billion hike authorized in 2012, it contained an even larger amount of spending cuts, $917 billion. It did not, however, include any new revenue from higher taxes or tax reform. Obama was so eager to make a deal that he simply caved in on that demand. In their appraisal of the "terrible deal," the *New York Times* called it "a nearly complete capitulation to the hostage-taking demands of Republican extremists" that would "hurt programs for the middle class and poor, and hinder an economic recovery."[61]

But even that act of surrender wasn't the worst of it. Another big feature of the Budget Control Act was a ticking time bomb: the creation of the Joint Select Committee on Deficit Reduction, or "Super Committee"—twelve members of Congress, six from each party—given the task (because Simpson-Bowles had worked so well!) of producing by November 23, 2011, a grand plan to reduce the deficit by $1.5 trillion. Congress was then charged with voting on the plan, with no amendments or filibuster permitted, by December 23.

But here was the real kicker: If Congress did not agree to the Super

Committee's recommendations, a round of nondebatable, across-the-board "sequestration" cuts of $1.2 trillion over the next eight years (2013 to 2021) would automatically kick in on January 1, 2013—one-half of the cuts in nondefense spending; one-half at the Pentagon.[62]

The logic behind the Super Committee was simple, if flawed: These proposed wholesale cuts would be so bad, so destructive, so draconian, so ill-informed, so harmful to the military, as well as to important social programs, that Congress would never, never, never let them kick in. They were bound to approve the Super Committee report, no matter how odious.

That was the logic. So simple, yet so hopelessly naïve. Because what Obama and others miscalculated was that for Tea Party Republicans, this was exactly the opportunity they were looking for. Obama had "thrown them into the briar patch," as it were. They had come to Washington to shrink the government, if not destroy it, and this was their chance. They didn't care about the military, and they certainly didn't care about social programs. They were more than willing to gut both military and social spending with no consideration of which programs were worth saving and which were not. Their number-one goal was to shut the entire government down.

America remained on edge while the Super Committee got down to work, but it wasn't long before it became apparent that the grand strategy had failed. Democrats insisted on a "balanced" approach of spending cuts and new revenue. Republicans demanded spending cuts only, and again rejected any new sources of revenue as raising taxes. Not even the sword of Damocles, aka "sequester," hanging over their heads could force the two sides to bridge their differences.

On November 21, members of the Super Committee threw in the towel with a statement that began: "After months of hard work and intense deliberations, we have come to the conclusion today that it will not be possible to make any bipartisan agreement available to the public before the committee's deadline." The committee was formally disbanded on January 31, 2012, and the $1.2 trillion sequester—those terrible, no-good, draconian cuts that Obama assured us Congress would never let happen—became the law of the land, effective January 2013.[63]

The deep, across-the-board sequestration cuts also paved the way for the next potential economic disaster: the "fiscal cliff" of January 2013, when the weak economic recovery risked being further undermined by the double blow of expiring tax cuts (meaning less personal spending) and the sequester kicking in—less government spending, too.

Campaigning for re-election in 2012, President Obama and members of Congress had spent most of their time trading accusations about which party was responsible for failure to reach a budget deal. When they returned to Washington in mid-November, the bickering only intensified. Neither side would budge. The deep sequester cuts were only a month away. It looked like Armageddon. Yet, just when we were about to go over the cliff, President Obama caved to the hostage-takers again, and made yet another bad deal with Republicans.

At midnight on January 1, 2013, the very day the government would run out of money and the dreaded sequester cuts were supposed to kick in, Congress passed the American Taxpayer Relief Act of 2012, which President Obama signed into law the next day. The ATRA provided some temporary relief, by keeping the government running and delaying the sequester for two months, until March 1. But it also contained many deeply harmful provisions, both to the economy in general and to middle-class Americans in particular.

Most notably, while the ATRA ended certain tax privileges for millionaires and billionaires, it still left 82 percent of the original Bush tax cuts in place. These cuts were made permanent for single people making less than $400,000 per year and couples making less than $450,000 per year—not exactly the middle class—and eliminated for those above the line. According to the Congressional Budget Office, that move cost taxpayers $2.8 trillion from 2013 to 2022. In other words, it didn't reduce the deficit, it actually added $2.8 trillion to the deficit.[64]

With his signature on the ATRA, President Obama adopted lower tax rates for dividends and capital gains—which was excellent news for the Mitt Romneys of the world—and left the vast majority of the Bush tax cuts, originally scheduled to sunset in 2010, permanently locked in place. Yes, those same tax cuts candidate Obama had pledged to eliminate. Under Bush, they were one of the major factors in shifting from a surplus to a deficit economy. Now, under Obama and his successors, they would continue to add to the deficit for years to come. No wonder conservatives rejoiced while Democrats cringed. "After more than a decade of criticizing these tax cuts," crowed Republican Dave Camp of Michigan, then-chair of the House Ways and Means Committee, "Democrats are finally joining Republicans in making them permanent."[65]

What puzzled and angered progressives was why Obama signed the ATRA in the first place. So what if Republicans were threatening to shut the government down? Let them do so, many Democrats advised Obama. Led by Speaker Newt Gingrich, Republicans tried that once, in 1995, under Bill Clinton, and it blew up in their faces. People will clearly blame Republicans if they shut down the government again.

Besides, even if he didn't realize it, Obama was dealing from strength. He'd just handily won re-election by campaigning with a pledge to raise taxes on anyone making over $250,000 a year. So why not call their bluff? Dare Republicans to shut down the government. Let them take us over the cliff—and then watch them deal with the public's wrath. Instead, he folded, made a bad deal, and let Republicans off the hook by raising taxes only on individuals making over $400,000 a year, Obama's new definition of middle class.

Meanwhile, the dark cloud of "sequestration" loomed larger and larger. Every day, cabinet secretaries and other top administration officials would come into the White House briefing room and outline for us reporters the disasters that would befall their agencies—Transportation, Health and Welfare, Housing, Education, Homeland Security, Environmental Protection—if the $1.2 trillion sequester cuts actually happened. But nobody believed them. Republicans tried to amend the sequester legislatively by dropping cuts to the military. But Obama vowed to veto any such legislation, absent a "balanced" deficit reduction plan of spending cuts and new revenue to replace it. If you don't want the hatchet to fall, Obama admonished legislators, "work with a scalpel" to come up with a better plan.[66]

Of course, they didn't. D-Day, March 1, arrived full of doom and gloom. With no deal reached, President Obama signed an executive order late in the day making the sequester cuts official and triggering $85 billion in program cuts between March and September. The impacts were immediate and widespread: Federal employees in every agency were forced to take furloughs with no pay; control towers in 149 regional airports were closed (although Congress later passed emergency legislation exempting air traffic controllers); national parks closed visitor centers or opened for fewer hours; White House tours were canceled; navy ships stayed in port; the air force grounded pilots and training flights; two of five mine-safety offices were closed; and federal unemployment checks were cut by 10 percent.[67]

According to a report issued by Congresswoman Rosa DeLauro (D-Conn.) and Congressman George Miller (D-Calif.), more than fifty-seven thousand children were dropped from the early education program Head Start in 2013 because of sequestration; and more than 5 million fewer meals were served to seniors living in poverty through the Meals on Wheels program. Speaking of severe cuts to education and innovation, MIT president Leo Rafael Reif called sequestration "the single biggest threat to our future success."[68]

The worst part is, although its short-term impact was somewhat mitigated by the budget deal brokered by Senator Patty Murray and Congressman Paul Ryan in January 2014, the sequester is still with us—and will be, unless Congress has a sudden change of heart, for the next decade. Which means that every federal agency—Justice, Agriculture, Education, FDA, Commerce, Homeland Security, NIH, the Pentagon, you name it—will be forced to operate under artificial spending caps and cut back essential services. Because they often need the help the most, these cuts will fall especially hard on the backs of the poorest Americans, though everyone will feel the pinch, from cancer patients to preschool kids to our men and women in uniform.

Under "sequestration," cuts must be made across the board, with no consideration of which programs work and which ones don't. All of which is already having serious side effects on the economy: reduced purchasing power by federal employees; fewer contracts available for private companies doing business with the government; generally lower consumer spending; and higher unemployment. According to the Congressional Budget Office, sequestration cuts cost as many as 1.6 million jobs through 2014 alone, with a reduction in GDP of 0.7 percent.[69]

A sad, ironic footnote to all the years wasted and damage caused by deficit hysteria is the tale of Harvard economists Carmen Reinhart and Kenneth Rogoff. In early 2010, Professors Reinhart and Rogoff published an enormously influential study, "Growth in a Time of Debt," which looked at the economic performance of various countries around the world and asserted that, once the debt of a nation reaches 90 percent of its GDP, its economy basically stops growing—"median growth rates fall by 1 percent, and average growth falls considerably more." At the time, America's debt-to-GDP ratio was 100 percent. "The sooner politicians reconcile themselves to accepting [fiscal] adjustment," the two economists concluded in an op-ed based on their study, "the lower the risks of truly paralyzing debt problems down the road." Even though Reinhart and Rogoff were using publicly available data— the historical record—no other economists could match their findings. But no matter—the Reinhart-Rogoff study said exactly what deficit hawks wanted to hear, and soon this report was being brandished all over Washington by Simpson-Bowles, Paul Ryan, and sundry other deficit scolds. High debt kills economic growth—Harvard said so! We have to cut, cut, cut![70]

Except there was a big problem—several, in fact. After three years of devastating austerity both here and abroad, graduate students at University of Massachusetts-Amherst attempting to re-create Reinhart and Rogoff's findings asked the two economists for their data set. They found that the study suffered from a simple Excel coding error that drastically changed the results when fixed. Instead of stagnating or shrinking as Reinhart-Rogoff claimed, economies with a 90 percent debt-to-GDP load grew at an average of 2.2 percent—quite a difference! Even more troubling, the data had been selectively weighted, and many examples that ran counter to the "high debt equals no growth" hypothesis had just been inexplicably left out.[71]

In April 2013, Thomas Herndon, Michael Ash, and Robert Pollin wrote a rebuttal exposing these fundamental errors in the Reinhart-Rogoff report, setting off a firestorm in the economics world. "Did an Excel coding error destroy the economies of the western world?" queried Paul Krugman of "the Excel Depression." "How much unemployment was caused by Reinhart and Rogoff's arithmetic mistake?" asked Dean Baker of the Center for Economic and Policy Research.[72]

So did Washington's deficit hawks hang their heads in shame at this news? Of course not. "I have obviously read the [Reinhart-Rogoff] report and have referenced it a number of times," said Erskine Bowles of the dynamic Simpson-Bowles duo. "What [this revelation] doesn't change is the common sense and my own personal experience in both the public and private sector that when any organization has too much debt," etc., etc. For his part, Paul Ryan had cited the "conclusive empirical evidence" of Reinhart-Rogoff as justification for his absurdly retrograde budget—as the U-Mass economists pointed out, it was the only study he cited to make his case that high debt damages growth. He did not recant, either. (Of course, back in 2000 when President Clinton had created a budget surplus, Paul Ryan used to fret that the national debt wasn't big enough—"It's too small. It's not big enough to fit all the policy we want"—so his credibility on these issues has always been only a little north of zero.)[73]

This would all be a tempest in a teapot if not for one sad fact: Reinhart-Rogoff was a favorite of the Obama administration, too. "I don't think it's too much of an exaggeration to say that everything follows from missing the call on Reinhart-Rogoff," Peter Orszag exclaimed in 2011. "I didn't realize we were in a Reinhart-Rogoff situation until 2010." After the study was exposed in April 2013, Richard Eskow of Campaign for America's Future told of a closed-door August 2010 meeting where Treasury secretary Tim Geithner argued that Social Security just had to be cut, so America could fall below the magic 90 percent debt threshold. Geithner, recalls Eskow, "was fixated on lower debt as a percentage of GDP. That's pure Reinhart/Rogoff." "Eight months after the 90 percent figure was published," Eskow sums up, "it had already become an article of faith in Washington, D.C. . . . their inaccurate paper fueled and amplified a debt panic among leaders and advisors in both parties, and helped the tide in favor of austerity."[74]

And now, sequestration and artificial spending cuts appear to be here to stay. Despite a modest increase in defense spending in the 2016 budget deal, the sequester has, in fact, become the new normal. For all intents and purposes, as David Dayen put it in the *New Republic*, it is a never-ending government shutdown. The sequester, he writes, is "already redefining the role of government, rolling back the ambitions of the past, and constraining needed investments in the future." We may have learned to live with it, but the sequester remains a serious drag on growth. As long as sequestration cuts remain in force, the economy will never fully recover.[75]

And it's all part of Barack Obama's legacy. The sequester may not be what he wanted, but it happened on his watch. He was the one willing to compromise. He signed the legislation. And he bears responsibility for the budgetary calamity we still live under.

Government Shutdown

Naturally, as deep as they were, not even the meat-ax sequester cuts were enough to satisfy the zealotry of Tea Party Republicans. With another debt ceiling deadline looming in October 2013, they threatened to take the nation over the cliff again and shut down the government unless they got their way with another round of deep spending cuts, including no funding for the Affordable Care Act and no compensating revenue from taxes.

This time, Democrats in Congress held firm. And, more surprisingly, so did President Obama, perhaps burned too often after five years in office, or perhaps—finally—taking his cue from President Bill Clinton. In 1995, facing a similar threat from House Republicans led by Speaker Newt Gingrich over cuts in Medicare, Clinton refused to budge. The federal government shut down for a total of twenty-seven days. And the whole move backfired against Republicans. In an *ABC News* poll, 46 percent of Americans blamed Newt Gingrich and House Republicans for the shutdown; only 27 percent blamed Clinton.[76]

Fearing a repeat of 1995, many Senate Republicans worked hard in

2013 to avoid a shutdown. So did Speaker John Boehner. But freshman Texas senator Ted Cruz, the Tea Party's hero, successfully lobbied
conservative House Republicans to buck Boehner. Unable to reach a
deal, Congress again shut down the federal government, this time for
sixteen days, October 1 through October 16, with severe cutbacks in
public services. Eight hundred thousand federal employees were furloughed; another 1.3 million were required to go to work with no guarantee of when they would get their next paycheck. The Grand Canyon,
the Statue of Liberty, the White House, Washington's World War II Memorial, and other iconic parks and monuments were closed. National
parks received 8 million fewer visitors in 2013, which cost neighboring
communities an estimated $414 million in lost tourist revenue.[77]

The shutdown triggered a bitter debate between House Republicans and the Senate. A bipartisan majority in the Senate endorsed a
plan to lift the debt ceiling and leave spending at the new, low sequester
levels. House Republicans, goaded on by Ted Cruz, insisted they would
accept no deal that did not include defunding Obamacare. After years
of negotiating with President Obama, they were accustomed to taking
hostages and getting rewarded for it. But this time, Senate Democrats
and Republicans rejected their demand. So did President Obama, who
vowed to prevent "one faction, of one party, in one house of Congress,
in one branch of government, [from shutting] down major parts of the
government—all because they don't like one law."[78]

Finally, on October 16, Speaker Boehner broke with his caucus and
scheduled the compromise Senate bill for a vote in the House, where
it was approved 285–144, with the help of 198 Democrats and only 87
Republicans.[79]

The government shutdown of 2013 was over, but not without dealing
a major hit to the economy. In a statement released on October 17, the
financial ratings agency Standard & Poor's estimated the shutdown had
taken "$24 billion out of the economy," or $1.5 billion a day, and "shaved
at least 0.6 percent off annualized fourth-quarter 2013 GDP growth."[80]

As in 1995, Republicans' approval ratings took a big hit, too. According to an NBC News/Wall Street Journal poll, 53 percent of Americans blamed Republicans for the shutdown, while only 31 percent

blamed Obama—an even greater margin than Bill Clinton enjoyed in 1995. Approval ratings for Congress sank to a near all-time low, at 11 percent. And only 24 percent said they had a favorable view of the Republican Party. The president's approval rating remained at 44 percent, exactly where it was before the shutdown began. And, curiously enough, the battle over funding the Affordable Care Act only increased its public approval, from 31 percent to 38 percent. (More on that law in the next chapter.) As it turned out, America didn't take kindly to the Republicans' hostage-taking—if only Obama had learned that lesson sooner.[81]

The Incredible Shrinking Deficit

Since the government shutdown of 2013, the economy has limped along in a slower recovery than what's needed while Congress, through a succession of short-term continuing resolutions, or "CRs," has kept the government sputtering along at record-low sequester rates—and while the Obama administration holds out as "Austerity Central," maintaining its primary focus on deficit reduction, not economic growth.

Meanwhile, a strange thing happened. Because of a combination of factors—some new tax revenue, a pickup in the economy, the Affordable Care Act, and, yes, spending cuts—the deficit shrank more and more until, the CBO reported in October 2015, it had reached the lowest point since 2007.[82]

At that point, on February 4, Obama dispatched Jason Furman, chairman of the Council of Economic Advisers, to meet with us reporters in the White House Briefing Room and brag about the administration's success. But the longer I listened to Furman touting success in reducing the deficit, the more I wondered why they were still on such an austerity kick. Which led to this exchange:

Press: "You said we are now at 4.1 percent of GDP with the deficit, and heading toward 2.6 percent. What is the ideal considered among economists as a percent?"

Furman: "The most important thing is that you're getting your debt down as a share of the economy, and that—that it's on a downward path says that you're fiscally sustainable. And deficits under 3 percent of GDP are generally consistent with getting your debt down."

Press: "So I guess my question is, if you're already at 4.1 percent and you're heading to 2.6 and you've got 15 million Americans out of work, why the fixation on more deficit cutting? Why not an emphasis on more stimulus or more spending to boost the economy? It seems you can afford it. You've succeeded in getting the deficit down."

Furman: "Again, if you looked at the State of the Union, the President was talking about things like more investment in infrastructure, about other fiscal policies that would help growth and help job creation. And in the past, we've always shown how you can do that while also, over the medium and long run, dealing with your deficit."[83]

Pure talking points! In other words, Furman was saying, you can have it both ways. You can have stimulus and deficit reduction at the same time. You can be both John Maynard Keynes and Milton Friedman at the same time. Except you can't.

By the way, the deficit has continued to shrink. Furman returned to the briefing room in December 2014 to report that the budget deficit for November was $56.8 billion, down 58 percent from the $135.2 billion reported one year earlier. By January 2015, President Obama could rightly brag that the deficit had dropped by two-thirds since he took office. Unfortunately, the size of the deficit was never even close to being our real economic problem during his tenure. A lower deficit may make the Simpsons and Bowleses of the world sigh in satisfaction, but it is cold comfort for all those left jobless, hungry, and desperate by years of inadequate recovery.

Ironically, Obama's obsession with deficit reduction failed in another way, too. As noted, one of the reasons President Obama shifted so dramatically from growing the economy to reducing the deficit was that Peter Orszag and others convinced him that this was one way to win over swing voters, who were turned off by too much government spending. There was zero evidence to support that premise, but this is something that so-called Serious People in Washington tend to believe, all evidence to the contrary.

Once attempted, of course, it had just the opposite effect. In February 2014, with the deficit at its lowest point in six years, a *Huffington Post* poll showed that 54 percent of Americans thought the budget deficit had actually increased since Obama took office—and blamed him for it. Only 19 percent of respondents knew it had decreased. From a political point of view, all that compromise and pain had been for nothing.[84]

Wall Street Rules

While the economy limped along at its very sluggish pace, there was another part of President Obama's response to the 2008 financial crisis that perplexed and outright infuriated many progressives. The entire collapse of the economy was triggered by reckless, if not illegal, trading of worthless securities by some of the nation's biggest financial institutions. Yet what did President Obama do to crack down on the malefactors of Wall Street? Almost nothing.

His first attempted reform of any kind, in July 2010, was to sign the Dodd-Frank Wall Street Reform and Consumer Protection Act, aka simply "Dodd-Frank." This may have been the toughest legislation reformers were able to get out of Congress, though many would argue otherwise, but it still did nothing to punish those responsible for the crash. Indeed, it left all the major players and institutions in place, thereby offering zero protection against the same calamity happening again.

In July 2013, former senator Ted Kaufman, a member of the Senate Banking Committee during his brief time serving the remainder of Vice President Joe Biden's term, was asked to assess the results of Dodd-Frank for *USA Today*. "Three years later," Kaufman concluded, "Dodd-Frank is a failure."[85]

Kaufman listed two main problems with Dodd-Frank:

1. Delay in new regulations. Rather than lay out new rules for Wall Street, the legislation left that task up to various federal agencies,

which, as a result of either bureaucratic inertia or intense pressure from Wall Street lobbyists, were in no hurry to get the job done. When Kaufman penned his article, only 155 of 398 new rules required by Dodd-Frank had been finalized. The legislation's crown jewel, the so-called Volcker Rule, designed to limit risk-taking by banks, was not finalized until December 2013, more than three years after the bill was signed into law.

2. Banks are still gambling with FDIC-insured money. Because of a giant loophole in the law, Wall Street firms can still trade in the same kind of derivatives that contributed to the crash of 2008— as long as they do so in overseas markets and not in the U.S.A. JPMorgan Chase learned that the hard way in 2012 when one of its London traders, quickly dubbed the "London Whale," lost $6.2 billion for the company and shareholders through trading in worthless securities.[86]

Despite progressives like Senators Elizabeth Warren and Bernie Sanders pointing out that Obama has actually done quite little to re-regulate financial institutions, the White House still views reform of Wall Street as one of the signature achievements of the Obama administration. On October 6, 2014, Press Secretary Josh Earnest told us reporters: "The President has been pleased with the progress that the regulators have made in implementing the law. The implementation of Wall Street— well, let me start at this place. The passage of Wall Street reform is actually going to be one of the most prominent aspects of President Obama's legacy."[87]

It's hard to see what that confidence is based on. For the most part, Wall Street firms are as little regulated as ever. Most of the banks and financial institutions that created the fiscal crisis of 2008 are still up to the same old tricks. The same CEOs are still at their posts. If anything, banks are bigger and badder and making more money than ever before. And there is no guarantee that the whole house of cards could not collapse again at any moment.

An interesting insight into Obama's unwillingness to stand up to

Wall Street is revealed in *A Fighting Chance*, a memoir published by the new Massachusetts senator Elizabeth Warren in April 2014. As a consumer activist and Harvard professor, she was the first to talk about the need for a Consumer Finance Protection Bureau, which became a key element of Dodd-Frank. And Obama hired her at the White House as an adviser on the legislation.

It was widely assumed that Obama would name Warren herself, "mother" of the CFPB, as its first chair. But in 2010, according to Warren's memoir, Obama called her into the Oval Office and informed her he dared not appoint her to that position because she made Senate Republicans and Wall Street bankers "very nervous."

A few weeks later, Warren recounts, Obama called her back in and asked her to do the setup work for the new agency—even though, again, she would never lead it. When she declined, Obama told her testily: "Elizabeth, you're jamming me." He wanted the political appearance of cracking down on Wall Street, without the actual crackdown.[88]

As weak as it had been, Dodd-Frank got even weaker in December 2014 when congressional Republicans, yet again, took the economy hostage to further their policy goals. This time, they added a rider gutting one of Dodd-Frank's major provisions in the so-called $1.1 trillion "Cromnibus" bill, hammered together—in another eleventh-hour desperation move—to fund the federal government through September 2015.

"Cromnibus" represents the worst of Washington-speak. It's the amalgam of a Continuing Resolution, or CR, to keep the government funded, plus an omnibus budget package. Under the proposed Republican amendment, reportedly written by Citibank lobbyists, taxpayers would once again be on the hook, responsible for bailing out banks for any losses suffered from gambling in derivatives—the very practice that caused the 2008 fiscal collapse.[89]

Progressives in Congress denounced the amendment as a "Wall Street give-away." Former congressman Barney Frank condemned Republicans for trying to gut the regulatory legislation he had coauthored. Opposition in both the House and Senate was led by new Massachusetts senator Elizabeth Warren, who thundered from the Senate floor:

"Who does Congress work for? Does it work for the millionaires, the billionaires, the giant companies with their armies of lobbyists and lawyers, or does it work for all the people?"[90]

In this case, apparently, Congress worked for the billionaires. And so did President Obama. Any strength of the opposition collapsed when the president announced he would sign the Cromnibus bill, with its pro–Wall Street amendment attached. He defended his decision as demonstrating his willingness to compromise—which, in fact, had never been in question. In fact, he even personally lobbied for the bill, as did Jamie Dimon, the head of JPMorgan Chase.[91]

Most shocking of all, in the wake of the 2008 recession, not one Wall Street executive has been charged with a crime, even though they knowingly peddled worthless securities to trusting investors and drove this nation into the worst fiscal crisis since the Great Depression.

In contrast, after the Savings and Loan scandal of 1990, the FBI opened up over 5,400 criminal investigations, which resulted in 1,100 prosecutions and more than 800 convictions. This time around, nobody went to jail except Bernie Madoff, who was running his own Ponzi scheme, and was not really one of the big bankers responsible for the collapse of the national economy. He made the mistake of stealing from other rich people. President Obama, meanwhile, continued to hold special meetings at the White House with the same crowd of financial CEOs who had toppled the American economy through greed and outright corruption.[92]

At first, when people started to ask whether anyone would be held responsible, we were assured that the Department of Justice was on the case. At a 2009 Finance Committee hearing, then–assistant attorney general Lanny Breuer assured senators that high-level prosecutions were being "pursued and investigated." It just takes time, he explained. "The folks who perpetrated a lot of these crimes, to the degree they were crimes, took a long time in hatching and developing them, and bringing the cases will take a long time, but they will be brought."[93]

That was then, this is now. The DOJ has successfully filed a number of civil lawsuits against financial institutions, including Bank of America, Goldman Sachs, and Citigroup—and won as much as $66 billion in fines. That, to these megabanks, is a mere pittance—just the cost of doing illegal business.[94]

However, despite widespread evidence of wrongdoing, not one criminal case has been filed against those on Wall Street most responsible for the activities that directly caused the collapse of 2008. In both Iceland and Ireland, bankers were charged, tried, convicted, and imprisoned for the same kind of criminal activities that wrecked their economies. Yet in this country—after taxpayers spent $700 billion bailing out Wall Street and saving it from total collapse—not one major Wall Street executive has been charged or gone to jail for knowingly selling worthless securities. Quite the contrary, they've been continually invited to White House meetings.[95]

JPMorgan CEO Jamie Dimon made sixteen visits to the White House during Obama's first term, meeting with Obama himself three times. He was, in fact, known as Obama's "favorite banker" until JPMorgan's embarrassing "London Whale" trading loss in 2012. And today, Dimon and his Wall Street friends are still on the job, making more money than ever, with little government oversight.[96]

"It's a gross miscarriage of justice," says Dennis Kelleher, president of the financial reform group Better Markets. "How can you have the biggest crash since 1929, causing the worst economy since the Great Depression, and not a single person at a major, politically-connected, too-big-to-fail Wall Street bank is held accountable?"[97]

Failure to act was bad enough. Attorney General Eric Holder twisted the knife when he tried to explain why. On March 6, 2013, in testimony before the Senate Finance Committee, he told Iowa senator Charles Grassley: "I am concerned that the size of some of these institutions becomes so large that it does become difficult for us to prosecute them when we are hit with indications that if you do prosecute, if you do bring a criminal charge, it will have a negative impact on the national economy, perhaps even the world economy. And I think that is a function of the fact that some of these institutions have become too large."[98]

Holder later tried to walk his comments back, but it was too late. Senator Elizabeth Warren had already tagged him—and President

Obama—for believing that Wall Street banks were not only too big to fail, they were now also "too big to jail."

The HAMP Disaster

One of the least successful aspects of President Obama's economic program was also one of the least reported-on: the administration's initiatives to deal with the home mortgage crisis.

The housing bubble was a major contributor to the 2008 recession: Millions of Americans who had been granted fantasy loans to buy homes with no money down soon found themselves "underwater" and unable to keep up with mortgage payments, while their worthless loans were being repackaged and sold as derivatives by Wall Street banks.

In 2009, to address this problem head-on, President Obama created the Home Affordable Modification Program, or HAMP, as a follow-up to the Wall Street bailout known as TARP. Launched with much fanfare, its announced goal was to help homeowners get back on their feet by being able to renegotiate terms on their home mortgage. But that's not how it worked out. In the end, HAMP made it easier for banks to squeeze money from troubled home mortgage loans, but often only made things worse for homeowners. Contrary to what HAMP promised, in other words, bankers got bailed out, homeowners did not.

By 2012, even the Treasury Department acknowledged that HAMP had fallen far short of its goal of helping 3 to 4 million homeowners avoid foreclosure. Only slightly more than five hundred thousand home loans had been renegotiated under the program, 40 percent of which Treasury expected to default anyway. Far more borrowers dropped out of the program, or were denied eligibility, than successfully achieved loan modifications. Those who did end up with a new loan, along with those who would later default, were often left with larger outstanding debt, worse credit scores, and less home equity.[99]

The problem, as reported by economics writer David Dayen in *The Guardian*, was how the program was structured. Instead of just giving struggling borrowers the cash they needed to better handle their mortgage payments, HAMP offered incentive payments to banks and their mortgage servicers to modify the loans. That left the decision on whether to accept homeowners into the program, and at what rates, entirely up to the banks—which sometimes saw more profit in kicking people out of their homes. Dayen calls it "the government program that failed homeowners."[100]

By 2014, five years after its creation, 1.3 million homeowners had benefited from modified mortgages under HAMP, but 350,000 of them defaulted again on their mortgages and were evicted from their homes. By early 2015, fewer than one million homeowners remained in the HAMP program—just a quarter of its original target—and 28 percent of all modified loans had slipped back into default, including nearly half of those loans modified in 2009, at the height of the foreclosure crisis.[101]

When confronted with such dismal results, Treasury Department officials insisted that their actual goal was not to help 4 million people stay in their homes, but only to delay foreclosures until the market could better absorb the glut of vacant homes—which, again, did nothing to help beleaguered homeowners. In other words, originally sold as a plan to help homeowners, HAMP was actually a program to help banks deal with the flood of foreclosures—and then–Treasury secretary Tim Geithner admitted as much. In his book, *Bailout: How Washington Abandoned Main Street While Rescuing Wall Street*, former TARP inspector general Neil Barofsky recounts a 2009 meeting between Geithner and Elizabeth Warren, who was then head of the Congressional Oversight Panel. When Warren pressed Geithner for what impact HAMP would have on banks, Geithner explained: "We estimate that they can handle ten million foreclosures, over time . . . this program will help foam the runway for them."[102]

This was the moment we learned that HAMP was actually designed to help banks, not homeowners. In fact, homeowners were quite beside the point. Regardless of how bad off they were, in Geithner's world, they would end up just one of 10 million foreclosures. By setting up HAMP, Treasury's goal was merely to space out the foreclosures and give banks time to earn their way back to health, mostly through the other parts of the bailout, which enabled them to earn profits.

In any case, there was no sense of urgency to help homeowners. By mid-2010, only $250 million of an earmarked $75 billion had been spent on the homeowner program. By 2013, just $3 billion. As part of President Obama's plan to help homeowners recover from losses suffered in the crash of 2008, HAMP was a colossal failure. Which is probably why he never talks about it.[103]

As for bringing banks to justice for widespread mortgage and foreclosure fraud—manifestly criminal behavior which included forging documents and titles to more easily evict Americans from their homes—Obama and his advisers opted for another pittance of a settlement. Once again, nobody went to jail, and the bad behavior continued.

The Bottom Line

By law, it seems, every article on the economy must end with the phrase "bottom line." So here goes.

Bottom line: President Obama's record on the economy is a series of missed opportunities.

Yes, he inherited the worst financial crisis since 1929, but he made the mistake of hiring a team of Wall Street insiders who could not be counted on to solve it, and his ensuing economic record is a string of serious mistakes and costly compromises.

Yes, he saved the country from a second Great Depression, but the stimulus, his initial response, was far too timid and far less than what the situation demanded, or what he could have achieved at the time. He fell short, in other words, by not reaching high enough.

Yes, he tried to bring leaders of both parties together, but he ended up swallowing the Republican Kool-Aid, buying into voodoo economics, and accepting Republican claims that, in light of our economic problems, our number-one priority should be deficit reduction, not job creation.

Yes, he was always willing to compromise, but that's the problem. He was always willing to compromise, even when the other side was not, and he therefore wasted too much time trying to get them to make a deal and settled for many bad ones. In the end, there was, sadly, little

Obama did not compromise on, including extending the Bush tax cuts and even supporting cuts in Social Security and Medicare, ignoring his campaign promises not to.

Yes, the economy has recovered some from the crash of 2008, but only very slowly and unsteadily. Seven years later, some economists still say we will never fully recover. There are some positive signs: The unemployment rate continues to drop; more than 13 million new private-sector jobs have been created since October 2010; new housing starts are up; the Dow and the S&P averages have soared to record highs, more than doubling under President Obama. Yet 8 million Americans are still out of work; millions more are underemployed in part-time work, but would prefer to work full-time; except for top white-collar workers, wages for those lucky enough to have a job remain stagnant; and the federal government is still operating under strict sequester limits that cripple the economy, prevent many government agencies from doing their jobs, endanger our military readiness, and have put hundreds of thousands of Americans out of a job.[104]

For a while, it was convenient for President Obama to blame George W. Bush for our economic problems. But that no longer works. While it was Bush who put us in the hole, it's Obama who's been too slow in bringing us out of it. And the American people sense that. In an October 2014 CNBC survey, only 24 percent of Americans said they are extremely or quite confident in President Obama's economic leadership. Forty-four percent said they had zero confidence in Obama on the economy. And, in that supposed fifth straight year of recovery, only 18 percent saw the economy as excellent or good.[105]

Perhaps the most devastating indictment of Barack Obama's economic stewardship is that income inequality—which he once called "the defining challenge of our time"—has only grown worse during his time in office.

In July 2014, MSNBC contributor Timothy Noah reported on the findings of the nonpartisan Tax Policy Institute on the widening income gap: "The top one percent gobbled up 22.46% of the nation's collective income in 2012, the last year for which we have data. The comparable figure for 2009 was 18.12%."[106]

Noah also noted another measure of the rise in income inequality, known as the "Gini Index." He explains: "The Gini measures equality of distribution on a scale of zero to one. Zero would mean everybody received the identical income; one would mean a single person received all the income, leaving nothing for anybody else. For U.S. households, the Gini was 0.477 in 2012. In 2009, it was 0.468. That's a significant increase." In layman's terms, under Obama, the rich have been getting ever richer in comparison to everybody else.[107]

No less a figure than Federal Reserve chair Janet Yellen has joined the chorus of alarm over income inequality. In an October 2014 speech at the Federal Reserve of Boston, she revealed that the gap between the very wealthy and everybody else had widened to the greatest point since the nineteenth century, the days of John D. Rockefeller. She told the Boston bankers: "By some estimates, income and wealth inequality are near their highest levels in the past hundred years, much higher than the average during that time span and probably higher than for much of American history before then."[108]

Yellen also pointed to data compiled by the Fed showing that the bottom half of homeowners by wealth lost more than 60 percent of their home values between 2007 and 2013, while the wealthiest 5 percent lost only 20 percent of their home equity.[109]

That point was underscored in May 2015, when New York mayor Bill de Blasio, Senator Elizabeth Warren, and Nobel Prize–winning economist Joseph Stiglitz unveiled a National Progressive Agenda at the National Press Club. "Why are we all so focused on inequality all of a sudden?" Stiglitz asked. "Part of the answer is it's gotten so much worse." He pointed out that 90 percent of all gains in the three years after 2009 went to the richest Americans and that the minimum wage, when adjusted for inflation, had fallen to about where it was forty-five years ago.[110]

The facts don't lie. Under Obama's presidency, income gains have been concentrated at the very top, and are practically nonexistent for those Americans in the middle and at the bottom. That may not be entirely Obama's fault, there are many economic factors involved, but he has done little to slow down or reverse the trend.

Again that bottom line: On the budget and economy, Barack Obama's performance fell far short of what was expected from the great liberal hope of 2008. And former Treasury secretary Tim Geithner has his own theory on why that was so.

In *Stress Test*, his memoir of his days in the Obama administration, Geithner writes: "Sometimes I thought he wore his frustration too openly. He harbored the overly optimistic belief that since his motives and values were good, since his team was thoughtful and well-intentioned, we deserved to be perceived that way."[111]

Geithner's observation might be a reflection of the entire Obama presidency. But it clearly rings true here. On the economy, good intentions were not enough. Bold leadership was needed. But Barack Obama did not provide it. And the economy still suffers.

TWO

Health Care

The legislative history of the Obama administration has already been written. For better or for worse, Barack Obama's domestic record will be primarily remembered for one signature achievement: the Affordable Care Act, or Obamacare.

Whether it's women's rights, workers' rights, caring for the poor, or protecting the environment, progressives march under a lot of different banners. But if there's one cause that has united all progressives under the same standard for the last hundred years, it's universal health care. Health care, we progressives believe, is a right, not a privilege—and should be available to all Americans by birthright.

Over those hundred years, both Republican and Democratic presidents, with varying degrees of intensity—Teddy Roosevelt was the first; Harry Truman and Bill Clinton went all out; George W. Bush hardly mentioned it—had embraced the goal of making sure that all Americans are protected by health insurance.

And after many failed attempts, it looked in 2008 as if Barack Obama would finally be the president to achieve universal health care. He made it one of the central issues of his campaign. He embraced it as his first and most important presidential initiative, after securing passage of the stimulus to deal with the immediate fiscal crisis. He made it the centerpiece of his first term in office.

And many would argue he delivered with the Affordable Care Act. But let's be honest: What he delivered was far from the dream of universal health care liberals had long fought for.

I was there with a horde of White House reporters on March 23,

2010, when Obama signed the bill into law. For an hour, it felt as if the stately East Room had become a high-school gym cheering on the home team. About 150 Democratic members of Congress and administration officials were giddy with excitement. Applause broke out every time somebody connected with the legislation walked into the room.

Vice President Joe Biden pumped up the crowd even more with his effusive introduction of Obama, repeating the phrase over and over: "This is a historic day." To members of Congress, he said: "History is made when you all assembled here today take charge to change the lives of tens of millions of Americans. You've made history." To President Obama, he gushed: "You've done what generations of not just ordinary, but great men and women, have attempted to do." And again: "Mr. President, you are literally about to make history." Then, as the crowd roared, Biden capped it off with perhaps the most widely heard "off-the-mike" comment in history, telling Obama: "This is a big fucking deal!"[1]

For his part, Obama didn't hesitate to wrap himself in the mantle of historic achievement. His first sentence confirmed that he, too, believed that this was a big fucking deal: "Today, after almost a century of trying; today, after over a year of debate; today, after all the votes have been tallied—health insurance reform becomes law in the United States of America. Today!"[2]

Standing behind the president as he signed the bill were leaders of Congress who'd been fighting for health-care reform for years: Senators Tom Harkin, Dick Durbin, Harry Reid, and former senator Chris Dodd; and House leaders Nancy Pelosi, Steny Hoyer, James Clyburn, and Sandy Levin. Also alongside the president, most fittingly, were Vicki Kennedy and Patrick Kennedy, widow and son of Senator Ted Kennedy, who'd carried the torch of universal health care for so long.

But it finally happened on Barack Obama's watch. With the Affordable Care Act, he accomplished more than any other president on health care since Medicare and Medicaid were created under Lyndon Johnson. And the ACA's already done a lot of good: by reining in the worst of insurance company abuses, expanding the number of Americans insured—either under Obamacare or under expanded Medicaid—and bringing down the costs of health care.

That's the good news. But notice that Obama said "health *insurance* reform" and not "health *care* reform." The bad news is that Obamacare remains a flawed plan and a boondoggle for private insurance companies. And with 9 percent of the population still uninsured as of August 2015, the ACA still falls short of the goal of universal health care, long fought for by progressives.[3]

Even with all the improvements it's made, the fact is that the Affordable Care Act could have been so much better—more inclusive and comprehensive, less bureaucratic and loophole-ridden. It could have resulted in far fewer headaches and much more affordable coverage, with even greater savings for the economy at large. But, once again, as we saw with the economy in the last chapter, Obama was willing to settle for half a loaf on health care—before even fighting for a full loaf. He aimed low, and ended lower.

Single-Payer Health Care

For liberals, the goal was never just universal health care (although that, too, would have been closer to the mark than what we ended up with under Obamacare). The goal was "single-payer health care," where the government pays doctors and hospitals directly for medical care, and the insurance companies currently profiting from people's misery as middlemen are left out of the picture entirely.

It's not "socialized medicine" like they have in the U.K., no matter how many times conservatives call it that. In the U.K., the government actually owns the hospitals, and doctors and nurses are government employees. In the single-payer plan, the government just pays the bills. Basically, it's an expansion of Medicare—from its current base of seniors only to the general population, with no age restrictions. Call it "Medicare for Everybody."

Progressives were always in favor of a single-payer plan. And, for a while, so was Barack Obama. Indeed, for a while, single-payer proponents were encouraged by a video of remarks made by then–state senator Obama back in June 2003, when he was just gearing up to run for the U.S. Senate. He told an AFL-CIO conference on civil, women's, and human rights: "I happen to be a proponent of a single-payer universal health care program. I see no reason why the United States of America, the wealthiest country in the history of the world, spending 14 percent of its gross national product on health care, cannot provide basic health insurance to everybody . . . everybody in, nobody out. A single-payer health care plan, a universal health care plan. That's what I'd like to see."[4]

It wasn't long, however, before Obama changed his tune. Ever the pragmatist, he came to believe that rounding up enough votes in Congress for a full-bore single-payer system would be impossible. In February 2004, after interviewing all Illinois candidates for the U.S. Senate, the Associated Press reported: "Obama says he supports the idea of universal health care but does not think a single-payer government system is feasible." Instead, he now backed some kind of public/private hybrid.[5]

Three years later, as he began his campaign for president, the *Chicago Tribune* once again noted that Obama had fallen off the single-payer bandwagon: "Obama has pledged that, if elected, all Americans would have health-care coverage by the end of this first term. He has said he is reluctant to switch to a 'single-payer' national health insurance system because of the difficulty in making a quick transition from the employer-based private system."[6]

And, once elected, Obama stuck with his new position against single-payer. On July 1, 2009, just as health-care reform legislation started moving in the House and Senate, President Obama cautioned a group of Democrats in Annandale, Virginia: "For us to transition completely from an employer-based system of private insurance to a single-payer system could be hugely disruptive, and my attitude has been that we should be able to find a way to create a uniquely American solution to this problem that controls costs but preserves the innovation that is introduced in part with a free-market system."[7]

Declaring any discussion of "single-payer" off the table was Obama's first mistake on health care. It was an instant replay of his mistake on the stimulus. Where the economy needed some $1.5 trillion in stimulus spending, he made his opening bid $787 billion—and could only go down from there. He settled for a half-measure before even fighting for what was needed. Same with health care. He started by rejecting the best possible way to achieve universal health care—and thereby guaranteed that, whatever final product we ended up with, we'd have to play catch-up.

Obama's reasoning for abandoning single-payer had three main flaws. First, he argued it would have been difficult, if not impossible, to round up enough votes in Congress to pass single-payer legislation, and probably impossible to find the sixty votes necessary to overcome a filibuster in the Senate. Wrong! Difficult, perhaps, but not necessarily impossible. The fact is, as has been proven true on many occasions, you never know how many votes you're going to get until you try—especially when the vote is to expand an already enormously popular program like Medicare. And, besides, the ACA was amended in the Senate in order to be considered under rules of reconciliation, where only fifty-one votes were needed. In the end, there was no need to fear the filibuster, but Obama had already thrown single-payer out the window.

Second, by removing the single-payer option from consideration, Obama guaranteed that whatever health-care plan was finally adopted by Congress would tilt heavily toward private insurance companies. And that's exactly what happened. His version of universal health care became a mandate for every American to purchase insurance from a private insurance company—subject, with few exceptions, to their rates and conditions—or else pay a penalty! No other industry has ever enjoyed that kind of mandate: government forcing you to buy their product. And by building his entire plan around private insurance, Obama also institutionalized many of the problems with coverage already inherent in the existing system.

Third, Obama summarily turned his back on what had been proven to be, in country after country—England, Canada, Sweden, France, Norway, the Netherlands—the best way of containing costs and delivering quality health care at the same time. So what if some people call it "socialized medicine"? It still works, and those same people call the Affordable Care Act "socialized medicine," anyway. Again, as many progressives pointed out at the time, Obama should have stuck with single-payer and simply called it Medicare Part E—"Medicare for Everybody"—something everybody was familiar with and could readily understand.

For supporters of the single-payer system, there was only one bright spot in the Affordable Care Act. Congressmen John Conyers and Dennis Kucinich managed to shoehorn into the final version of the bill an amendment allowing individual states, if they so chose, to experiment with a single-payer plan. Taking advantage of that opening, state legislators in nine states—California, Hawaii, Illinois, Massachusetts, Minnesota, Montana, Oregon, Pennsylvania, and Vermont—introduced single-payer legislation. In every state but one, after an onslaught of lobbying by private hospitals and the insurance industry, the bills failed to pass the legislature or were vetoed by the governor. Vermont was the sole exception.[8]

Under legislation signed into law by Governor Peter Shumlin in May 2011, Vermont began moving forward to establish by 2017 what they called "Green Mountain Care"—a single-payer plan that would have bypassed insurance companies and set up a government-managed insurance system to collect all health-care fees and pay out all health-care costs.

For a while, health-care reformers held out hope that Vermont would prove to be the national pacesetter for single-payer. As its plan kicked in and proved successful, they figured, other states would take notice and pass their own single-payer plan—until, state by state, America had built an effective, nationwide single-payer system. But that wishful thinking imploded three years later, in December 2014, when Governor Shumlin—unable to devise a financing plan that did not require a big hike in taxes—suddenly shelved plans for "Green Mountain Care."

It was still the right thing to do, he told reporters, but Vermont just couldn't afford it at that time: "Pushing for single payer health care when the time isn't right and it might hurt our economy would not be good for Vermont and it would not be good for true health care reform. It could set back for years all of our hard work toward the important goal of universal, publicly-financed health care for all."[9]

Progressives like me were disappointed with Shumlin. And now, unfortunately, with Vermont out of the picture, any possibility of a statewide single-payer plan seems more remote than ever. To put in place what all evidence shows is the cheapest and easiest-to-use health-care plan available will require federal leadership to get past all the entrenched interests profiting mightily from the current, broken system. And any possibility of a national and truly universal plan, thanks to President Obama, seems dead for at least a generation.

A Right-Wing Idea

Having denied Democrats what they most wanted in health-care reform—a single-payer system—Obama decided to give Republicans what they most wanted in health-care reform, instead: a market-driven, private-sector solution. His naïve political strategy, again, was that if only he played nice with Republicans, they would play nice with him. Which proved to be as wrong in health care as it was in budget negotiations.

To that end, Obama turned to the old files of the Heritage Foundation, Washington's leading conservative think tank, and lifted directly from them a proposal they'd cobbled together during the Clinton administration as an alternative to what conservatives dubbed "Hillary-care." Under the Heritage plan, every American would be protected by health insurance—but only because the government would force all those who did not receive coverage from their employer to buy it from a private insurance company or pay a stiff fine. This requirement to buy insurance became known as the "individual mandate." Under the plan, government subsidies would also be available to help low-income and middle-class Americans who could not afford the cost of insurance on their own obtain coverage.[10]

For Obama, the Heritage proposal had one other advantage: It had already been tried, with reasonable success, by Republican governor Mitt Romney of Massachusetts. In fact, when he signed the new legislation in April 2006, Romney bragged to reporters that he had stolen the health-care issue from Democrats: "Issues which have long been the province of the Democratic Party to claim as their own will increasingly move to the Republican side of the aisle."[11]

In theory, this was a brilliant, Machiavellian move for Obama. By embracing the health-care plan crafted by the prestigious Heritage Foundation and already enacted by Governor Mitt Romney, Obama had settled on a proposal that Democrats would now have to get behind, because he had adopted it as his own. But Republicans would have to get behind it, too, because it had originally been theirs. Granted, it may not have been the best plan out there by any means, but Obama felt this course was the wisest one in terms of political expediency.

Of course, that theory backfired. Democrats never liked the plan, because it relied too much on private insurance companies. And Republicans were quick to disown the plan, once Obama put his stamp of approval on it.

Public Option

With single-payer off the table and a Republican plan adopted in its place, Obama had to find some way to keep progressives on board. So, borrowing an idea from Yale professor Jacob Hacker, he settled on the idea of a public plan option.[12]

Don't like dealing with private insurance companies? You don't have to. You have another choice: enrolling in a "public insurance option," or simply "public option," a government-run health-insurance agency that would compete with other, private health-insurance companies within the United States. It would be, for all practical purposes, an expanded form of Medicare, available to consumers of all ages. Again, as already noted, it would have been best from the start if Obama had just called it "Medicare for Everybody."

Obama not only endorsed the public option plan, he championed it in health-care rallies across the country, forcefully making the argument that a public option was an essential part of any health-care legislation and would accomplish two goals: provide competition in the marketplace and put pressure on insurance companies to cut costs and keep rates low. Health-care staffers at the White House preached the same message. And his advocacy campaign worked. Consumer organizations and labor unions rallied to the cause. Polls showed that 60 percent of Americans supported the public option, while only one-third of voters supported the overall health-care legislation. For progressives, in fact, the public option soon became the number-one reason for supporting the Affordable Care Act—which, otherwise, they weren't too happy with.[13]

And then, in another show of weakness and confusion over health care, as quickly as Obama had embraced the public option, he suddenly dropped it. Just like that. With no explanation or excuse. One day it was "key," the next day it was gone. Obama raised the white flag and stopped insisting the public option was an essential part of any plan, even after the House of Representatives, under Speaker Pelosi, passed a version of the health-care law including it.[14]

At first, liberals were confused. The White House only shrugged, explaining they had to drop the public option because they couldn't round up sixty votes for it in the Senate. To which liberals responded: You'll never get sixty votes for anything if you don't fight for it! And, besides, as already noted, the final bill was amended through reconciliation anyway, which required only fifty-one votes, not sixty. "This has been a complete and utter failure of White House leadership," wrote the *Washington Post*'s Ezra Klein of Obama's mercurial public option stance. "The White House has stayed quiet—and confusing . . . the worst of all worlds."[15]

But progressive confusion soon turned to anger when we learned what apparently caused President Obama's sudden change of heart. It was former Senate majority leader Tom Daschle, a key adviser on Obamacare, whom President Obama had originally wanted to name as secretary of Health and Human Services, who ultimately spilled the beans.

In an interview with Igor Volsky at *Think Progress*, Daschle revealed that the public plan option was dropped, not because it lacked support in Congress, but because it was part of a backroom deal Obama made with hospital lobbyists, whereby hospitals would agree to accept $155 billion in payment reductions over ten years, in return for which the Senate legislation would aim to cover at least 94 percent of Americans and Obama would jettison the public option, because it would have reimbursed hospitals at a lower rate than private insurance companies. In other words, in one of the first tests of his new presidency, Obama caved in to the very special interests whose undue influence in Washington he had pledged to end.[16]

As Daschle explained it to Volsky, "It was taken off the table as a result of the understanding that people had with the hospital association, with the insurance industry (AHIP), and others. . . . The premise was you had to have the stakeholders in the room and at the table. . . . They wanted to keep those stakeholders in the room and this was the price some thought they had to pay."[17]

What's most troubling is that, according to Daschle, the whole deal to dump the public option was struck in July 2009, at the very same time the White House was vigorously denying rumors it was backing away from the provision. "Nothing has changed," insisted Linda Douglass, then communications director for the White House Office of Health Reform, in August. "The president has always said that what is essential is that health insurance reform must lower costs, ensure that there are affordable options for all Americans, and it must increase choice and competition in the health insurance market. He believes the public option is the best way to achieve those goals."[18]

Douglass was absolutely right. That's what the president had always said. But, apparently, he changed his mind.

Obama's decision to jettison the public option, on top of rejecting single-payer, represented not only a cowardly sellout to special interests. It was also a classic case of mismanagement. He and his team bungled the messaging from the start. There was no need to rev up public support for something brand-new called the "public option." Since 1965, Americans have had a public option. It's called Medicare. Americans know it, they like it, they can't wait to sign up for it. A plan to expand Medicare in order to include more Americans, and allow voluntary buy-ins to the program, would have been far more popular and more readily understood than the wonkily named "public option."

After word of Obama's 180-degree change of direction became public, the White House redoubled their insistence that President Obama didn't want to abandon the public option, but he had no choice because of the lack of support in Congress. He was forced into dropping the public option, they argued, by hardliners in the Senate like Joe Lieberman. To which plain-speaking Senator Russ Feingold and others quickly cried bullshit. The president wasn't forced into anything, they countered. He got exactly what he wanted. "This bill appears to be legislation that the president wanted in the first place, so I don't think focusing it on Lieberman really hits the truth," Feingold told reporters. "I think they could have been higher. I certainly think a stronger bill would have been better in every respect."[19]

Big Pharma

But, wait! That wasn't the only sweetheart deal that Obama made with K Street lobbyists. He also pulled the rug out from under progressives on prescription drug prices.

For decades, as part of their demand for universal health care, liberals had been calling for an end to the stranglehold that pharmaceutical companies hold over the price of drugs in this country. Americans have been forced to pay double what Canadians pay for the same brand-name drugs. By law, the federal government—by far the largest purchaser of prescription drugs—cannot even negotiate with drug companies for discount, wholesale prices for patients on Medicare or Medicaid.

Lower prices for prescription drugs were a necessary component of any progressive health-care legislation, and would have been included in the Affordable Care Act—if Obama had not cut a deal with Big Pharma.

As the *Huffington Post* reported in August 2009: "In return for $80 billion in projected cuts—and $150 million in supportive television ads—Obama has apparently sworn to protect the pharmaceutical industry from congressional efforts to, among other things, let the government use its bargaining power to lower prescription drug costs."[20]

What a difference a year makes. President Barack Obama made that dubious deal with Billy Tauzin, former congressman from Louisiana, then serving as CEO of the Pharmaceutical Researchers and Manufacturers of America, or PhRMA, and chief lobbyist for the pharmaceutical industry—the same man Barack Obama had once personally excoriated as the epitome of everything that's wrong with Washington.

Just one year earlier, in April 2008, the Obama presidential primary campaign released this ad:

"The pharmaceutical industry wrote into the prescription drug plan that Medicare could not negotiate with drug companies. And you know that the chairman of the committee, who pushed the law through, went to work for the pharmaceutical industry making 2 million dollars a year. Imagine that. That's an example of the same old game playing in Washington. You know, I don't want to learn how to play the game better. I want to put an end to the game playing."[21]

Later, that pledge to take on the pharmaceutical industry and end its stranglehold on drug pricing became one of the central planks of the Obama/Biden campaign. Here's the language of their official campaign document:

"Allow Medicare to negotiate for cheaper drug prices. The 2003 Medicare Prescription Drug Improvement and Modernization Act bans the government from negotiating down the prices of prescription drugs, even though the Department of Veterans Affairs' negotiation of prescription drug prices with drug companies has garnered significant savings for taxpayers. Barack Obama and Joe Biden will repeal the ban on direct negotiation with drug companies and use the resulting savings, which could be as high as $310 billion, to further invest in improving health care coverage and quality."[22]

Now that promise—to challenge the long-held supremacy of the big drug companies and save taxpayers money—was bold enough in itself. But Obama didn't stop there. In a campaign appearance in Parma, Ohio, on March 4, 2008, he vowed to conduct his negotiations with pharmaceutical lobbyists on national television, so everybody could watch the give-and-take.

"But here's the thing. We're going to do all these negotiations on C-SPAN.

"The American people will be able to watch these negotiations, so if they start seeing a member of Congress who is carrying the water for the drug companies instead of for their constituents, and says 'Oh, you know. We can't negotiate for the cheapest available price on drugs because the drug companies need these profits to invest in research and development,' I'll say 'OK, let me bring my health care expert in here.' And on TV, we'll ask my health care expert, 'What do you think about what the drug companies are saying?'"[23]

"Anyway, you get my point. Open this. Transparency. You will hold me accountable, you will hold Congress accountable. That's how we'll get health care reform passed."[24]

Sounds good. Sounds great, in fact. Except that's not at all how it happened. On July 7, 2009, before he brought a final health-care reform bill to Congress, and without even testing to see if he could round up enough votes in Congress to end the ban on negotiating lower drug prices, Obama conducted his negotiations with Billy Tauzin and the pharmaceutical companies behind closed doors at the White House—and, once again, gave away the store. The White House agreed to oppose any congressional efforts to use the government's leverage to bargain for lower drug prices or import drugs from Canada. In return, as reported by the *Huffington Post*, Pharma agreed to cut costs by $80 billion and pony up $150 million for television ads supporting the Affordable Care Act.[25]

Nobody was more blindsided by this deal than then-Speaker Nancy Pelosi, longtime champion of lower drug pricing, who broke with Obama on the issue, vowing she was not bound by any deal she was not a party to. Senators Sherrod Brown and Byron Dorgan led opposition in the Senate. But, in the end, Obama carried the day, and his oft-made campaign promise of cracking down on the pharmaceutical industry never made it into the final legislation.[26]

Stand up to the drug industry and conduct all negotiations out in the open? That was then, and this was now. Within just a few months of taking office, Obama had not only learned how to play the Washington insider game, he played it to benefit Big PhRMA—and hurt American consumers.

The Revolving Door

If there were any doubt that a backroom deal with PhRMA was in the works from the very beginning, consider the strange case of Elizabeth Fowler and the revolving door.

Revolving doors are nothing new to Washington, of course. They're spinning wildly everywhere you look, especially in federal buildings. Senators or representatives leave office and go to work for the very interests they used to oversee as members of Congress, pushing, or even opposing, the very legislation they wrote in their previous jobs. Case in point: Billy Tauzin. The door spins the other way, too. Former lobbyists are hired to write legislation favoring the same special interests they used to represent on Capitol Hill.

And that's where Elizabeth Fowler comes in. The legislation that eventually became known as "Obamacare" originated in the Senate Finance Committee under Chairman Max Baucus. It was Baucus, a low-key, conservative Democrat and consummate dealmaker, who steered it through the Senate. But, as Baucus himself freely admitted, its architect—the person who wrote the bill—was Fowler.[27]

Curiously enough, and so illustrative of the way Washington works, Fowler started out as a Senate staffer, working for Senator Baucus. She left the Senate to join WellPoint, the nation's largest health-insurance provider, where she eventually served two years as vice president for public policy and external affairs—before she returned to the Senate, charged with writing the new health-care legislation. And—wouldn't you know it?—the person she replaced as chief health counsel in Baucus's office, Michelle Easton, was already working as a lobbyist for WellPoint in the law firm of Tarplin, Downs, and Young. How cozy.[28]

It was bad enough that the Senate hired a former health-insurance executive to craft legislation only health-insurance providers could love: requiring everyone to buy private insurance, with no public option available. But, once the bill passed, the White House hired Fowler to oversee implementation of the Affordable Care Act. Despite complaints from public-interest groups about an obvious conflict of interest, she became special assistant to the president for health-care and economic policy at the National Economic Council: the top person at the White House for health care. Obama had put the fox in charge of the henhouse.

Then, in 2012, Fowler took another spin through the revolving door, returning to—where else?—the pharmaceutical industry, as a senior executive in Johnson & Johnson's government affairs and policy group. Johnson & Johnson's a big-time member of PhRMA, which, as we have seen, strongly supported passage of Obamacare and, through the deal Billy Tauzin cooked up with Obama, ended up one of the major beneficiaries of the bill drafted by Fowler.[29]

Elizabeth Fowler's insider back-and-forth dance from the health-care industry to the halls of power represents all that's wrong with Washington: the closed-door, special-interest, pay-to-play game that Obama explicitly vowed to transform. Instead, he practiced and perpetuated it.

The Bill at Last

In one sense, given the partisan gridlock in Washington, it's surprising Congress was able to pass any health-care legislation at all. It certainly wasn't easy, not just because of the hostility between Democrats and Republicans but also because of the tension between House Democrats and Senate Democrats, and between both of them and the White House.

Henry Waxman, chairman of the House Committee on Oversight and Government Reform, accused Senate Finance chair Max Baucus of dragging his feet and spending too much time trying to make a deal with Republicans. Both Baucus and Waxman complained that the White House kept undercutting them by making its own deals.[30]

Still, the health-care train ground slowly forward in Congress, thanks mostly to the determination of Speaker Nancy Pelosi to get a bill passed. But then, on January 19, 2010, the whole exercise came close to collapsing when Republican Scott Brown was elected to fill the seat vacated by the death of Massachusetts senator Teddy Kennedy, longtime undisputed champion of universal health care. While Kennedy was still alive, even some Republicans were willing to compromise on health-care legislation, out of respect and friendship for him. With his death, all bets were off. Democratic congressmen Barney Frank and Anthony Weiner even told MSNBC that health care was dead. And, at the White House, as first reported by Jonathan Cohn in the *New Republic*, Chief of Staff Rahm Emanuel advised Obama to dump the Affordable Care Act and settle for a smaller bill that protected children only.[31]

More than any other factor, Cohn adds, it was the iron will of Speaker Nancy Pelosi that saved the day. Pissed at having spent so much time rounding up votes for a comprehensive bill only to be told, after moving heaven and earth, to settle for less, she raised hell with Obama and, with support from Senate Democratic Leader Harry Reid, convinced him not to throw in the towel. She then pushed her caucus to grit their teeth and sign on to the more limited Senate version of the bill, along with a package of amendments that was passed on the Senate side through reconciliation. That we got any health-care reform at all is a testament to her leadership and refusal to give up.[32]

In the end, the Affordable Care Act pleased few. To conservatives, it represented the textbook case of big government run amok, the twenty-first-century equivalent of "socialized medicine." To liberals, it was a sellout, a patched compromise that came nowhere close to the goal of universal health care. In a word, it was a missed opportunity.

To be fair, Obamacare is a definite improvement over the days when the coverage, cost, and availability of health insurance were controlled entirely by private insurance companies. It extends coverage beyond the 60 percent of Americans lucky enough to have health insurance through their jobs. It eliminates some practices that progressives had long railed against, like denying coverage because of a pre-existing condition. And some experts predict that, simply by pooling millions of people together in exchanges and expanding coverage under Medicaid and Medicare, Obamacare itself will create an organized constituency for additional reform: The more people in the system, the more people who will want to be in the system; the more on Medicare or Medicaid, the more who will want to join; the more people covered, the greater the movement toward single-payer. Which, of course, may all be wishful thinking.

I'll now turn the floor over to Connecticut congresswoman Rosa DeLauro to tell us what's right about the Affordable Care Act. In September 2013, she gave one of many speeches trumpeting the "Benefits of Obamacare." In her words:

- Because of the Affordable Care Act, men, women, and children can no longer be denied coverage because of a pre-existing condition.
- Women's health is now on an equal footing. Women are no longer charged more than men for the same coverage.
- Young people all across the country can now stay on their parents' plans until age 26, and seniors are getting much-needed help in the prescription drug "donut hole."
- Pediatric and maternity care are now covered. And Americans can now get access to key preventive health services, like cancer and STD screenings and contraception, with no out-of-pocket costs.
- Individuals, families, and small businesses are able to take advantage of federal subsidies to help pay for their coverage.
- Consumers shopping for a family plan now benefit from unprecedented transparency about what is and is not covered by plans.
- In sum, the Affordable Care Act will help save lives, reduce health care costs, and help families attain the quality of life they deserve.[33]

And the ACA has already made a positive difference in the lives of millions of Americans. Often lost in the debate over Obamacare is the fact that, in its first year, over 8 million people who never before had health insurance for themselves or their families signed up for plans on either the federal or state exchanges and paid their premiums—and millions of them now renewed their plan. They're in. They're covered.

On March 19, 2015, David Blumenthal, president of the Commonwealth Fund, testified before the Senate Finance Committee on the status of the Affordable Care Act, five years after it became law. As of that date, according to the Commonwealth Fund, "more than 25 million people are estimated to have health insurance under the provisions of the ACA. About 11.7 million have selected a plan through the insurance marketplaces, 8.8 million through the federal website healthcare.gov and 2.8 million through state-based marketplaces. An additional 10.8 million have enrolled in Medicaid or the Children's Health Insurance Program, or CHIP. Finally, nearly 3 million more young adults are covered under their parent's plan compared to 2010."[34]

Blumenthal also outlined the ACA's broader impact: "As a result, the number of uninsured adults has fallen. This week, the U.S. Department of Health and Human Services reported that 16.4 million previously uninsured people had gained coverage since the law passed in 2010. Similar gains in coverage have been documented in a number of government and private-sector surveys. Furthermore, groups that historically have been most likely to lack insurance—young men and women, and adults with low or moderate incomes—have experienced among the greatest gains in coverage. These gains have occurred across racial and ethnic groups."[35]

Unfortunately, Republican governors in twenty-one states, taking advantage of a Supreme Court ruling, have refused to accept the expansion of Medicaid—purely out of political spite.[36]

So, you can't deny that Obamacare has done a lot of good. But it's still a half-baked measure that falls far short both of what is needed and of what was politically possible. Its main provision is to force people to buy health insurance from a private insurer if they're not already insured by their employer. That is certainly not a progressive idea. In fact, government forcing people to buy a product from a private company is not even a good *conservative* idea.

Here, in brief, is what's wrong with the Affordable Care Act:

- It's no single-payer plan, which has proven in many countries to be the best way to deliver universal quality health care and lower costs.

- It does not achieve the goal of "universal health care." It does not cover everybody. For years to come, it will leave some 30 million Americans, the vast majority between the ages of eighteen and forty-four, without health insurance, either because they can't afford it or because they choose not to buy it.[37]
- It offers no public option, no alternative to buying insurance from private insurance companies.
- It is therefore a huge bonanza for private insurance companies, forcing millions of Americans to buy their product—with little competition and no price controls.
- It leaves those who do purchase health insurance vulnerable to annual increases in premiums by their insurance carrier.
- It does not allow the federal government to negotiate with pharmaceutical companies for discount prices for prescription drugs, nor allow consumers to purchase drugs cheaper in Canada.
- Policyholders have to renew their insurance policy every year, with no guarantee that their existing plan will still be available, that premiums won't go up astronomically, or that the federal subsidies they now enjoy will still be available.

Writing in the *New York Times* on the day before the plan took full effect on January 1, 2014, liberal filmmaker Michael Moore, whose documentary *Sicko* helped build the constituency for universal health care, confessed: "Let me begin with an admission: Obamacare is awful." Yes, it's the closest we have come to universal health care, Moore acknowledged, but it was still "awful." Its problems, he said, stemmed from one fatal flaw: "The Affordable Care Act is a pro-insurance-industry plan implemented by a president who knew in his heart that a single-payer, Medicare-for-all model was the true way to go."[38]

Website Chaos

As imperfect as the ACA is, we all at least expected the president's team to do their best in launching it. But that didn't work out, either.

Over three years, ACA benefits slowly went into effect, but the un-
veiling of the centerpiece of the plan—the new health-insurance exchanges designed to bring down costs and give Americans access to
more, better plans—was delayed. That gave Republicans two election
cycles, 2010 and 2012, to blabber on about "Big Government Social-
ism," without anyone having the chance to try the new system out.

At last, and with great fanfare, the exchanges were finally launched
on October 1, 2013. The website was open for business. People were
urged to sign up. President Obama assured consumers that buying
health insurance on HealthCare.gov would be as easy as buying airline
tickets on Kayak. And then, as quickly as it opened, in a monumental
embarrassment, the whole system collapsed. And remained shut down
for two months.

The Centers for Medicare and Medicaid Services, or CMS, a divi-
sion of the Health and Human Services Agency, had spent three and a
half years and $300 million creating the Obamacare website. It was like
Amazon or ProFlowers going online for the first time, except worse.
Because, unlike buying a new book or a dozen roses, consumers didn't
have a choice about buying health insurance. They were required to do
so by law.[39]

So, there was no room for error. The website had to work. But it
didn't. In fact, only three out of ten people who tried to access the website were able to connect, and most of those who made it were soon
tossed off because of other bugs in the system. Even in the midst of a
damaging and idiotic government shutdown brought on by conservative hardliners, the failure of the website became the biggest news story
for weeks—and the butt of late-night comics' jokes.[40]

Every day at our White House briefings—where reporters glee-
fully pulled out their laptops and demonstrated their inability to join
HealthCare.gov—Press Secretary Jay Carney sounded like a broken
record, repeating over and over, "We know there's a problem, but
they're making improvements every day." Except they, whoever "they"
were, were not making any progress at all. By November 13, six weeks
later, only 26,794 had managed to sign up for coverage—90 percent
fewer than HHS had predicted by that date.[41]

Inside the White House, near panic set in. Their silly attempts to blame problems with the website on its surprising success—"More people rushed to sign up for Obamacare than we ever thought possible in our wildest dreams"—fell flat. It was clearly much more serious than that. There were fundamental problems with the underlying technology. As Steve Brill later reported in *Time* magazine, in every prelaunch meeting at the White House, CMS officials assured President Obama and White House chief of staff Denis McDonough that the technology was up and running. The problem is, before the public launch, nobody on the White House staff had taken the time to test it.

With nobody at HHS or CMS willing to take ownership of the problem, Obama realized he couldn't trust his health-care team any longer. So he summoned Jeff Zients, head of the National Economic Council—whom he'd earlier entrusted with the job of rescuing the "Cash for Clunkers" program—and anointed him "Mr. Fix-It." As a sign of how bad things were, Obama's first question to Zients reportedly was: Is it even possible to fix this mess, or do we have to toss it out entirely and start from scratch?[42]

Obama's loss of confidence in his own health policy officials was nowhere more apparent than in his appearance in the Rose Garden on October 21, which I attended as part of the White House press corps. He began by stoutly defending the act. He then went on to reassure the American people that problems with the website were only a momentary bump in the road, well on their way to being fixed, and that all Americans would soon be able to realize their dream of obtaining health coverage they could never before afford. In the front row sat then–HHS secretary Kathleen Sebelius. He didn't recognize her. He didn't thank her for her work in overseeing the ACA. He never even mentioned her name.[43]

For his part, Zients turned to the people the administration should have started with in the first place: Obama's get-out-the-vote tech team from his 2012 campaign. Having succeeded in getting their man reelected by developing the most pinpoint voter identification program in history, their job now was to save his political butt. They flew in from around the country, camped out in Washington, worked around the clock (unlike your typical Washington consultants), and, within six weeks, had worked their magic. By December 1, the website could handle fifty thousand visitors at one time. Which would make even Jeff Bezos, head of Amazon, proud. By mid-February, 1.9 million Americans had signed up for coverage.[44]

In July 2014, the Government Accountability Office, the nonpartisan investigative arm of Congress, released its report on the website failure—which it blamed on pure bureaucratic incompetence by the CMS. There was no "effective planning or oversight practices" for development of HealthCare.gov, the GAO found. As a result, the administration kept changing contractors' marching orders, creating widespread confusion and adding tens of millions of dollars in costs. The cost for the website sign-up system, for example, ballooned from $56 million to more than $209 million. The cost of the electronic backroom for verifying information submitted by applicants jumped from $30 million to almost $85 million.[45]

In the understatement of the year, CMS administrator Marilyn Tavenner told members of Congress: "The website has not worked as well as it should."[46]

By then the website was fixed, but the damage was done. Public confidence in Obamacare had been grossly undermined. Who knows how many people never even tried to sign up because they didn't trust the system? Equally undermined was public trust in the government's ability to do anything right. Everybody wondered: Why didn't they just subcontract it out to Google or Amazon? And, most significantly, Obama himself had suffered an embarrassing blow, with legitimate questions now being raised about whether he was up to the job.

But no sooner had Obama dealt with the disastrous rollout of the website than another health-care-related fiasco blew up.

"Keep Your Plan"

During debate over passage of the Affordable Care Act, one problem kept coming up: People lucky enough to already have a good health-insurance plan were afraid they'd lose it once the ACA became the law of the land. In fact, the reverse was true. Because it mandated that more benefits had to be covered as standard, the ACA would force insurance companies to improve coverage on a lot of lousy plans, or drop them. But, valid or not, this fear felt by many people—of having to jettison a good, existing plan in favor of a substandard one bought through the state or federal exchange—became such a drag on support for the bill that President Obama decided he needed to clear the air.

He first did so in his weekly TV and radio address on June 6, 2009: "If you like the plan you have, you can keep it. If you like the doctor you have, you can keep your doctor, too. The only change you'll see are falling costs as our reforms take hold."[47]

In case that wasn't clear enough, he made his point again at a presidential news conference on June 23: "If you like your plan and you like your doctor, you won't have to do a thing. You keep your plan. You keep your doctor."[48]

When Obamacare opponents—and people who had read and understood the bill—continued to warn people they might lose the health insurance they'd already paid for, a frustrated president took to the road to set the record straight. On July 29, he told a town hall audience in Raleigh, North Carolina: "I have been as clear as I can be. Under the reform I've proposed, if you like your doctor, you keep your doctor. If you like your health care plan, you keep your health care plan. These folks need to stop scaring everybody. Nobody is talking about forcing you to change your plans."[49]

A couple of weeks later, on August 15, at a town hall in Grand Junction, Colorado, showing a little more frustration, Obama repeated: "I just want to be completely clear about this. I keep on saying this but somehow folks aren't listening—if you like your health care plan, you keep your health care plan. Nobody is going to force you to leave your health care plan. If you like your doctor, you keep seeing your doctor."[50]

And they were not the only times Obama or a top administration official made the same claim. The Pulitzer Prize–winning website *Politifact* identified thirty-seven different occasions on which Obama reassured the American people, almost word for word: "If you like the health plan you have now, you can keep it." There's only one problem: It wasn't true. Which the whole world learned in the fall of 2013, when health-insurance companies started sending cancellation notices out to over 4 million policyholders.[51]

At which point, rather than offering an apology for getting it wrong, Obama confused things even further by offering, instead, a clarification of his previous clarification. At a speech on November 4, 2013, Obama insisted he never made a flat-out "you-like-it, you-keep-it" promise. The media had just reported it wrong. As he explained to leaders of Organizing for America, his campaign organization, what he really said was: "Now, if you have or had one of these plans before the Affordable Care Act came into law and you really like that plan, what we said was you can keep it if it hasn't changed since the law passed."[52]

Now, to a certain extent, Obama was right. Indeed, under the Affordable Care Act, all health-insurance policies must cover a certain list of benefits, including emergency care, maternity care, mental health, and prescription drugs. In many cases, where those benefits were not already covered, insurance companies had to add them to existing plans. In which case, by law, insurers were required to give policyholders ninety days' notice that their old, substandard, policy was being dropped—and offer them alternative plans for continued coverage. Those were the letters people started receiving in the mail.

Even though this was an exception to the rule, affecting only those Americans who had purchased individual policies on the open market, an estimated 5 percent of those with health insurance (the vast majority get health insurance at work), it nonetheless flew in the face of Obama's repeated claim of "If you like it, you can keep it."

For Obama, the trouble was that while he might have meant to say "you can keep it if it hasn't changed since the law passed," that's not what he actually said. Again, *Politifact* found thirty-seven times where Obama made the "like it, keep it" promise. They could not find one single instance in which he added the caveat "as long as your plan hasn't changed since the law was passed."

Obama's claim that everybody could keep his own plan and doctor was so far from true that *Politifact* actually gave it the worst possible designation: "Pants on Fire." Later, they added insult to injury by recognizing Obama's oft-repeated promise—"If you like your health care plan, you can keep it"—as the "Lie of the Year for 2013." It was a sad chapter in what should have been Barack Obama's hour of triumph.[53]

The Employer Delay

While the administration was trying to end confusion over the individual mandate provision of Obamacare—Who had to enroll? And when?—another problem unfolded over the employer mandate.

Under the terms of the Affordable Care Act, small businesses with fewer than fifty employees are off the hook. They do not have to provide coverage for their employees. But companies with fifty or more employees that didn't already do so were required to offer health insurance to all full-time employees by January 1, 2014, the day the ACA took effect, or face a fine of $2,000 per employee.

When many business leaders and trade organizations protested the employer mandate, arguing they wouldn't have time to make necessary changes before the January 2014 deadline, the administration caved—twice in one year. Larger companies of one hundred or more, which represent seven out of ten American workers, were given a year's delay—until 2015—by which time they would have to offer health insurance to 70 percent of their full-time employees, instead of the original mandate of 95 percent. Small companies, with fifty to ninety-nine workers, received an even bigger break. They were given until 2016 to offer health insurance, two years longer than the ACA originally required, with no federal penalty.[54]

Business groups applauded the move, but consumer groups denounced it as one more delay on the road to universal health care and one more case of President Obama's caving in to big business while ignoring the plight of the middle class. After all, lobbyists for big business tried but failed to remove the employer mandate provision from the ACA as it moved through Congress. Why should they get a free pass from Obama, now that the ACA was already federal law?

The Legacy of Obamacare

The combination of a less-than-perfect law and its botched execution left the crowning achievement of Barack Obama's legacy badly scarred and widely unpopular, despite its upsides.

By early 2015, the Department of Health and Human Services announced that 11.7 million people were enrolled in health insurance through the marketplace exchanges (up from 8.1 million who had originally selected plans). Some 4 million young people between the ages of nineteen and twenty-five had been covered through their parents' plan, and an additional 7.5 million people had gained health-care coverage through the expansion of Medicaid in twenty-seven states and the District of Columbia. That's a good start, but far from the 32 million Americans the Congressional Budget Office estimated would obtain coverage under the law by 2017.[55]

In many ways, the problems with the website exemplified everything that was wrong with Obamacare: It started out with the highest of expectations, but ended up a colossal disappointment. Not a disaster, perhaps, but nothing to cheer about, either. Which created a problem for Democrats and provided much welcome ammunition for Republicans in the midterm elections of 2014.

Democrats, who had counted on making the Affordable Care Act the centerpiece of their re-election strategy—"We promised to deliver universal health care, and we did!"—barely mentioned the reforms at all. Instead of bragging about Obamacare, they found themselves on the defensive, insisting: "Yes, there are problems with it, but it's better than nothing, and I'm going to make sure we fix it." Or: "Yes, I voted for it. It's not perfect, but it's a lot better than the way it used to be, when insurance companies were in charge." All of which is true, but still a tougher political sell.

Republicans, meanwhile, routinely repeated their promise to repeal Obamacare entirely, which—after some fifty-five meaningless repeal votes in the House—nobody took seriously. Otherwise, they shifted the bulk of their attacks to what they portrayed as Obama's weak response to the double threats of Ebola and ISIS. The combination apparently worked, especially after, as we will see, Obama failed to live up to his promises on immigration reform on time. As a result, the president got most of the blame for the Democratic loss of the Senate on November 4.[56]

For his part, President Obama continues to insist that the Affordable Care Act is as close to universal health care as we could possibly get today, given all the ugly gridlock in Congress. As more and more people sign up, he says hopefully, stories about its benefits will far outweigh stories about its shortcomings, and the success of the ACA will be apparent to all. At that point, jokes the president, Republicans will stop calling it "Obamacare," because they won't want to give him any credit at all.

On October 27, 2014, the *New York Times* took an in-depth look at the good and bad of the Affordable Care Act, thirteen months after the launch of HealthCare.gov. They summed it up in one sentence: "The law has largely succeeded in delivering on Obama's main promises, even as it has fallen short in some ways and given birth to a new and powerful conservative movement." And, according to the *Times*, the ACA ended up hurting the Democratic Party the most: "Politically, the law has also not served Mr. Obama or his party well, fueling the anger that helped spawn the Tea Party movement. And while demands for repeal have faded, the law still stands as a symbol of everything that conservatives consider wrong with government."[57]

Even its supporters acknowledge that Obamacare will never lead to universal coverage. The Department of HHS admits, in fact, that some 30 million Americans will remain uninsured for years to come. Those who bought policies through the exchanges must renew them every year and face the threat of soaring premiums. At the same time, health-insurance companies, pharmaceutical manufacturers, and health-care providers are enjoying a business bonanza. In effect, the federal government forced every American to buy their products. That means more customers—and higher profits.

Meanwhile, most remarkably, Obamacare has survived two major challenges before the conservative Roberts Supreme Court. On June 28, 2012, Chief Justice John Roberts himself wrote the majority opinion in *National Federal of Independent Business* v. *Sebelius*, which challenged the very heart of the Affordable Care Act, the individual mandate. By a five-to-four vote, the Court ruled the mandate fell under the taxing powers of Congress and was therefore constitutional. Unfortunately, the justices also ruled that individual governors could opt out of the Medicaid provisions of the ACA by refusing to offer extended Medicaid to residents of their state. Twenty-one red-state governors chose not to.[58]

Almost exactly three years later, on June 30, 2015, Chief Justice John Roberts again led the Court in endorsing the Affordable Care Act by a six-to-three vote, rejecting specious arguments by several state attorneys general that, because of a minor drafting error in the law, federal subsidies should be available only to those who bought health insurance through a state, and not a federal, exchange. Within hours of their decision, President Obama came out to the Rose Garden and proudly declared: "After multiple challenges to this law before the Supreme Court, the Affordable Care Act is here to stay."[59]

That is good news, but also a glass half-full. For progressives, the Affordable Care Act will always stand as a colossal missed opportunity. Given the best chance of any president in over one hundred years to deliver basic, quality health care to every American family, President Obama fell short. He settled instead for a hodgepodge, public/private halfway measure that fattens the profits of private insurance companies while leaving 30 million Americans still without health care. Sadly, it may be decades before we get another crack at it.

THREE

National Security

It's hard to tell who was more surprised in a San Francisco federal courtroom, back in early February 2009, only a few days after Obama had been sworn in as forty-fourth president of the United States: the judge or the plaintiff's attorneys.

The case was a lawsuit brought by the ACLU in 2007, on behalf of five foreign detainees, against Jeppesen DataPlan, a subsidiary of Boeing. Plaintiffs charged that Jeppesen, under contract with the CIA, had flown suspects to countries where they were routinely tortured under the Bush administration's "extraordinary rendition" program. Back in February 2008, the Bush administration, using the all-encompassing "state-secrets" argument, had convinced a district court judge to block the suit.[1]

Now, with a new administration in place, the ACLU had confidence in reinstating the lawsuit. And with good reason. After all, candidate Barack Obama had denounced the Bush administration's wholesale use of the "state-secrets" argument "to get cases thrown out of civil court." And his new attorney general, Eric Holder, had promised during his confirmation hearing to review "significant pending cases in which DOJ has invoked the state-secrets privilege," and to work with DOJ attorneys "to ensure that the United States invokes the state secrets privilege only in legally appropriate situations."[2]

Given Holder's comments, bringing back the lawsuit against Jeppesen DataPlan was a slam dunk. Right? Wrong! Imagine the surprise in the courtroom when Obama DOJ lawyers resurrected the Bush administration's claim that allowing that case to go to trial would reveal state secrets. And exactly what "state secrets" might those be? As detailed in their court papers, and never disputed by government lawyers: an appalling level of torture inflicted on the plaintiffs, after they had been "rendered" by the CIA, including the detail that one of the detainees, Binyam Mohamed, had had his "genitals . . . sliced with a scalpel."[3]

As horrifying as these accounts of torture may have been, however, they were hardly news. And they were clearly not state secrets. Stories of terrorist suspects "rendered" by the CIA—seized and flown to secret "black sites" in friendly countries, where they were routinely tortured—had by then been widely reported in journals around the world, including the front pages of the *Washington Post* and the *New York Times*. A former Jeppesen employee told the *New Yorker*'s Jane Mayer: "We do all of the extraordinary rendition flights—you know, the torture flights. Let's face it, some of these flights end up that way."[4]

Apparently, according to the Bush administration's state-secrets doctrine, the only place the torture of prisoners could not be discussed was in a federal courtroom. Why not? Not because it would reveal state secrets, but because it would embarrass the U.S. government for having knowingly violated international law against torture and attempting to cover it up.

What was really shocking was that this cover-up had now become the official doctrine of the brand-new Obama administration. And that was just the first indication that, despite all his campaign promises to abandon the Bush-Cheney policy of "anything goes" in the war on terror, Obama would, for the most part, not only continue down that same path, but expand it.

Indeed, perhaps the area where liberals held out the most hope for change under Barack Obama was on national security matters. After all, in the wake of September 11, George W. Bush, egged on by Dick Cheney, had embraced an unapologetic agenda of unconstitutional overreach: extraordinary rendition, secret prisons or "black sites," torture, waterboarding, unmanned drone attacks, massive NSA spying, and endless warfare—all in the name of the "war on terror." Any concerns about personal privacy or international law were swept aside by asserting yet-untested presidential authority under the Patriot Act, or the Authorization for the Use of Military Force (AUMF)—both rushed through Congress in the immediate aftermath of the 9/11 attacks.

Yet, this is arguably the area in which progressives are most disappointed in the Obama presidency.

Back in the day, candidate Obama promised a radical change from the simplistic, militaristic, cowboy approach to national security practiced by George W. Bush and Dick Cheney. "No more illegal wiretapping of American citizens," Obama explicitly declared in 2007. "No more ignoring the law when it is inconvenient."[5]

Clearly, his supporters believed, those abhorrent, absurd, unconstitutional, and often blatantly un-American activities pursued by the Bush administration would be the first thing to change under President Barack Obama. Except it didn't turn out that way. Instead, Obama increased the bulk surveillance of Americans by the NSA, condemned Americans to death without a fair trial, expanded the use of drones as killing machines, even of innocent civilians, and hunted down journalists who dared report on national security abuses. In the end, the place progressives anticipated the most change is where, to their shock and chagrin, they found the least.

In September 2014, reflecting the despair of many progressives, former *Washington Post* columnist and senior writer for *The Intercept* Dan Froomkin summed up: "In a lot of ways, we're worse off today than we were under George W. Bush. Back then, Bush's extremist assault on civil liberties, human rights and other core American values in the name of fighting terror felt like an aberration. The expectation was that those policies would be quickly reversed, discredited—and explicitly outlawed—once he was no longer in power. Instead, under President Barack Obama, they've become institutionalized."[6]

Tortured Reasoning

Barack Obama didn't wait to reach the Oval Office before vowing to end the practice of torture by agents of the United States. As *The Guardian*'s investigative reporter Glenn Greenwald pointed out in

2012, Obama repeatedly vowed as a candidate that he would outlaw torture and, "without engaging in 'partisan witch-hunts,' instruct his attorney general to 'immediately review' the evidence of criminality in the conduct of torture because 'nobody is above the law.' "[7]

As president-elect, he took the first steps toward fulfilling these promises. At a news conference in Chicago on January 9, 2009, where he introduced his nominee for CIA director, former Clinton chief of staff Leon Panetta, the president-elect announced he'd already given Panetta his marching orders: "I was clear throughout this campaign and was clear throughout this transition that under my administration the United States does not torture. We will abide by the Geneva Conventions. We will uphold our highest ideals."[8]

On January 22, two days after his inauguration, Obama followed through by signing a series of executive orders banning the use of torture, ending so-called extraordinary rendition flights, and closing secret torture prisons in Poland, Thailand, Morocco, and Britain's naval base on Diego Garcia. So far so good. But there were already clouds on the horizon.[9]

Even while ending torture, Obama refused to hold responsible those who had authorized or practiced it, starting with the former president of the United States. At his first major news conference, on February 9, Obama typically tried to have it both ways. He began by stating he had little interest in pursuing Bush, Cheney, or anybody else in the chain of command of Bush's "war on terror" for what were clearly war crimes: "Generally speaking, I'm more interested in looking forward than I am in looking backwards." Neither I nor anyone else pointed out that prosecution of any crime is, in a sense, "looking backwards."[10]

At that conference, however, Obama did leave the door open to the possibility of criminal charges against some malefactors: "Nobody is above the law and if there are clear instances of wrongdoing, people should be prosecuted just like ordinary citizens." Progressives took heart. It still looked as if the administration might actually act to prosecute U.S. personnel, high and low, responsible for widespread use of torture.[11]

But no sooner had Obama opened the door than he closed it

halfway. In April 2009, he declared absolute immunity for any official—from higher-ups in the White House to CIA agents in the field—involved in torture so long as they had acted in accordance with the extraordinarily permissive guidelines issued by the Bush Department of Justice. Only "rogue" operators—whatever that meant—would be held responsible, promised Obama, ever trying to straddle the fence.[12]

In making this announcement, Obama also scolded those progressives who had been urging him to hold Bush administration officials responsible for their war crimes. "This is a time for reflection, not retribution," chided the president. And then added: "Nothing will be gained by spending our time and energy laying blame for the past. . . . We must resist the forces that divide us, and instead come together on behalf of our common future."[13]

As Glenn Greenwald observed: All those Obama supporters, myself included, who argued for years that the rule of law should apply equally to all Americans, even those in high political office—and who at one time thought Obama himself agreed with us—were now cast off as among "the forces that divide us."[14]

In August 2009, Attorney General Eric Holder announced that the Department of Justice would investigate whether to file criminal charges against those involved in the practice of torture, but—in accordance with Obama's directive—only for those who went "beyond the techniques that were authorized" in the official Bush administration torture orders. Which was as bad as, or perhaps even worse than, doing nothing.[15]

By focusing only on "rogue" suspects, those who had allegedly exceeded the precise letter of Bush's orders on torture, Holder and Obama were, in effect, condoning torture itself. They were giving Bush and Cheney a free pass. They were endorsing wholesale and repeated violations of the Geneva Convention rules against torture. "It is vital," conservative blogger Andrew Sullivan had written, "that the Obama administration does nothing to imply that what was authorized within the rules under the Cheney torture program is in any way legal, defensible or moral." But that's what they did.[16]

Reportedly, the cases the DOJ did choose to look into included those of a CIA officer who brought a gun into an interrogation room to convince a suspect to talk; another who threatened to kill a suspect's children; yet another who suggested the suspect would have to watch his mother being sexually molested; a torturer who went "overboard" on waterboarding (as if all waterboarding was not overboard to begin with); and those responsible for the deaths of two suspects while they were undergoing torture, one at a secret CIA prison outside Kabul in Afghanistan, the other at the notorious Abu Ghraib prison in Iraq.[17]

But, in the end, Holder dropped even those attempts to crack down on persons responsible for torture. In August 2012, he announced he was ending the DOJ investigation without filing criminal charges against anyone. Not one single person. His action, editorialized the *New York Times* the next morning, "eliminates the last possibility that any criminal charges will be brought as a result of the brutal interrogations carried out by the CIA." Just as on Wall Street, nobody went to jail. So much for no one being above the law.[18]

And nobody could deny there had been brutal actions. Holder's cop-out flew in the face of the official Pentagon investigation led by Major General Antonio Taguba of possible war crimes. He found evidence that official U.S. personnel had tortured and abused detainees in Iraq, Afghanistan, and Guantanamo Bay, using beatings, electrical shocks, sexual humiliation, waterboarding, and other cruel practices. In his own June 2008 report, Taguba didn't hold back. "After years of disclosures by government investigations, media accounts and reports from human rights organizations, there is no longer any doubt as to whether the current administration has committed war crimes," Taguba wrote. "The only question that remains to be answered is whether those who ordered the use of torture will be held to account." Under Barack Obama and Eric Holder, apparently not.[19]

Taguba also left no doubt who was responsible: "The commander in chief and those under him authorized a systematic regime of torture." His findings were echoed by retired general Barry McCaffrey, who told reporters: "We tortured people unmercifully. We probably murdered dozens of them during the course of that, both the armed forces and the CIA."[20]

Holder's decision to walk away from any prosecutorial pursuit of torture cases was met with disbelief and anger by progressives and civil libertarians nationwide. Jameel Jaffer, deputy legal director of the ACLU, spoke for many when he said: "That the Justice Department will hold no one accountable for the killing of prisoners in CIA custody is nothing short of a scandal. . . . The decision not to file charges against individuals who tortured prisoners to death is yet another entry in what is already a shameful record."[21]

The question remains: How was General Taguba able to discover evidence of war crimes where Eric Holder was not? Clearly, the answer was that Holder and Barack Obama didn't want to. They'd already made up their minds they were not going to pursue criminal prosecution of those responsible for torture.

But their whitewashing efforts didn't stop there. Obama even went so far as to oppose and successfully quash a congressional investigation into the use of torture. His administration went to great pains to delay and redact the Senate Intelligence Committee's report on the CIA's torture program, which publicly revealed for the first time some of the techniques used, including repeated waterboarding and locking suspects inside small, closed boxes for hundreds of hours. The report also documented five cases of forced "rectal rehydration," in which a prisoner's lunch tray "consisting of hummus, pasta with sauce, nuts, and raisins was pureed and rectally infused."[22]

The administration also pressed Spain and Germany to drop their investigations into the torture of their citizens by U.S. officials, intervened to prevent British courts from disclosing details of torture, and, as shown in one notable case at the opening of this chapter, invoked the doctrine of state secrets to protect Bush officials from civil cases.[23]

Obama's failure to pursue a criminal prosecution of anybody connected with the use of torture, of course, had far greater implications than merely letting Bush, Cheney, and their foot soldiers off the hook. Because, by declining to hold torturers and their superiors accountable, Obama left the door wide open for leaders of a future administration, faced with a new terrorist threat, real or perceived, to resume the use of torture—again, with impunity. Now the precedent has been set.

Obama refused to act even in one notorious case in which Bush and Cheney's apparatus tortured the wrong guy. Maher Arar, a dual citizen of Canada and Syria suspected by both Canada and the United States of being an al Qaeda operative, was seized at JFK airport in 2002 and whisked off on a rendition flight to Syria, where he was tortured for the next ten months, including beatings with electrical cables. After a Canadian government–led inquiry found Arar completely innocent and having nothing at all to do with terrorism, Canadian officials released him without charges.[24]

What a contrast between how the two countries that had ordered his arrest and torture acted next. Canada created a commission to investigate the screwup, issued Arar an official apology, and paid him $9.8 million in damages.

The Obama administration, meanwhile, refused to apologize to Arar and never acknowledged any wrongdoing. Instead, once again invoking the "state-secrets privilege," the Department of Justice successfully blocked Arar's attempts to get a trial in the United States, first at the Second Circuit Court of Appeals and later at the Supreme Court. Georgetown University law professor David Cole, one of Arar's attorneys, wrote: "In twenty-five years as a civil rights and human rights lawyer, I have never handled a case of more egregious abuse. U.S. officials not only delivered Arar to Syrian security forces that they regularly accuse of systematic torture, but did everything in their power to ensure that Arar could not get to a court to challenge their actions while he was in their custody."[25]

For progressives, Obama's reluctance to hold the architects of torture to the law was just the beginning of his overall disappointing record on national security. In the end, Obama not only did *not* repudiate Bush's national security policies, he continued and expanded them. He signed an extension of the Patriot Act. He defended the NSA's massive domestic spying program. He vastly increased the use of drones, even to kill American citizens on foreign soil. He aggressively pursued whistle-blowers and journalists who published stories based on leaks by government officials. And he bypassed Congress in launching military strikes against Libya and the Islamic State.

And all the while, Gitmo, the most notorious site of George Bush's war on terror, remained open for business.

Close Gitmo

In January 2002, as part of that "war on terror," President George W. Bush established a military prison at Guantanamo Bay Naval Base in Cuba. At the time, Defense Secretary Donald Rumsfeld said it was created to house extraordinarily dangerous criminals (as if we were suddenly facing super-villains who couldn't be kept in regular maximum security), interrogate detainees in a secure setting, and prosecute suspects for war crimes.

Rumsfeld named the prison "Camp X-Ray," but with its harsh conditions, denial of basic rights, and rumors of torture, the prison at Guantanamo Bay, or "Gitmo," soon gained the reputation as "The Gulag of Our Times" and became a recruiting tool for terrorist groups around the world. This is what the United States is really all about, they charged: Americans preach equal justice for all, yet throw people in prison for years with no access to a lawyer, no charges filed, no access to a fair trial, and no opportunity to defend themselves in court.[26]

Shutting down Gitmo therefore became a goal of many liberals and progressives, and a common theme of Democratic candidates for president in the 2007–2008 primaries. And few were more outspoken on the issue, on more occasions, than Barack Obama.

On June 3, 2007, Obama first raised the issue during a Democratic presidential debate. "Our legitimacy is reduced when we've got a Guantanamo that is open, when we suspend habeas corpus," he argued. "Those kinds of things erode our moral claim that we are acting on behalf of broader universal principles."[27]

On November 15, 2007, he chose the setting of another debate to pledge to do something about it: "We're going to lead by shutting down Guantanamo and restoring habeas corpus in this country so that we offer them an example."[28]

On November 16, 2008, President-elect Obama told the nation on

60 Minutes that closing Gitmo would be one of his first priorities: "I have said repeatedly that I intend to close Guantanamo, and I will follow through on that."[29]

But for Obama it turned out to be another promise made, another promise broken.

To be fair, you can't say he didn't try. As on so many issues, he just didn't try hard enough. And in the end he just gave up.

On January 22, two days after taking the oath of office, Obama signed an executive order suspending military commissions at Gitmo, initiating a review of charges against all prisoners, and ordering that the facility be closed down exactly one year later, in January 2010. And all hell broke loose. Even though this was hardly an unexpected move, and even though Democrats controlled both the House and Senate, Congress quickly moved to kill the plan. Nobody wanted to see a campaign ad accusing them of being weak on terror. In May 2009, the Senate voted ninety-to-six to block all funds necessary for the release or transfer of prisoners from Gitmo.[30]

Obama's response to the cowardly Senate vote shocked even his most die-hard supporters. Speaking to reporters, Obama said that nobody would have to worry about the most dangerous prisoners at Gitmo, because some detainees would be held without trial indefinitely. "We are going to exhaust every avenue that we have to prosecute those at Guantanamo who pose a danger to our country," vowed the president. "But even when this process is complete, there may be a number of people who cannot be prosecuted for past crimes, but who nonetheless pose a threat to the security of the United States."[31]

In other words, said Obama, we're just going to slap some people in prison and throw the key away, without ever filing charges against them or bringing them to trial. In the United States of America! That was a promise you might expect to hear from Dick Cheney, but never from Barack Obama—and it stirred the ire of civil libertarians and constitutional scholars. "My question is not only what happens to those people who may be perpetually in prison, but what kind of precedent does that set for the future," said Michael Ratner, president of the Center for Constitutional Rights. "It's not one I find constitutional or acceptable. Opening that door even for a few Guantanamo detainees is anathema."[32]

Of course, one of the main reasons some detainees could never be brought to trial is that a judge might rule that their testimony was inadmissible because it was obtained through torture. Another strike against the widespread use of torture by the CIA, for which no one was held responsible.

Ironically, one of the strongest condemnations of a continued policy of indefinite detention would come from Obama himself. Three years later, in April 2013, he told a formal White House news conference: "The notion that we're going to continue to keep over a hundred individuals in a no-man's-land in perpetuity, the idea that we would still maintain forever a group of individuals who have not been tried— that is contrary to who we are, it is contrary to our interests, and it needs to stop."[33]

Sitting with fellow reporters in the East Room, I was stunned. It was almost as if Obama forgot that the very policy he was denouncing was one he himself had promulgated for the entirety of his first term. The only difference was that he would have a group of prisoners held indefinitely without trial on U.S. soil, instead of at Guantanamo Bay.

Curiously enough for a professor of constitutional law, Obama did not reveal under what legal authority he was able to create a new category of detainees who cannot be tried in court, but must be nevertheless held in cages indefinitely. Nothing in American jurisprudence would justify denial of such a basic right. But Obama didn't spell out his legal reasoning, and has not since.

Going back to 2009, the Gitmo saga took another turn in December, when Obama signed another executive order designating Thomson Correctional Center in Illinois as the new home of all remaining Gitmo prisoners.

But, for Obama, that was the end of the road. Faced with continued opposition from Congress and the failure of other countries to accept prisoners released from Gitmo, Obama, in effect, walked away from the fight. In January 2011, he officially threw in the towel by signing the 2011 Defense Authorization Act, which included restrictions

on transferring prisoners from Guantanamo Bay to American soil or
to foreign countries, thereby guaranteeing that Gitmo would remain
open. Which it still is today.

The Pentagon, meanwhile, has sought to transfer prisoners out
of Guantanamo, providing it can find a country that will take them.
Uruguay, for example, accepted six prisoners in November 2014,
which leaves 114 detainees at Gitmo, including 53 already approved
for release—if the administration can find any country willing to accept them. This is all part of Obama's new goal to get the population of
Gitmo down to double digits, in the hope that, at that point, Congress
will repeal the law prohibiting their transfer to American soil.[34]

Yet, as those efforts go forward ever so slowly, it now seems all too
likely that Gitmo will remain open long after President Obama leaves
office, an embarrassing public contradiction of America's pledge of justice for all.

Until and unless the law is changed, failure to close the prison at
Guantanamo Bay will count among the biggest failures of the Obama
administration—for which Obama, naturally, lays all the blame on
Congress. Even though he wanted to, "they would not let us close it," he
said. Which is not true. A closer reading of the law shows that Obama
has the authority to shut down Guantanamo—if he really wanted to,
and if he were willing to take the heat.

In blaming Gitmo on Congress, Obama cites the National Defense
Authorization Act of 2012 (NDAA), which confirms the president's
power to wage war against al Qaeda—power originally given him in
the Authorization for Use of Military Force (AUMF), passed in the
wake of September 11. The NDAA also authorizes the president to de-
tain enemy combatants, but expressly prohibits him from transferring
Gitmo detainees to American soil.

But the act also contains a loophole big enough to drive a truck
full of Gitmo detainees through. To my knowledge, Max Fisher of the
Washington Post and Eric Posner of *Slate* were the first to point out that
Section 1021(c)(1) allows for "detention under the law of war without
trial until the end of the hostilities authorized by" the AUMF against al
Qaeda. Note the key phrase: "until the end of hostilities." And when are

hostilities against al Qaeda over? When the president says they are! Only Congress can authorize a war, but the president can end a war any time he wants—as Obama himself already did in Iraq and Afghanistan.[35]

In other words, President Obama could shut down Guantanamo Bay any time by declaring the war against al Qaeda over—and then transferring remaining detainees to their home country, or any country that would take them, as long as they agree not to torture them. Sure, he'd generate a storm of criticism from some members of Congress who'd insist the "war on terror" is still going strong, but the point is: He could still unilaterally shut down Gitmo IF he wanted to.

But, even though he boasts of having destroyed the core body of al Qaeda, Obama doesn't want to declare war with al Qaeda or the AUMF over. Why? Because, as we shall soon see, he has cited the AUMF as legal justification for the expanded use of drones and for U.S. air strikes against ISIS in Syria, without having to seek new authorization from Congress. So he's willing to take the political heat for not closing Gitmo rather than give up his extrapresidential powers under the AUMF. Just like the ring in *The Lord of the Rings*, Obama has decided he does not want to give up these powers.

End result: George Bush's prison at Guantanamo Bay remains open. Barack Obama broke his promise to close it. And not because Congress wouldn't let him close it, but because he decided that closing it might interfere with other priorities of his national security strategy—such as launching more drones.

A Kettle of Drones

The use of torture and drones were two Bush-initiated practices that progressives were confident would end with President Obama. How naïve. Yes, torture disappeared—as far as we know—although no one was ever held accountable. But, under Obama, there were suddenly more drones, on more lethal, and questionably legal, missions than ever before.

President Obama's ban on torture theoretically eliminated extraordinary rendition to secret prisons run by torture-friendly countries. But since there were still enemy agents out there, Obama came up with another solution. In place of rounding up suspected terrorists and whisking them off to "black sites" to be waterboarded, the Obama administration simply assassinated them with drones wherever they happened to be, instead. Quicker, cheaper, and simpler. You don't have to pay for secret prisons. You don't have to feed the prisoners, or clean up those messy torture chambers. You don't have to send any more personnel to the Middle East, not even any pilots. CIA agents can operate drones with a joystick from their stations on American soil, kill a few terrorist suspects, and maybe even a few innocent civilians, and still get home in time for dinner with the wife and kids.

And, yes, President Obama also decided to entrust conduct of America's drone war to the CIA, and not the Pentagon, which raises serious public policy issues. The CIA, after all, is an intelligence agency, not a military agency. Its purpose is to spy on America's perceived enemies and not, at least since political assassinations were banned by President Gerald Ford in 1976, to kill them. Further, their decisions about killing targets are based, not on solid evidence, but on intelligence information, which is notoriously unreliable. Remember those "weapons of mass destruction" in Iraq? Nor is intelligence data, by its nature, subject to cross-examination or judicial review.

At first, according to reports, Obama merely shrugged those problems off. In one Situation Room meeting, Mark Mazzetti reports in *The Way of the Knife*, General James Cartwright, vice chairman of the Joint Chiefs of Staff, asked why the United States was, in effect, "building a second air force" in the form of the CIA's expanding fleet of drones. Obama's cold response: "The CIA gets what it wants." Obama later regretted his decision and proposed moving drone operations to the Pentagon, but thus far Congress has blocked these efforts.[36]

The use of drones as killing machines escalated so dramatically under Obama that, in a special 2013 report commissioned by the Council on Foreign Relations, investigator Micah Zenko asked: "What is the difference between George W. Bush and Barack Obama on drones?" His answer: "Zero."[37]

Zenko found that President Bush authorized a total of about fifty nonbattlefield drone strikes. President Obama, with more unmanned drones available, launched more than five times as many strikes, in Pakistan, Afghanistan, Yemen, and Somalia. According to Zenko, by the end of 2012, the count was 411 strikes and 3,430 dead—which included many innocent civilians and bystanders. But nobody really knows the exact number.[38]

Despite Obama's oft-repeated pledge to lead "the most transparent administration in history"—and despite congressional pressure to issue an annual update—the Obama administration has steadfastly refused to divulge the number of people killed each year by drones, their identities, the number of civilian casualties, or the legal rationale behind each strike.

So estimates vary. In a 2013 study, the United Nations reported 2,200 killed in Pakistan by drone strikes, including 400 civilians. On January 23, 2014, the fifth anniversary of the first drone strike under President Obama, the Bureau of Investigative Journalism reported that at least 2,400 people had been killed by drones under Obama. In Pakistan alone, they concluded, between 416 and 951 civilians had been killed, including 168 to 200 children. Amnesty International, in its 2013 report, estimated 900 civilians had been killed by drones.[39]

In one set of documents obtained by reporter Jeremy Scahill for *The Intercept*, the Pentagon itself acknowledged a significant percentage of innocent civilians killed. According to those Pentagon papers, in "Operation Haymaker," a special operation in northeastern Afghanistan between January 2012 and February 2013, air strikes killed more than 200 people, of whom only 35 were the intended targets. During one five-month period of the operation, according to the documents, nearly 90 percent of those killed were not the intended targets.[40]

Again, no precise numbers are available from the Pentagon, but one expert, Larry Lewis of the Center for Naval Analysis, estimates that U.S.-led drone strikes in Afghanistan are ten times more likely to cause civilian deaths than are strikes by traditionally piloted military aircraft. Former president of Afghanistan Hamid Karzai cited continued civilian killings by U.S. drones as one of his reasons for refusing to sign a ten-year security agreement between his country and the United States, once all American combat troops left Afghanistan in the summer of 2014.[41]

Today, we still don't know how many drones are deployed by the CIA, where they're used, who their targets are, or how many actual terrorist or civilian deaths they're responsible for. And the CIA has many ways of making sure we'll never know, such as classifying all men of military age as "enemy fighters." So defined, any males killed in a drone strike, even innocent bystanders, were by definition "combatants," not civilians, and therefore legitimate military targets. In short, "black sites" have been replaced by "black drones."

In October 2013, members of Congress, for the first and only time, heard from a family of civilian victims of drone attacks at a special congressional hearing convened by Florida congressman Alan Grayson. Only five members of Congress—Grayson, Jan Schakowsky, Rick Nolan, Rush Holt, and John Conyers, all Democrats—showed up. They heard powerful testimony from a Pakistani schoolteacher, whose mother was killed by a drone as she gathered okra in a field with two grandchildren.[42]

"Nobody has ever told me why my mother was targeted that day," Rafiq ur Rehman told the stunned panel through a translator. "Some media outlets reported that the attack was on a car, but there is no road alongside my mother's house. Others reported that the attack was on a house. But the missiles hit a nearby field, not a house. All of them reported that three, four, five militants were killed." Instead, he said, only one person was killed that day: "Not a militant, but my mother."[43]

Rehman testified that his mother was just one of dozens of people in his own tribe killed by drones over the years, including many women and children. Even the translator broke down and wept as Rehman expressed his difficulties, as a teacher, dealing with his mother's death: "My job is to educate," he explained. "But how do I teach something like this? How do I explain what I myself do not understand? How can I in good faith reassure the children that the drone will not come back and kill them, too, if I do not understand why it killed my mother and injured my children?"[44]

Asked what he wanted from the United States, Rehman had one simple request: "In the end I would just like to ask the American public to treat us as equals. Make sure that your government gives us the same status of a human with basic rights as they do to their own citizens. We do not kill our cattle the way the U.S. is killing humans in Waziristan with drones."[45]

The Obama administration refused to send a representative to the congressional hearing. In response to Rehman's testimony, a Pentagon spokesman would say only that the drone campaign is conducted "consistent with all applicable domestic and international law." Yet the administration has cited no law, outside an exceedingly broad interpretation of the post–September 11 Authorization for the Use of Military Force, or AUMF, that would justify the use of killer drones. Nor has the administration commented on what would be our response if any other country employed drones to kill its perceived enemies in a third country.[46]

For progressives, the problem is not only Obama's expanded use of drones to track down foreign terrorist suspects. He ratcheted things up even higher by asserting authority to assassinate American citizens, on foreign soil or at home in the United States, merely because the government suspected them of being involved, or planning to get involved, in a terrorist plot. For the Obama administration, no actual act of terrorism was necessary. There would be no arrest, no charges filed, no trial, no evidence presented in court, and no chance for a possible suspect to defend himself. There would only be death dropped from the sky. One drone attack would do it all, eliminating any possibility that person might ever commit a terrorist act. And that lethal drone attack could be carried out anywhere on the planet, regardless of national borders, because under this new doctrine, the whole world is a battlefield.

White House lawyers insist that this broad new power is perfectly legal under the AUMF and not subject to any oversight by Congress or the judiciary. Not even Bush and Cheney dared go that far.

In September 2011, Obama's zealous pursuit of assassination by drones erupted in controversy with news of the killing of Muslim cleric and American citizen Anwar al-Awlaki, born in New Mexico, who was living in Yemen and suspected of actively plotting to kill Americans. He had at least talked about terrorist attacks against the United States, but had not yet been charged with any crime. Al-Awlaki was one of four Americans killed overseas between 2009 and 2013 by U.S. drones. The others were his sixteen-year-old son, targeted two weeks later; Samir Khan, killed in the same attack as al-Awlaki; and Jude Kenan Mohammed, killed later in a drone strike in Pakistan.[47]

Civil liberties groups assailed the attacks and questioned the government's legal authority to kill an American anywhere without a trial. "The targeted killing program violates both U.S. and international law," declared Jameel Jaffer, deputy legal director of the ACLU. Jaffer explained: "This is a program under which American citizens far from any battlefield can be executed by their own government without judicial process, and on the basis of standards and evidence that are kept secret not just from the public but from the courts."[48]

They were not alone in raising questions. Several foreign allies also voiced their concern about whether the United States might fly killer drones over their own sovereign territory and challenged our authority to do so under international law. Two years later, President Obama finally addressed the controversy in a May 2013 speech at the National Defense University.

Obama began by admitting that the wholesale use of drones raised "profound questions" for the United States, such as "who is targeted, and why; about civilian casualties, and the risk of creating new enemies; about the legality of conducting such strikes under U.S. and international law; about accountability and morality." And he acknowledged the responsibility of the United States to set a clear policy for all actions taken in the so-called war on terror before it was too late: "So America is at a crossroads. We must define the nature and scope of this struggle, or else it will define us. . . . From our use of drones to detention of terrorism suspects, the decisions that we are making now will define the type of nation—and world—that we leave to our children."[49]

Obama ended by assuring the world that the United States was adopting new, strict guidelines for the use of drones. From that point on, promised Obama, lethal force by drones would be used only "to prevent or stop attacks against U.S. persons, and even then, only when capture is not feasible and no other reasonable alternatives exist to address the threat effectively." The targeted person, Obama added, must also pose "a continuing, imminent threat to U.S. persons." The Justice Department would have to review and approve every proposed assassination. And that's when Obama also announced his intent to (finally) transfer operation of the drone program from the CIA to the Pentagon, a move Congress later prevented.[50]

It was a good speech, parts of which could have been written by the ACLU. But it didn't make much difference in Obama's actions. A year later, little had changed in the U.S. deployment of drones. Civilians were still being killed. Human rights still did not figure in the calculation. Location and casualties of drone attacks were still kept secret. And American citizens were still being targeted.

In February 2014, the Associated Press reported that the administration was again debating the use of a drone to assassinate another American living in Pakistan and suspected of terrorist activity. In accordance with the new guidelines, the White House had asked DOJ for its blessing, which it promptly received—Eric Holder was not about to deny his friend permission. But Pakistan threw a wrench into the works by announcing it would oppose any action taken by the U.S. military on its soil.[51]

Whatever the outcome, it put the White House in the embarrassing position of having to defend the fact that the United States was once again deciding whether to send an unmanned drone to kill an American citizen, living in another country, who had not been charged with any crime.

Problems in operating under the new guidelines became even more manifest in April 2015, when President Obama came into the White House Briefing Room to announce that the United States had "accidentally" killed two civilian aid workers—American Warren Weinstein and Italian Giovanni lo Porto—in an attack on a suspected al Qaeda compound in the Afghanistan/Pakistan border area. (One of the targets was also an American—al Qaeda member Ahmed Farouq.) "As president and as commander in chief," he added, "I take full responsibility of all of our counter-terrorism operations, including the one that inadvertently took the lives of Warren and Giovanni."[52]

Later, White House Press Secretary Josh Earnest explained that the operation was carried out with "near-certain intelligence" that there were no civilians in the near vicinity of the compound. Despite days of surveillance, the CIA never discovered that two hostages were being held there by al Qaeda operatives. Earnest said the tragic consequences of this strike, ordered by a senior counterterrorism official at the CIA, would trigger a review of the new drone guidelines. But neither he nor President Obama, while apologizing for its results, would even acknowledge that the attack had been carried out by a drone.[53]

In announcing the botched operation resulting in the deaths of Weinstein and lo Porto, the White House also revealed for the first time that yet another American, an al Qaeda recruit named Adam Gadahn, had been killed by a drone strike in January 2015—with, again, no attempt to capture him and bring him to trial.[54]

These latest incidents once again raised perhaps the most troubling question of America's drone warfare: Who decides who's a legitimate target and who's not? In most cases, it was President Obama himself.

As reported by the *New York Times* and other publications, for some time Obama met with his national security team every Tuesday in the Situation Room, on what some aides in the White House dubbed "Terror Tuesday," to review and approve nominations for drone attacks. That offered up, noted the *Times*, the unbelievable scenario of a "liberal law professor who campaigned against the Iraq war and torture, and then insisted on approving every new name on an expanding 'kill list,' poring over terrorist suspects' biographies on what one official called the macabre 'baseball cards' of an unconventional war: 'When a rare opportunity for a drone strike at a top terrorist arises—but his family is with him—it is the president who has reserved to himself the final moral calculation.'"[55]

Shades of George W. Bush, who kept a list of two dozen senior terrorist suspects in the Oval Office and reportedly drew an X over their photographs when he received word that they'd been eliminated or imprisoned. Progressives expected it from Bush, but not from Obama.

The practice is so unbelievably contrary to the Constitution that only late-night comedian Stephen Colbert could capture its absurdity: "Trial by jury, trial by fire, rock, paper, scissors, who cares? Due process just means that there is a process that you do. The current process is apparently, first the president meets with his advisers and decides who he can kill. Then he kills them."[56]

And, of course, those decisions are made in secret White House meetings by the president alone with zero transparency, zero accountability, and no checks or oversight of any kind by Congress or the courts. It's a stunning and troubling use of imperial presidential power.

In August 2009, for example, CIA director Leon Panetta informed the president they had an opportunity to take out Baitullah Mehsud, leader of the Pakistani Taliban. Doing so, however, meant the "near certainty" of innocent civilians being killed also, because he was with his wife at a family gathering at his in-laws' home. Nevertheless, Obama gave the order. Mehsud was killed, along with his wife and possibly other family members. According to a report by the human-rights group Reprieve, that was the seventh attempt to kill Mehsud by drone. All seven together resulted in 164 deaths.[57]

After seven years of drone warfare by the Obama administration, one thing is clear: While it's supposed to be part of an effort to capture or kill terrorist suspects, there's little effort put into the capture department. For Obama, drones are a convenient way to escape the pesky complications of capture found at Gitmo: Where will suspects be housed? Where will they be tried? You never have those problems when you just send a drone to assassinate them.

In fact, while thousands of suspects have been killed by American drones, the *Times* reported in May 2012 that only one suspect—one!—has been taken into custody. The administration will never admit this is its goal, but one top Republican has. "Their policy is to take out high-value targets, versus capturing high-value targets," said former senator Saxby Chambliss, who served as ranking Republican on the Senate Intelligence Committee. "They are not going to advertise that, but that's what they're doing."[58]

In one sense, drone warfare has served the Obama administration well. Dennis Blair, former director of national intelligence, points out: "It is the politically advantageous thing to do—low cost, no U.S. casualties, gives the appearance of toughness. . . . It plays well domestically, and it is unpopular only in other countries. Any damage it does to the national interest only shows up over the long term."[59]

And yet, the use of drones as killing machines has serious short-term and long-term consequences for the United States. In the Middle East, drones have become a provocative symbol of unchecked American power, resented by both enemies and allies. With so many civilian casualties, they undercut any American claims to just war or moral authority. With operations located so far from the battlefield, they eliminate any sense of responsibility or accountability. They set a dangerous precedent for other countries to send their own drones over borders, anywhere on the planet, to kill their enemies. And they raise a yet-untested, but fundamental question, as posed by the *New Yorker*'s Steve Coll: "Is a program of targeted killing, conducted without judicial oversight or public scrutiny, consistent with American interests and values?"[60]

One thing is for sure: Sitting in the White House, unilaterally deciding who will be killed by remote-controlled drones, is the last thing progressives expected to see from constitutional law professor Barack Obama.

Of course, we didn't expect he'd be listening in on our phone calls, either.

NSA Listens In

Equally as troubling as Obama's expanded use of drones was his embrace of wholesale domestic eavesdropping by the National Security Agency. While no one died as a result, it affected many millions more, both here and abroad, and it continues, in only a somewhat limited form, to this day.

On domestic spying, civil libertarians reeled from one shock to another. During the previous administration, they were outraged to learn that President George W. Bush had authorized the NSA to eavesdrop on phone calls made overseas by American citizens without even seeking authorization of the FISA Court, as required by law. They were further shocked when Edward Snowden revealed to *The Guardian*'s Glenn Greenwald in June 2013 that under President Obama, NSA spying not only had continued with his full blessing, but had been vastly expanded. With the cooperation of Verizon and other communication companies, the NSA was now collecting "metadata" on every phone call, domestic and foreign, made by every American citizen—as well as every email sent out of the country.[61]

In sum, Obama had not only failed to rein in America's intelligence agencies, as promised during his presidential campaign, he had given them practically unlimited freedom to operate, without regard to the right of privacy.

News of Verizon's cooperation with the NSA was just the first of a series of blockbuster revelations by Snowden that trickled out from the pages of *The Guardian* and other news outlets over the next year. Six months after Greenwald's first story, the *National Journal* tallied up all we had learned from Snowden. Here's their report verbatim:

- June 5: Verizon on "an ongoing, daily basis" provides the NSA information on telephone calls within the U.S. and between the U.S. and other countries. (*The Guardian*)
- June 6: A secret program known as PRISM that began in 2007 collects foreign communications traffic from the servers of nine leading U.S. Internet companies, namely Microsoft, Google, Yahoo, Facebook, PayTalk, YouTube, Skype, AOL, and Apple. (*Washington Post*)
- July 31: XKeyscore, the NSA's self-described "widest-reaching" intelligence system, is a software tool that allows analysts, reportedly without authorization, to search through enormous databases containing emails, online chats, and the browsing histories of millions of individuals. (*The Guardian*)
- August 29: The government's top-secret "black budget" details the allocation in fiscal 2013 of $52.6 billion for 16 federal spy agencies that comprise the U.S. intelligence community. (*Washington Post*)

- October 30: In tandem with the British Government Communications Headquarters, a program known as MUSCULAR secretly infiltrates and copies data flows across fiber-optic cables transporting information among data centers of Yahoo and Google. (*Washington Post*)
- November 26: The NSA gathers records of online sexual activity and visits to porn sites in an effort to discredit the reputations of those believed to be jihadist radicalizers. (*Huffington Post*)
- December 4: The NSA is tracking 5 billion records a day that monitor the location of cell phones around the world. "In scale, scope and potential impact on privacy, the efforts to collect and analyze location data may be unsurpassed among the NSA surveillance programs." (*Washington Post*)
- December 9: Agents working for the NSA and Britain's GCHQ are infiltrating the virtual realities of online video games such as World of Warcraft and Second Life in an effort to catch and foil possible terrorist plots. (*New York Times*)
- December 10: The NSA uses Google-acquired "cookies," relied upon by Internet advertisers to track preferences of consumers, to locate targets for hacking. (*Washington Post*)
- December 20: The NSA paid RSA, a large computer security firm, $10 million to build and promote a flawed encryption system that left open a "back door" through which the agency's intelligence analysts could access data on computers around the world. (Reuters)[62]

Attorney General Eric Holder immediately charged Snowden with three violations of the U.S. Espionage Act, even though he had not given his secrets to the enemy. But, in his own initial response to the Snowden revelations, Obama seemed to play down the leak of information. I was there in the White House Briefing Room on June 7, 2013, when he told reporters: "Now, the programs that have been discussed over the last couple days in the press are secret in the sense that they're classified, but they're not secret in the sense that when it comes to telephone calls, every member of Congress has been briefed on this program."[63]

As many journalists, including this one, soon discovered, that statement was simply not true. All members of Congress had *not* been briefed on the NSA's megadata phone collection program. Not even all members of the House and Senate intelligence committees had been briefed. Only the chairs and ranking members. I interviewed several members of Congress in the weeks following the president's remarks. Not one of them knew of the NSA's expanded activities until Edward Snowden unveiled them.

The president went on to cite continuing judicial overview. "So in summary, what you've got is two programs that were originally authorized by Congress, have been repeatedly authorized by Congress. Bipartisan majorities have approved them. Congress is continually briefed on how these are conducted. There are a whole range of safeguards involved. And federal judges are overseeing the entire program throughout."[64]

By "federal judges," of course, Obama meant the Foreign Intelligence Surveillance Court, or FISA Court, which everybody knows is a joke. Established by Congress in 1978, as a result of the Church Committee hearings, it was intended to ensure judicial oversight and approval of intelligence activities. Alas, it has since become nothing but a rubber stamp for the CIA, NSA, and other agencies—where all deliberations are held in secret and there was no public advocate—until the Senate amended the Patriot Act in June 2015.

Any notion that the FISA Court was a true deliberative body was crushed years earlier, when the *New York Times* revealed that, in the wake of September 11, President George W. Bush had broken the law by authorizing the NSA to eavesdrop on telephone calls made by Americans without obtaining a warrant from the FISA Court. After conducting my own research at the time, I remember reporting that Bush had needlessly gone out of his way to bypass FISA—because the court seldom, if ever, turned down any request made by an intelligence agency. In fact, *Salon* magazine reported, the very day of Obama's news conference: "Since the start of the War on Terror more than 11 years ago, the court has denied just 10 applications, and modified several dozen, while approving more than 15,000." Russell Trice, a former NSA analyst, told *The Guardian* the FISA Court "is a kangaroo court with a rubber stamp."[65]

So for President Obama to tell Americans their privacy was protected by the FISA Court was also simply not true.

But Obama wasn't done trying to minimize the importance of Snowden's revelations. In that same news conference, he first reassured Americans they had nothing to worry about: "Nobody is listening to your phone calls." But Obama then went on to issue a warning he had never made before. There were "some trade-offs involved" in keeping Americans safe, Obama insisted. "You can't have 100 percent security, and also then have 100 percent privacy and zero inconvenience."[66]

That flatly contradicted Obama's previous statements on government snooping and personal privacy. As candidate for president in August 2007, Senator Obama pledged: "The Bush administration puts forward a false choice between the liberties we cherish and the security we provide. I will provide our intelligence and law enforcement agencies with the tools they need to track and take out the terrorists without undermining our constitution and our freedom."[67]

In his inaugural address, President Obama reiterated: "As for our common defense, we reject as false the choice between our safety and our ideals."[68]

Now, here was the same Barack Obama offering up the same old false choice, defending the NSA's massive data collection as legal, approved by the FISA Court, and necessary to track down terrorists— while condemning Snowden for releasing documents detailing the NSA's massive overreach. The White House routinely denounced Snowden as a felon and demanded that he be returned to the United States from exile in Russia so he could stand trial (and probably spend the rest of his life in federal prison, like poor Chelsea Manning).[69]

It should have come as no surprise, therefore, when Obama also defended the next Snowden bombshell: that, in addition to monitoring phone calls of American citizens, the NSA was also snooping on calls made by friendly foreign leaders on their personal cell phones, including German chancellor Angela Merkel and Brazilian president Dilma Rousseff. Both responded with outrage. An angry Merkel called

Obama to complain. Rousseff canceled a planned state visit to the United States.[70]

At first, the White House dismissed complaints about foreign eavesdropping by insisting it was no big deal: Yes, we spy on them, but "they also spy on us." But when criticism from foreign capitals failed to subside, Obama convened a panel of five intelligence experts to review the NSA's procedures and recommend any necessary changes.

In their final December 2013 report to the president, the Review Group on Intelligence and Communications Technologies found that the NSA was, indeed, abusing its authority under the law, thereby undermining the right of privacy of all Americans, and recommended forty-six changes in the way the NSA collects and stores data. They also concluded that the data produced by years of massive spying on our phone calls by the NSA "was not essential to preventing attacks and could readily have been obtained in a timely manner using conventional" methods.[71]

One month later, the government's own Privacy and Civil Liberties Oversight Board came to the same conclusion. On January 23, 2014, the board released its report on the NSA's surveillance program revealed by Edward Snowden and recommended the program be ended as illegal and ineffective. Federal agencies would still be able to obtain phone and other records under court orders in cases involving an individualized suspicion of wrongdoing, concluded the board, but there would be no storehouse, private or public, of telephone data beyond what the phone companies keep in the course of their normal business activities.[72]

Most notably, the Privacy Board determined that the NSA program "lacks a viable legal foundation" and concluded: "We see little evidence that the unique capabilities provided by the NSA's bulk collection of telephone records actually have yielded material counterterrorism results that could not have been achieved without the NSA's Section 215 program."[73]

In effect, the president's own commission and the official Privacy and Civil Liberties Oversight Board both concluded that Edward Snowden was right: The NSA was out of control and its wholesale collection of phone call data yielded little or nothing of value. Yet President Obama largely ignored both panels' recommendations and made only minor adjustments to the program.

To this day, after an official presidential inquiry, extensive media scrutiny, and several congressional hearings, nobody has concluded that anything—not one single detail—about the NSA revealed in the Snowden documents is wrong. Nor has the White House provided evidence of any damage to America's national security resulting from the Snowden documents.

Nevertheless, having charged Snowden with two counts of espionage, the Obama administration continues to pursue him as a criminal, not as the whistle-blower he is. Obama, in fact, denounced whistle-blowers in general in a January 2014 speech to the Justice Department: "Our nation's defense depends in part on the fidelity of those entrusted with our nation's secrets. If any individual who objects to government policy can take it in their own hands to publicly disclose classified information, then we will not be able to keep our people safe, or conduct foreign policy." In fact, Snowden reported concerns to his superiors at NSA several times, to no effect. Had he persisted, it is hard to imagine he would have been met with anything but hostility, if not criminal charges.[74]

Note: Once he left office, Eric Holder told *Yahoo News* he thought Snowden, while breaking the law, had actually performed a public service in drawing attention to the NSA's overreach. Not only that, he suggested there might be a deal whereby Snowden could return to the United States and admit guilt in return for serving a light sentence. But, speaking for the administration, FBI Director James Comey quickly shot down that possibility: "There will be no deal for Edward Snowden."[75]

As it is, Snowden remains in exile in Moscow, charged with three felonies and blocked by the United States from flying anywhere outside Russia. After all, said former White House press secretary Jay Carney, "He is not a human rights activist, he is not a dissident. He is accused of leaking classified information."[76]

The Obama administration's drive to put Edward Snowden behind bars stands in stark contrast to the sweetheart deal the Justice Department gave to David Petraeus, another American charged with revealing state secrets. According to his indictment, Petraeus, former director of the CIA and former commander of U.S. forces in Afghanistan, admitted giving Paula Broadwell, his biographer and lover, eight notebooks full of "classified information regarding the identities of covert officers, war strategy, intelligence capabilities and mechanisms, diplomatic discussions, quotes and deliberative discussions from high-level National Security Council meetings . . . and [his personal] discussions with the president of the United States." Yet, in March 2015, the Justice Department agreed that Petraeus would receive a sentence of only two years' probation and a fine of $100,000. No jail time.[77]

That contrast was not lost on famed whistle-blower Daniel Ellsberg, the first person charged under the Espionage Act for leaking the Pentagon Papers, who told *The Guardian*'s Trevor Timm: "The factual charges against Edward Snowden are not more serious, as violations of the classification regulations and non-disclosure agreements, than those Petraeus has admitted to, which are actually quite spectacular."[78]

The White House still insists all it wants to do is return Snowden to the United States so he can be granted a fair trial—like Private Chelsea Manning, who is now serving thirty-five years in federal prison for leaking devastating documents about the Iraq War to Wikileaks. But Edward Snowden's not the only one who knows that the promise of a fair trial for him, or any NSA whistle-blower, is a joke.

In *Citizenfour*, the powerful Oscar-winning Laura Poitras documentary about Snowden, there's a clip of Jay Carney telling us reporters at the White House: "Mr. Snowden has been accused of leaking classified information and he faces felony charges in the U.S. He should be returned to the United States as soon as possible, where he will be accorded full due process." At which point, in the theater where I saw the film, the audience erupted in laughter.[79]

As we will see in the next section, not only have other whistle-blowers been similarly pursued by the Justice Department, but so have reporters they talked to, such as James Risen of the *New York Times* and James Rosen of *Fox News*.

Meanwhile, even as they condemned and harassed whistle-blowers,

White House officials stood by James Clapper, appointed by Obama as director of national intelligence—after he had blatantly lied to Congress. At a March 2013 hearing of the Senate Intelligence Committee, Oregon senator Ron Wyden, the Senate's chief NSA critic, publicly asked Clapper a question he had given him advance warning of, the day before: whether the NSA collects "any type of data at all on millions or hundreds of millions of Americans."[80]

Clapper lied through his teeth. "No, sir," he replied, before adding, "Not wittingly." He was lying, and everybody on the committee knew he was lying. If anyone else had so openly perjured himself before a congressional committee, he'd be in federal prison today. But Clapper's still on the job, stoutly defended by both intelligence chair Senator Dianne Feinstein and President Obama.[81]

In fact, nobody was more blindsided by President Obama's Bush-like hard line on the NSA than Wyden, who was, for a while, chief sidekick of freshman senator Barack Obama on national security issues. In his keynote address to the 2004 Democratic National Convention, the speech that made him a national celebrity, one of Obama's most memorable lines was his criticism of big government snooping: "We worship an awesome God in the blue states, and we don't like federal agents poking around our libraries in the red states." Once in the Senate, Obama joined Wyden in opposing renewal of the Patriot Act and in sponsoring legislation to curb the NSA's massive snooping powers under George W. Bush. In a speech on the Senate floor, Obama declared that the NSA's expanded power under the Patriot Act to seize phone and library records "seriously jeopardizes the rights of all Americans and the ideals America stands for."[82]

Imagine Wyden's surprise, then, on his first visit with his former colleague in the Oval Office. Wyden had requested the meeting in order to discuss the NSA's spying practices with Obama, Attorney General Eric Holder, and Director of the National Counterterrorism Center Matthew G. Olsen. As recounted by Ryan Lizza in the *New Yorker*, Obama stunned Wyden by asserting that, on national security issues, he would defer to Olsen—chief of the very intelligence agencies whose overreach Obama had repeatedly challenged as a senator. In admirable understatement, Wyden told Lizza: "I realized I had a lot more to do to show the White House that this constant deferring to the leadership of the intelligence agencies on fundamental policy issues was not going to get the job done."[83]

In other words, Wyden was shocked to discover that President Obama disagreed with Senator Obama on national security issues.

The whole issue of NSA's surveillance program came to a head in the spring of 2015 because of two events: a court decision and a legislative deadline. On May 7, a federal appeals court ruled that the NSA's once-secret phone program was illegal. In a unanimous ruling, the United States Court of Appeals for the Second Circuit held that Section 215 of the Patriot Act, under which the NSA justified its phone data collection, "cannot bear the weight the government asks us to assign to it, and that it does not authorize the telephone metadata program."[84]

The court's ruling was particularly timely, given that Section 215 was due to expire on May 31. If Congress did not act to extend Section 215, the NSA phone collection operation would shut down. The battleground over national security was set.

There were those—including Senate Leader Mitch McConnell and, originally, President Obama—who wanted to simply reaffirm Section 215 and keep the NSA in business as usual. But the votes were not there. There were others, led by Kentucky senator Rand Paul, who wanted to seize the occasion to kill the program altogether. But the votes weren't there for that, either.

The result, instead, was a historic, middle-of-the-road, bipartisan compromise, which received 338 votes in the House and 67 votes in the Senate. Coauthored by Democrat Patrick Leahy and Republican Mike Lee, the USA Freedom Act accomplished two main goals: clipping the wings of the NSA and removing some of the secrecy of the national security court, or FISA. After six months, phone companies, not the NSA, would store the bulk phone data—any part of which the NSA could access, but only after obtaining a specific warrant from the FISA Court. And, for the first time, a special panel of outside experts would be added to the FISA Court, to represent the public by reviewing and challenging government requests for access to information.[85]

With those relatively minor changes, and with Obama's blessing, telecom companies continue to collect and store data on every phone call made and every email sent by every American citizen—a storehouse of private information to which the NSA, through the FISA Court, has ready access.

In the end, what Senator Frank Church predicted would happen back in 1975 has come true. At the conclusion of his hearings on intelligence agencies, Church warned: "The NSA's capability at any time could be turned around on the American people, and no American would have any privacy left, such is the capability to monitor everything: telephone conversations, telegrams, it doesn't matter. There would be no place to hide."[86]

That's exactly what's happening today. And you thought *1984* was a novel! Even reporters found themselves being spied on.

Freedom of the Press

It's a rare occasion to get the White House press corps together on a Saturday afternoon. But members did gather on Saturday, October 25, 2014, to celebrate the work of four veteran White House reporters who had spent more than forty years on the job: Thomas DeFrank, now with the *National Journal*; Ann Compton, *ABC Radio News*; Bill Plante, *CBS News*; and Mark Knoller, *CBS Radio*.[87]

However, what was planned as a festive, celebratory event suddenly took on a harder edge. At one of two panels organized by the WHCA, former and current members of the White House press corps discussed the unique challenges of covering the Obama presidency.

Several other reporters had earlier noted that the Obama administration, which reporters initially greeted as a welcome change from the hostile days of George Bush and Dick Cheney, had, in fact, become even less open to the press. "This is the most secretive White House I have ever dealt with," fumed then–*New York Times* executive editor Jill Abramson. *CBS News Face the Nation* host Bob Schieffer also expressed his frustration with trying to get answers out of the White

House. "When I'm asked what is the most manipulative and secretive administration I've covered, I always say it's the one in office now."[88]

Schieffer told former *Washington Post* executive editor Leonard Downie this as part of a thirty-page report, "The Obama Administration and the Press," prepared by Downie for the Committee to Protect Journalists. "Every administration learns from the previous administration. They become more secretive and put tighter clamps on information. This administration exercises more control than George W. Bush's did, and his before that." *New York Times* reporter James Risen, personally targeted by the Obama Justice Department, put it more bluntly: "I think Obama hates the press."[89]

The highly respected and generally soft-spoken Susan Page, Washington bureau chief for *USA Today*, added a whole new dimension to tense dealings between the Obama administration and the media when she told our WHCA gathering that the current White House was not only "more restrictive," but also "more dangerous" to the press than any other administration in history. Not surprisingly, perhaps, and I was there: No one challenged her dismal characterization of the Obama White House.[90]

Indeed, as part of its determination to prevent government leaks, the Obama administration has waged an unprecedented war against investigative journalists, who were guilty of nothing more than doing their jobs: talking to sources and reporting what they had learned. In his October 13 report, Downie cited the "chilling effect" on freedom of the press when reporters learned that their phones had been tapped, their emails monitored, and their travel records seized. "The administration's war on leaks and other efforts to control information are the most aggressive I've seen since the Nixon administration, when I was one of the editors involved in the *Washington Post*'s investigation of Watergate," wrote Downie, now professor of journalism at Arizona State University.[91]

Heading the assault on press freedom was then–attorney general Eric Holder, whose Justice Department targeted six government employees and two contractors for prosecution under the 1917 Espionage Act on charges they had leaked classified information to the press. Only three such prosecutions had occurred under all previous presidents!

The first media organization targeted was the Associated Press, which discovered that the Justice Department had secretly collected phone records of several AP reporters in 2012 as part of a leak investigation. "It was a very large number of records that were obtained, including phone records from Hartford, New York, Washington, from the U.S. House of Representatives and elsewhere where AP has bureaus," according to AP lawyer David Schultz. "It included home and cellphone numbers from a number of AP reporters."[92]

Again, Schultz noted the negative impact the Justice Department's unprecedented actions would have on investigative journalism: "This sort of activity really amounts to massive government monitoring of the actions of the press, and it really puts a dagger at the heart of AP's news-gathering activities."[93]

Individual journalists who talked to alleged leakers were also targeted, most notably James Rosen of *Fox News* and James Risen of the *New York Times*.

Rosen was caught up in the Justice Department's investigation of State Department contractor Stephen Jin-Woo Kim, who pleaded guilty to leaking information about North Korea to the press and is now serving thirteen months in federal prison. As part of its investigation, the DOJ labeled Rosen a "criminal co-conspirator," and under that moniker were successful in obtaining search warrants that enabled them to monitor Rosen's activities by tracking his visits to the State Department through phone traces, timing of calls, and personal emails.[94]

Attorney General Eric Holder personally signed off on the search warrant calling Rosen a "criminal co-conspirator," an act for which he later expressed regret. In an October 2013 interview with NBC justice reporter Pete Williams, he confessed he was "not comfortable" with having issued the search warrant: "I don't like that, because it means me as an official who has great respect for the press, is in essence saying a reporter doing his or her job and doing that important job is somehow branded a criminal."[95]

He also admitted the Justice Department had probably gone too far and promised to fix the problem. "I'm a little concerned that things have gotten a little out of whack," he told Williams. "I think we can do a better job than we have. We can reform those regulations, reform those guidelines to better reflect that balance [between national security and press freedom]."[96]

In the end, fortunately, Rosen was not jailed or prosecuted, and the White House announced in May 2013 that he was definitely off the hook. No additional charges would be filed against him. That same month, shaken by backlash from the AP and Rosen stories, the Obama administration began to respond. The president, who declared that journalists should not be at legal risk for doing their jobs, called on Congress to pass a "media shield" law that would protect journalists from being forced to reveal their confidential sources. "Stop me before I threaten the press again!" Obama in effect implored Congress. But no such law was passed.[97]

And on May 30, Attorney General Holder held an unusual, ninety-minute meeting with Washington bureau chiefs, seeking their advice on new media guidelines for the Justice Department. According to those present, Holder again acknowledged that the department had over-reached in its leak investigations and would seek further procedural and legislative changes to protect the First Amendment rights of journalists. We will never know what actually transpired at the meeting, however, because Holder insisted that it be entirely "off the record." Which is why the New York Times and the Associated Press refused to attend.[98]

But even after that meeting, and all those good words, there was no smooth sledding, or apparent change of policy, for New York Times investigative reporter James Risen. The two-time Pulitzer Prize winner was still being pursued by the Justice Department for his reporting on "Operation Merlin," a failed CIA effort to undermine Iran's nuclear weapons program by providing them with false blueprints. Former CIA agent Jeffrey Sterling, charged with leaking information on the program to Risen, was convicted by a federal court and sentenced to forty-two months in prison.[99]

In pursuit of Risen, the government traced and monitored his phone calls, emails, and credit card and bank records. Again, all for just doing his job. He received his first subpoena to testify in the government's case against Sterling in 2008, which he successfully fought. That subpoena expired in 2009. Then, to the consternation of freedom of the press advocates, the Obama administration renewed Risen's subpoena in 2010, and this time Risen lost his appeal. He testified at a "moot" hearing in federal court on January 5, 2014. As agreed ahead of time, prosecutors did not ask Risen to name his source, but he still refused to provide any information other than to confirm that he had written a book and two articles, one of which mentions Jeffrey Sterling, about Operation Merlin. Finally, in January 2015—nearly seven years after his ordeal began—the Department of Justice informed Risen that he was off the hook, and would not be called as a witness against Sterling.[100]

As any veteran White House aide or reporter will acknowledge, there is always tension between the president and the press corps. Reporters want more access; the president—or at least the president's aides—wants less. The White House wants stories that paint the president's policies in the best light; reporters believe in telling the story, however it falls. Reporters want to know everything that's going on; the White House tells them only what it thinks they need to know. Reporters ask tough questions; the White House would prefer, if not easy, at least less intimidating ones.

That tension between reporters doing their jobs and White House officials, from the president on down, goes with the territory. And it's healthy. But not since Richard Nixon has a White House used the powers of the presidency to threaten or actually persecute journalists for seeking to uncover and report the truth. The Obama administration's war on journalists raises serious questions about how much freedom of the press really exists today. It's certainly not what progressives expected from the man who promised "the most transparent" administration in history.

Bush v. Obama

Bottom line: On national security issues, there's not a curve between the Bush and Obama administrations. There's a straight, even escalating line between the two.

With the notable exception of banning torture, on critical national security matters, there's little difference between Bush/Cheney and Obama/Biden. For the most part, Obama not only continued, but expanded, every executive action taken by Bush. He kept Guantanamo open. He vastly increased the number of drone strikes, personally approving every target on the CIA's "kill list." He even authorized drones to hunt down and kill American citizens on foreign soil.

And, of course, Obama failed to challenge or rein in the intelligence agencies he had so strongly criticized when he was a United States senator—which will have a lasting and pernicious effect. Because, in ratifying the Bush post-9/11 security state apparatus, Obama made it bipartisan, and thus even more powerful—just as, in an earlier era, Eisenhower made Social Security and the New Deal more secure by giving them his bipartisan stamp of approval.

There's a big difference, of course. Eisenhower's embrace of Social Security made Americans more secure. Obama's embrace of NSA put Americans more at risk—from their own government.

In sum, what the country was yearning for in 2008 was a radical break from the Bush/Cheney approach to national security, a reassertion of moral principles, the end of decision-making based on fear, and a return to respect for international law. But that's not what President Obama delivered.

There's no doubt that if the CIA's escalation of killer drones and the NSA's mass collection of phone and Internet data had happened during the presidency of George W. Bush, progressives would have been raising holy hell. As they should now under Barack Obama. Progressives can't condone or ignore the growth and intrusion of an oppressive, extralegal national security state simply because its current leader happens to be America's first black president.

FOUR

Foreign Policy

As badly as progressives wanted to see an end to the Bush national security state, they were also eager for the end of the Bush brand of foreign policy.

George W. Bush may not have been a Texan by birth, but he certainly brought to Washington a cowboy, shoot-from-the-hip approach to foreign policy: It's my way or the highway. You're with me, or you're with the terrorists. You can run, but you can't hide. Bring 'em back, dead or alive. Bush and his foreign policy team—Dick Cheney, Condi Rice, and Donald Rumsfeld—cooked up their plans in the White House and then gave orders to carry them out, with no consideration of, or consultation with, members of Congress or allies around the world—and zero respect for international law.

Bush so turned off allies and stoked anti-American sentiment among other nations that, when Barack Obama moved into the Oval Office, the United States was hated around the world by friend and foe. There were, literally, worldwide smiles when Obama was elected. In terms of international relations, there was nowhere to go but up.

So the stage was set for a new look and direction in foreign policy. Barack Obama had promised one, and, for a while at least, he delivered. He outraged conservatives by traveling to Cairo, into the belly of the beast, to reassure Arab nations that the United States was not engaged in war against Islam. (They're still calling this trip his "apology tour.") He rekindled important relationships with allies Bush had alienated. He carried through with his promise to withdraw all combat troops from Iraq by the end of 2011. He put together an international coalition to support Libyan rebels in the overthrow of Muammar Qaddafi. In 2009, he became perhaps the first person to be awarded the Nobel Peace Prize not for what he had already done to make the world a better place, but for what he was fully expected to do. No pressure![1]

But looking back now, in the twilight of his presidency, it's difficult, if not impossible, to define Obama's foreign policy. Because there was no overall, defining strategy. As *New Yorker* editor David Remnick, who authored a well-received critique of Obama's rise to the presidency, summed it up: "Obama has offered no full and clarifying foreign-policy vision."[2]

Under George Bush, there was no doubt what his foreign policy was: "American exceptionalism." The United States has the right to go anywhere, against any foe, any time it wants, no allies needed, and no apologies given. If you don't like it, you're a friend of Osama bin Laden's.

Under Barack Obama, the foreign policy seemed to be: "American leadership . . . sometimes." We are still the world's greatest leader. You *may* be able to count on us when you need us, but we won't be there in any hurry—or we may not show up at all. Meanwhile, if you do anything really bad, we'll respond with the full force of the United States—but, then again, maybe we won't.

Following that "on-again, off-again" approach to foreign policy, Obama threatened to bomb Syria if President Assad used chemical weapons against insurgents. But, once Assad did in fact deploy chemical weapons, Obama decided to ask permission of Congress, instead. That vote was ultimately postponed after Russia offered a diplomatic path forward. Speaking of Russia, Obama vowed to protect the territorial integrity of Ukraine. But, once Vladimir Putin seized Crimea, he effectively let him have it. Crimea's now part of Russia. Obama at first refused to send arms to the Syrian opposition. Three years later, he made them the centerpiece of America's anti-ISIS campaign.

Critics dubbed Obama's brand of foreign policy "leading from behind." Obama himself summed up his approach to world affairs in four little words: "Don't do stupid stuff"—which reportedly, inside the sanctity of the White House, came out in the more colorful version: "Don't do stupid shit." It's a policy one former White House insider, former secretary of state Hillary Clinton, didn't hesitate to criticize, once she left the administration. "Great nations need organizing principles," she told journalist Jeffrey Goldberg. "Don't do stupid stuff is not an organizing principle."[3]

Asked to defend what appeared to be an uncertain approach to foreign policy, Obama outlined his approach to world crises, exploring every possible economic and diplomatic lever before even considering the use of armed force. As he explained it to reporters in April 2014: "That may not always be sexy. That may not always attract a lot of attention, and it doesn't make for good argument on Sunday morning shows, but it avoids errors. You hit singles, you hit doubles; every once in a while we may be able to hit a home run. But we steadily advance the interests of the American people and our partnership with folks around the world."[4]

That deliberate, considered approach to world problems was assuredly preferable to George Bush's tendency to shoot first and ask questions later. But it still left the distinct impression that Obama's foreign policy—much like his domestic policy, in fact—was a game of small ball, in which he was never willing to swing for the fences. It's hard to inspire anyone, at home or abroad, when your stated goal is just to hit a blooper beyond the infield.

The Bad War: Iraq

As much as anything else, Barack Obama is president of the United States today because of the war in Iraq. As a state senator from Illinois, he opposed it in a speech to a Chicago antiwar rally in October 2002. As a United States senator from New York, Hillary Clinton voted for it on the Senate floor. And that made all the difference.

Even in that now-famous speech, Obama made it clear he was not opposed to all wars. "What I am opposed to is a dumb war," he told the crowd. "What I am opposed to is a rash war. . . . I know that an invasion of Iraq without a clear rationale and without strong interna-

tional support will only fan the flames of the Middle East." As a candidate for president, he promised to end the war in Iraq. As president,
he immediately set out to do so. On February 27, 2009, barely a month
after becoming commander-in-chief, he announced that the U.S. combat mission in Iraq would end by August 31, 2010, while a transitional
force of up to fifty thousand troops tasked with training Iraqi security forces would remain until the end of 2011. This news was hap-
pily received by Iraqi prime minister Nuri al-Maliki, who expressed
total confidence in the ability of his nation's security forces to maintain
order without U.S. military support. A confidence shared by President
Obama—which turned out to be woefully misplaced.[5]

Withdrawal of American troops from Iraq began soon after, and
continued in stages. On June 29, 2009, U.S. forces abandoned Bagh-
dad and handed over thirty-eight bases outside the capital to the Iraqi
military. In February 2010, to mark the transition, Defense Secretary
Robert Gates announced that "Operation Iraqi Freedom" was officially
over, to be replaced by "Operation New Dawn." The drumbeat of de-
partures continued apace until August 19, 2010, when the last U.S.
combat brigades crossed the border out of Iraq into Kuwait.[6]

Left behind until December 2011, as agreed, were fifty thousand
American troops assigned to train the Iraqi military. And that's where
trouble began. For the next year, negotiations dragged on about the
status of residual American troops, and whether they would be guaranteed immunity from Iraqi law while in the country. When al-Maliki
refused to consider immunity, President Obama abruptly pulled the
plug and declared that all U.S. troops and trainers would leave Iraq by
the end of 2011.[7]

The last American soldier to die in Iraq was killed by a roadside
bomb on November 14 of that year. The last U.S. troops left the country
on December 18, leaving behind twenty thousand embassy and consulate staffers, as well as some five thousand private military contractors.[8]

But, of course, as it turned out, the war in Iraq wasn't over; President Obama had just hit the pause button. In June 2014, three years
after American troops had left, the war flared up again when a largely
unknown terrorist organization called "The Islamic State in Iraq and

Syria," or ISIS, stunned the world by seizing Mosul, Iraq's second-largest city, having already occupied most of western Syria. By August, the United States had launched air strikes against ISIS targets in Iraq. In mid-September, air strikes were expanded to include ISIS installations inside Syria. And by mid-November—third verse same as the second—there were thirty-one hundred American troops back on the ground in Iraq, although President Obama insisted they were not "combat forces," but merely there to train Iraqi, Kurdish, and Syrian opposition combat forces. Yes, that's what they said in Vietnam, too.[9]

The new war against ISIS—the Iraq War, the Threequel—raises serious questions about our mission, strategy, chances of success, and legality of the operation—all of which will be discussed shortly. Meanwhile . . .

The Good War: Afghanistan

For President Obama, the war in Afghanistan was always the good war—a smart war, not a dumb one—one worth fighting and, even though the United States had long ago achieved its original mission of removing the Taliban from power, one worth finishing.

The problem was that when he took office, seven and a half years after President George W. Bush invaded Afghanistan, there were still 38,000 American troops in the country. Obama quickly allowed 21,000 more, already put in the pipeline by Bush, to be deployed. But military leaders warned that, without yet more ground forces, we could not win the war in Afghanistan.[10]

For a war-reluctant president, facing a war-weary nation in the first months of his presidency, that request posed a real dilemma. And how President Obama resolved it gave the nation the first exposure to his cautious approach to decision-making.

Obama was caught between two extremes. On the one hand, General Stanley A. McChrystal, the top military commander in Afghanistan, stated publicly that defeating the Taliban would take 500,000 troops and five years. More shades of Vietnam! Under pressure from the White House and Pentagon, McChrystal later reduced his absolute-must demand to 40,000 troops. On the other hand, Democrats in Congress opposed sending any more troops at all to Afghanistan, even on a temporary basis. We'd been there long enough, they said. Time to shut it down and bring all troops home.[11]

Thus began an agonizing, three-month-long review by the Hamletlike Obama. For us reporters, the lack of clarity provided at White House briefings reflected his uncertainty. Will he authorize more troops? If so, how many? Maybe none at all? Would he listen to the generals on the ground in Afghanistan or ignore them? The message seemed to change daily. It was certainly a far cry from George Bush's capacity to make an on-the-spot decision and never second-guess it. It maybe even reflected an inability to make any decision at all.[12]

Finally, Obama resolved the issue—in classic Obama fashion, by again trying to have it both ways. In a December 1, 2009, speech at West Point, in what he later described as "the most difficult decision of his presidency," President Obama announced he was sending 30,000 more American troops to Afghanistan—on top of almost 60,000 already there—but also announced those troops would start leaving the country in July 2011. Only Obama could announce a surge and a withdrawal from combat in the same breath.[13]

On schedule, American soldiers started coming home from Afghanistan in July 2011. Redeployments back to the States continued until, on September 21, 2012, Defense Secretary Leon Panetta announced that the surge was officially over, and a success: "The surge did accomplish its objectives of reversing the Taliban momentum on the battlefield and dramatically increasing the size and capability of the Afghan national security forces." A total of 33,000 troops had returned to the United States, leaving 68,000 still in Afghanistan—more than when Obama took office.[14]

By that time, the war in Afghanistan was already the longest, most expensive, and most meaningless war in American history. It was also one of the most unpopular. Public opinion on the conflict in Afghanistan had turned upside down. At the start of the war in October 2001, 88 percent of Americans supported the war; by December 2013, according to a CNN poll, only 17 percent supported the war, while 82 percent opposed it—which made it even more unpopular than the war in Iraq, opposed by 69 percent of Americans.[15]

As a result, despite repeated comeback spurts by the Taliban, the breakdown of Afghan security forces, evidence of massive corruption surrounding President Hamid Karzai, and a messy, if not crooked, election to choose his successor, President Obama insisted he would stick to his deadline of pulling all American troops out of Afghanistan by December 2014.

After a surprise visit to Bagram Air Field in Afghanistan over the Memorial Day weekend, President Obama appeared before reporters in the Rose Garden on May 27, 2014, and unveiled his final timetable for ending the war. After acknowledging that "Americans have learned that it's harder to end wars than it is to begin them," he announced that 32,000 American troops still in Afghanistan would be reduced to 9,800 by the end of 2014. That number would again be cut in half by the end of 2015, and by the end of 2016, all American forces would be gone— except for the small number necessary to protect the U.S. embassy in Kabul.[16]

On December 28, 2014, the Pentagon officially announced the end of all U.S. combat missions, which effectively concluded the war in Afghanistan. The American war George W. Bush started and waged for seven years, and Barack Obama continued for another six, finally stumbled to a close.

Or so we thought. Then, in October 2015, the Taliban suddenly raised its ugly head again and seized the major city of Kunduz. In response, President Obama again reluctantly changed course. All American forces would not come home by the end of 2016 after all. He directed a residual 5,500 American troops to remain in Afghanistan through the end of 2017, thereby prolonging a war that had already dragged on for fourteen years—and handing the problem over to his successor.

But with the Taliban still controlling vast areas of Afghanistan and no guarantee that any central government in Afghanistan will survive, many Americans are wondering why we went there in the first place, what we achieved in the long run, and why we stayed so long. President Obama could have pulled the plug on Afghanistan his first month in office. The end result would have been the same.[17]

The Nobel Peace Prize

After less than nine months as president, and while he was still struggling with his decision about whether to send any more troops to Afghanistan, President Obama received a surprise wake-up call from Press Secretary Robert Gibbs. Around six o'clock in the morning on October 9, 2009, Gibbs told Obama he'd been awarded the Nobel Prize for Peace. As Gibbs delighted in telling it privately, Obama's first, and natural, reaction was: "Shut the fuck up!"[18]

For the White House, Oslo's decision to single out Obama—"for his extraordinary efforts to strengthen international diplomacy and cooperation between peoples"—proved as embarrassing as it was unexpected. Everybody, starting with Obama, knew he'd done nothing to deserve the honor. The United States was, after all, involved in two wars and Obama was still trying to figure out how to deal with both. An angry White House chief of staff Rahm Emanuel—wasn't he always angry?—placed an early morning call to Norway's ambassador to the United Nations, accusing them of "fawning" over Obama and giving him the award only as a way of forcing the popular world figure to visit their country.[19]

But it was too late. The decision had already been made and announced. I was in the Rose Garden later that morning when Obama called a special press briefing to say he was "surprised" and "deeply humbled" by the award, which he did not feel he deserved, but that he would accept anyway. "I do not view it as a recognition of my own accomplishments," he noted, "but rather an affirmation of American leadership on behalf of aspirations held by people in all nations."[20]

Members of Norway's Nobel Prize committee may have had second thoughts when Obama gave his acceptance speech in Norway. In perhaps the most outrageous example of his trying to have it both ways,

Obama actually used the occasion of accepting the Nobel Peace Prize to make the case for a just war. And he did so almost forty-five years to the day after Martin Luther King, Jr., gave his own Nobel speech denouncing the use of war, period.

In some ways, it was a variation on his speech to the anti–Iraq War rally in Chicago years before, when he went out of his way to point out he was not opposed to all wars. While striving for peace, Obama told his Oslo audience, "We have to recognize that this is a dangerous world and that there are people who will do terrible things and have to be fought." He added: "The instruments of war do have a role in preserving the peace." Perhaps Alfred Nobel, the inventor of dynamite, would have been thrilled to hear it. Everyone else, not so much.[21]

Obama knew that everybody would be comparing him, America's first African-American president, to the first African-American who had received the Nobel Peace Prize, so he recognized the teachings of Martin Luther King, Jr., as "admirable"—yet not "practical or possible in every circumstance."(!) Then Obama went on to contradict what King said in his acceptance speech.

To Obama, war is inevitable:

"As someone who stands here as a direct consequence of Dr. King's life's work, I am living testimony to the moral force of nonviolence. I know there is nothing weak, nothing passive, nothing naïve in the creed and lives of Gandhi and King. But as a head of state sworn to protect and defend my nation, I cannot be guided by their examples alone. I face the world as it is, and cannot stand idle in the face of threats to the American people. For make no mistake: Evil does exist in the world."

In fact, King had anticipated and responded to this sort of riposte decades earlier. To King, then actively opposing the war in Vietnam, the very concept of war as inevitable is obsolete:

"So man's proneness to engage in war is still a fact. But wisdom born of experience should tell us that war is obsolete. There may have been a time when war served as a negative good by preventing the spread and growth of an evil force, but the destructive power of modern weapons eliminated even the possibility that war may serve as a negative good.

If we assume that life is worth living and that man has a right to survive, then we must find an alternative to war."[22]

As for Obama, his Nobel speech was yet another reflection of the frustration and disappointment progressives were starting to feel about Obama, even before he'd marked his first year in office. Before accomplishing anything as president, Barack Obama accepted the Nobel Peace Prize—and used it to justify war.

The Long-Distance War: Libya

Just as Barack Obama never expected to win the Nobel Peace Prize, Mohamed Bouazizi never expected to win the Sakharov Prize for his contributions to "historic changes in the Arab world." Nobody else did, either. But Bouazizi—a twenty-six-year-old Tunisian street vendor who, according to his family, had only one dream in life: to save enough money to buy a pickup truck—did, indeed, change the course of history in the modern Arab world.[23]

Early in the morning of December 17, 2010, in his hometown of Sidi Bouzid, a policewoman accused Bouazizi of peddling his goods without a license and not only demanded he pay a fine, but seized his electric scale and tossed aside his vending cart. Not having enough money to pay the fine, which street vendors knew was actually a form of bribe, Bouazizi went to municipal headquarters to get his scales back. When local officials refused even to talk to him, the angry and frustrated young man went to a nearby gas station and bought a gallon of gas. He then returned to the front of the city building, shouted "How do you expect me to make a living?," doused himself with the gasoline, and set himself on fire.[24]

Badly burned, Bouazizi lingered in a hospital until his death on January 4. But his dramatic actions sparked protests throughout Tunisia against the brutal and repressive dictatorship of President Zine El Abidine Ben Ali, whose corruption had recently been further exposed by Wikileaks. Those protests grew bigger and more widespread by the day, fueled by social media. By January 14, ten days after Bouazizi's death, the twenty-three-year reign of dictator Ben Ali came to an end when he fled the country—and the Arab Spring was born.[25]

Emboldened by Bouazizi's immolation and the rapid fall of the government in Tunisia, antigovernment protests sprang up throughout the Arab world: in Egypt, Jordan, Algeria, Kuwait, Sudan, Bahrain, Morocco, Yemen, and Libya. In most cases, the United States sided with prodemocracy protesters by urging dictators to step aside. (Bahrain, at the urging of Saudi Arabia, was one notable exception.) By September 2012, four Arab governments had actually been overthrown: in Tunisia, Egypt, Yemen, and Libya. But only in Libya did the United States actually get involved militarily in supporting the opposition.[26]

The war in Libya was President Obama's first war of his own choosing, and one in which he introduced a whole new way of waging battle. For the United States, this was very much a long-distance war. As part of a coalition of seventeen nations put together by Obama, acting with the support of UN resolutions against the government of Colonel Muammar Qaddafi, American forces lobbed cruise missiles from U.S. warships offshore and flew air strikes over Libya. But there were no boots on the ground and no American casualties.

Soon after Qaddafi was captured and murdered on October 20, 2011, the United Nations recognized the opposition's National Transitional Council as the new government of Libya—and the White House beamed with pride that President Obama had invented a new, bloodless kind of war, in which the United States could go into battle and conquer a foreign foe without suffering any consequences. The *New York Times* called it a potential "model for other efforts."[27]

There was only one problem: The war in Libya, from start to finish, was an illegal operation. President Obama had indeed invented a new kind of war: a war without congressional authorization, as required by the Constitution and the War Powers Act.

Article One, Section 8, of the Constitution gives Congress, and only Congress, the authority to declare war. Of course, President Obama's not the first president to violate that provision of the Constitution. Every president since Harry Truman has. But President Obama went even further. He violated the War Powers Act also.

Enacted in 1973, in the aftermath of the Vietnam War, the War Powers Act requires a president to notify Congress within forty-eight hours any time he sends American troops into battle. Which President Obama did. But it also sets a sixty-day deadline for the president to obtain approval from Congress for any military action. If he does not, the act requires that he cease all hostilities within thirty days. That requirement of the law President Obama simply ignored. In fact, in a highly questionable reading of the law, he overruled his own Justice Department and insisted he did not have to comply.[28]

Asked by the White House for its opinion, the Department of Justice's Office of Legal Counsel concluded that President Obama was bound under the War Powers Act to seek approval of Congress for the operation in Libya. But White House Counsel Bob Bauer disagreed. He came up with a different theory: that Obama could ignore requirements of the act because, since there were no "boots on the ground," the United States was not engaged in actual "hostilities."[29]

In other words, American sailors were firing cruise missiles from offshore and American pilots were bombing targets from the air, but, in the absence of ground forces, the war in Libya could not be defined as "hostilities." It was an outrageous, indefensible interpretation of the law. But ostensible constitutional law professor Barack Obama endorsed it—and never sought the authorization of Congress.

By flouting the law in Libya, President Obama engaged in a brazen expansion of his war-making powers and set a dangerous precedent that will allow future presidents to wage war at their own whim, in violation of the Constitution and the law, and free of any legislative checks and balances.

He also violated the standard for limited presidential powers he had laid down as a candidate for president. In 2007, he wrote: "The president does not have power under the Constitution to unilaterally authorize a military attack in a situation that does not involve stopping an actual or imminent threat to the nation. . . . History has shown us time and again, however, that military action is most successful when it is authorized and supported by the Legislative branch."[30]

Regardless, in the end, events have shown that the outcome of

Obama's war in Libya was not as bright and shiny as the White House first painted it. While it was never the scandal Republicans have tried to make of it, there were no American troops nearby to defend our consulate in Benghazi when it came under attack. Given the turmoil in Libya, that compound should have been better protected around the clock. And yes, Qaddafi's gone, but Libya is now hopelessly divided, torn by endless warfare between reformers, new terrorist groups, religious fundamentalists, and former Qaddafi loyalists. The country is in much worse economic shape than before, and is, for all intents and purposes, now a failed state. It has also become the second adopted home base of ISIS, far from Syria. Whether it was a new way of making war or not, it's hard to rate the war in Libya a success.[31]

The Sidelines War: Syria

To many observers, Syria represents the epitome of what's wrong with Obama's conduct of foreign policy. Teddy Roosevelt famously recommended: "Speak softly, but carry a big stick." Barack Obama has sadly practiced: "Speak softly, and carry a little stick—or, sometimes, no stick at all."

At best, Obama's response to Syria's civil war has been inconsistent and contradictory. After actively supporting dissidents in Tunisia, Egypt, and Libya as part of the emerging Arab Spring, the United States appeared suddenly reluctant when the Arab Spring moved on to Syria.

Yes, we expressed support for rebels seeking to overthrow President Bashar al-Assad—but no, we would not give them any military aid. Later, in 2013, we decided we would send them weapons, but small arms only—but then changed our mind once rebel factions started fighting with each other, and ended up sending no arms at all.[32]

Most troubling of all, Obama vowed military strikes against Syria if Assad ever crossed the "red line" by using chemical weapons. In August 2012, he said: "We have been very clear to the Assad regime, but also to other players on the ground, that a red line for us is we start seeing a whole bunch of chemical weapons moving around or being utilized."[33]

When Assad in fact did use chemical weapons against civilian populations, Secretary of State John Kerry condemned the attacks as a "moral obscenity" and promised a harsh response by the United States. But President Obama not only did nothing, he denied ever setting a red line. September 2013: "I didn't set a red line. The world set a red line."[34]

At that point, unlike his approach to Libya, Obama decided to ask Congress for authorization to bomb Syria. When Congress looked wobbly, Obama agreed to a hastily cobbled-together Russian plan for Syria to destroy its stockpile of chemical weapons. Assad appeared to have complied at the time—perhaps because it helped him remain in power, with a free pass to continue suppressing and murdering rebel forces. But by May 2015, there were reports of more Syrian "chlorine bombs" being used by Assad. A month later, John Kerry said he was "absolutely certain" the Syrian government was using chemical weapons on its own people again. Obama learned the hard way that a world leader can never set a "red line" for military action and then fail to follow through without being dismissed as weak or indecisive.[35]

Even liberals, certainly no hard-liners when it comes to foreign policy, expressed their dismay over Obama's wobbling on Syria. For liberals, of course, war is not necessarily the answer. But a forceful and coherent diplomatic strategy is. And we didn't even see that. *Time* magazine's Joe Klein complained that Obama's performance on Syria amounted to "one of the more stunning and inexplicable displays of presidential incompetence that I've ever witnessed."[36]

Meanwhile, in the Middle East, our strongest allies continue to be baffled and disappointed by Obama's indecision or lack of action against Assad. Saudi Arabian officials, for example, had urged Obama to intervene forcefully in the Syrian civil war, especially if Assad resorted to the use of chemical weapons. His failure to do so, complained Prince Turki al-Faisal, former intelligence chief of Saudi Arabia, amounted to "almost a criminal negligence." In a speech to the World Policy Conference in London, al-Faisal lashed out at Obama: "When that kind of assurance comes from a leader of a country like the United States, we expect him to stand by it." Al-Faisal added: "There is an issue of confidence."[37]

Partly as a result of Obama's indifference, the Syrian civil war continues to drag on—with both U.S. and Russian military right in the middle of it. More than two hundred thousand men, women, and children have been killed. The Syrian army continues bombing civilian population centers. Russian military aircraft are bombing Syrian opposition forces. U.S. planes are bombing ISIS targets. And Bashar al-Assad, now with the assistance of Russian fighter planes and ships, defiantly remains in power, thumbing his nose at the United States— while American forces are now, in effect, helping Assad by leading a military campaign to destroy ISIS, his number-one enemy.[38]

The Nonwar in Crimea and Ukraine

Nonetheless, by the spring of 2014, President Obama was feeling pretty good about his foreign policy agenda. The war in Iraq was over and the war in Afghanistan was winding down. At the time, it looked as if Secretary of State John Kerry was having success in bringing Israelis and Palestinians to the peace table after a long hiatus. And, in the biggest surprise, Iran, feeling the effect of tough U.S. sanctions, had agreed to sit down and discuss the dismantling of its nuclear weapons program.

Then everything fell apart: Vladimir Putin invaded Crimea, as foreplay to invading Ukraine; a dangerous new terrorist organization surfaced in Iraq and Syria; and President Obama suddenly faced the two most serious foreign policy tests of his presidency—one of which he flunked, while the other remains unresolved.

In Crimea, the Obama administration was caught sleeping at the switch by Vladimir Putin. The United States had given moral support to those protesting Ukrainian president Viktor Yanukovych's decision to change course and align economically with the Russian Federation, rather than the European Union. But when Yanukovych stepped down and fled to Moscow on February 21, nobody was prepared for what happened next. In a sudden series of carefully orchestrated, and illegal, moves, Putin for all intents and purposes invaded a neighboring country, seized part of its territory—and got away with it.[39]

Two days after the departure of Yanukovych, pro-Russian protesters demonstrated in the Crimean city of Sevastopol. Another two days and mysterious, unidentified armed forces, which everyone suspected were Russian troops, moved into Sevastopol. Putin later admitted they were his forces. The United States and other Western nations protested Putin's violation of international boundaries, but he simply ignored them, insisting he was just protecting Russian citizens who were still living in Crimea.[40]

On March 16, Crimean provincial officials held a referendum in which 96.7 percent of voters said they wanted to secede from Ukraine and rejoin Russia. Results of the referendum were denounced as illegitimate by the West. But, the very next day, Russia and Crimea made it official by signing a treaty that declared Crimea henceforward a Russian province.[41]

It all happened in less than a month, during which time President Obama repeatedly condemned Putin's invasion, denouncing the theory that "bigger nations can bully smaller ones to get their way." He demanded that Putin pull his troops out of Crimea and vowed never to recognize a Russian Crimea. But, in the end, Putin brazenly annexed Crimea and Obama did nothing about it. Granted, it wasn't worth starting World War III over, but it did make Obama look weak. And so did what happened next in eastern Ukraine.[42]

Emboldened by his cost-free annexation of Crimea, Putin next turned to Ukraine itself. By the end of August, unmarked tanks had rolled into the Donbass section of Ukraine to support local separatists who wanted to follow Crimea, secede from Ukraine, and become part of Russia. Again, Putin initially denied they were Russian forces, but satellite imagery and interviews with rebel leaders confirmed they were, indeed, Russian military. Violent clashes between separatists, backed by Russian troops, and the Ukrainian military soon broke out.[43]

On several occasions, President Obama strongly condemned Russia for its invasion of Ukraine and its role in hostilities, but rejected calls of many in Congress for the United States to intervene militarily. After speaking with German chancellor Angela Merkel, he told White House reporters: "We agree, if there was ever any doubt, that Russia is responsible for the violence in eastern Ukraine. The violence is encouraged by Russia. The separatists are trained by Russia, they are armed by Russia, they are funded by Russia. Russia has deliberately and repeatedly violated the sovereignty and territorial integrity of Ukraine, and the new images of Russian forces inside Ukraine make that plain for the world to see."[44]

At the same time, he ruled out any military options and proposed no shift in his response to Ukraine, which had yet to convince Moscow to halt operations against its far weaker neighbor.

Instead, Obama imposed a series of strong economic sanctions against Russia, but their impact was limited by France, Germany, and other European allies who, heavily dependent for their energy needs on Russian gas and oil, refused to impose sanctions of their own.

Fortunately for Obama, other economic factors rode to the rescue of his sanctions response. In the fall and winter of 2014, the global price of oil underwent a surprising collapse, from $110 a barrel to $45 a barrel by September 2015. As the third-largest oil producer in the world (after the United States and Saudi Arabia), Russia's economy was particularly hard hit, losing an estimated $2 billion for every dollar drop in the oil price. Soon, the ruble was falling, interest rates were rising, and Russia lurched toward recession.[45]

In his 2015 State of the Union address, Barack Obama was happy to take credit for Russia's economic woes. "Last year," the president proclaimed of Putin's aggression, "it was suggested as a masterful display of strategy and strength . . . today, it is America that stands strong and united with our allies, while Russia is isolated with its economy in tatters." The president's valedictory lap aside, most observers realize Obama had caught a lucky break: The halving of oil prices worldwide did the work his sanctions could not.[46]

Today, politically speaking, not much has changed. As of this writing, Russian troops are still stationed in eastern Ukraine, more than six thousand people have been killed since April 2014, sporadic fighting continues, and the fate of the Donbass region of Ukraine remains uncertain.

The United States may still be the world's preeminent superpower, but only if we dare use that power. In Ukraine, Barack Obama did not. Faced with a direct threat from Vladimir Putin, Obama blinked. The outcome of that decision is still being written, but it does not look good for the people of Ukraine. "Putin seems to have won his little war in Ukraine," Brookings' Marvin Kalb wrote in September 2015, "and his Western critics watch from the sidelines, sputtering with helpless rage."[47]

The Bad War: The Sequel

It was June 10, 2014. The war in Iraq, which ended three years earlier, was largely forgotten, when suddenly news broke that ISIS, a terrorist organization most Americans had never heard of, had seized control of Mosul. And soon American forces were deployed in yet another undeclared war in Iraq, which could last as long as the first one.[48]

Part of the confusion over ISIS was that it was so new, nobody knew what to call it. They originally called themselves the Islamic State in Iraq and Syria, or ISIS, but later changed their name to the Islamic State. The Obama administration, for whatever reason, insisted on calling them ISIL, or the Islamic State of Iraq and the Levant. Take your pick. Like most journalists, I prefer ISIS.

Actually, nobody should have been surprised by the emergence of ISIS, certainly not U.S. intelligence agencies with their vast surveillance apparatus. The group was formed in 2006, out of the remnants of al Qaeda in Iraq. It soon built a large following among Sunni tribal leaders resentful of the exclusive Shia government put together by Prime Minister Nuri al-Maliki. With the goal of creating a caliphate in Iraq and Syria under Sharia law, ISIS started acquiring territory and, by 2014, controlled most of western Syria and northern Iraq.[49]

Yet when ISIS took over Fallujah in January 2014, followed by Mosul and the Mosul dam, the Obama administration seemed to be caught asleep at the switch once again. (Which makes you wonder just who the NSA spends all day spying on.) President Obama, in fact, seemed to dismiss the threat of ISIS in an earlier interview with the *New Yorker*'s David Remnick. Asked directly about terrorist groups still operating in Iraq, Obama dismissed the idea that any of them were as big a threat as al Qaeda: "The analogy we use around here sometimes, and I think is accurate, is if a JV team puts on Lakers uniforms, that doesn't make them Kobe Bryant."[50]

By June, nobody was calling ISIS a "JV team" anymore, and Senator Dianne Feinstein, chair of the Senate Intelligence Committee, was accusing the administration of being caught off guard: "I mean, they crossed the border into Iraq before we even knew it happened. This is a group of people who are extraordinarily dangerous, and they'll kill with abandon." Indeed, ISIS was now identified as an even more serious threat than al Qaeda, because it had funding, territory, and heavy weapons, most of them American-made arms acquired from the Iraqi military when, in their first clash with ISIS, they dropped their weapons and fled.[51]

Recognizing the danger posed by ISIS was one thing. Knowing what to do about it was another. Which led to another agonizing, zigzagging decision-making process by President Obama. He said the goal of the United States was clear: "to degrade and destroy ISIS." But, for months, he never set forth any plan for achieving that goal. Instead, it was a series of stops and starts. He sent fifteen hundred American troops back to Iraq to assist the Iraqi military in confronting ISIS, but insisted they should not be called "boots on the ground," since they would not be directly involved in combat missions. On August 8, he ordered American air strikes against ISIS targets in Iraq, yet insisted that air strikes alone would not be enough to defeat ISIS.[52]

So what was his strategy? On August 28, Obama walked into the briefing room at the White House and famously fessed up to us reporters what was obvious to all: "We don't have a strategy yet." Which was a startling admission, even for Obama.[53]

A couple of weeks later, having finally figured out a strategy on ISIS, President Obama unveiled it in a speech to the nation. But the plan he outlined was doomed from the start. Air strikes would continue against ISIS targets in Iraq, he announced, noting that, in the future, air strikes might also be directed against ISIS installations in Syria. But, he warned, air strikes alone would never suffice. We could never degrade and destroy ISIS by air strikes alone. Success of the strategy instead depended on four factors: a stable, new, unified Iraqi government; a newly trained and armed Iraqi military; newly trained and armed moderate Syrian opposition forces; and active participation of military units from Sunni allies Jordan, Saudi Arabia, and the United Arab Emirates.[54]

As the president emphasized, these four elements were critical to success of the mission. They were the four legs of the table. If any one of them collapsed, there went the entire table. Yet not one of them was a sure thing. At that point, the new Iraqi government was only two weeks old and had still not included any Sunni representatives in its leadership. As noted above, in their first encounter with ISIS, Iraqi troops, trained and equipped by the U.S. Army, dropped their weapons and ran for the hills. Could they really be counted on to stand and fight the next time? As for the so-called moderate Syrian opposition, we weren't even sure who they were—and, once new camps were established, training them for combat would take at least six months. Finally, there was no sign that Jordan, Saudi Arabia, and the UAE would ever agree to fight openly against other Muslim forces, no matter how much of a threat to the region.

It was a perilous strategy, born of President Obama's determination to have it both ways: to defeat ISIS militarily without ever having any American combat boots on the ground—so he could never be accused of restarting a land war in Iraq he had once so bitterly opposed.

There were those who accused Obama of being responsible for the rise of ISIS because he'd refused to leave a residual force of five thousand troops behind in 2011, when American forces left Iraq, and because he had failed to arm the moderate Syrian opposition at the start of the civil war in Syria. That criticism came, not only from predictable war hawks like Senator John McCain, but even from Obama's former secretary of defense Leon Panetta, who bragged in his book *Worthy Fights*: "I privately and publicly advocated for a residual force that could provide training and security for Iraq's military, but the President's team at the White House pushed back, and the differences occasionally became heated. [Undersecretary of Defense for Policy

Michèle] Flournoy argued our case, and those on our side viewed the White House as so eager to rid itself of Iraq that it was willing to withdraw rather than lock in arrangements that would preserve our influence and interests."[55]

But, in this case, criticism of Obama is off the mark. The truth is, Obama also wanted a reserve of American troops to remain in Iraq, but Prime Minister al-Maliki refused to grant them immunity from local Iraqi law. Without that protection, it would have been irresponsible to leave American soldiers in the country. That was not only President Obama's position at the time, it was Panetta's, too—as he told the Senate Armed Services Committee on November 15, 2011: "If you're going to engage in those kinds of operations . . . you absolutely have to have immunities . . . I was not about to have our troops go there in place without those immunities."[56]

Panetta, McCain, and others seem to forget that the cause of the continuing instability in Iraq was not that Barack Obama didn't leave five thousand troops there in 2011, but that for eight long years al-Maliki stubbornly refused to include both Shia and Sunni leaders in his government, thereby leaving the country hopelessly divided—and that George W. Bush invaded Iraq in the first place, in a war based on a pack of lies about weapons of mass destruction.

As for the plan to train and arm the "moderate Syrian opposition," that turned out to be a total disaster. The original goal was to train 5,400 fighters in the first year. Yet, at the end of year one, in September 2015, the head of U.S. Central Command, General Lloyd Austin III, revealed to Congress that only 100 to 120 trainees were in the program, that only 54 had been trained, and that only 4 or 5 men were in the field against ISIS. As if that wasn't bad enough, two weeks later it was reported that the remaining 70 trained and equipped Syrian rebels in the program had surrendered and handed their weapons over to Jabhat al-Nusra, al Qaeda's branch in Syria. Whereupon the Pentagon promptly put the entire program on hold and promised to come up with a better plan. By the end of October, the Pentagon had abandoned the plan altogether. It was a total failure. And for American taxpayers, it was $500 million down the drain.

In late October 2015, President Obama upped the ante, sending fifty American special forces into Syria to assist local forces in fighting ISIS, even though the White House insisted they were not "combat troops" because they were there as advisers only and were not actually firing weapons themselves—which most observers recognized as a distinction without difference.

An even more serious criticism of Obama's strategy to "degrade and destroy" ISIS is that, once again, President Obama was engaging American troops in an undeclared, and perhaps illegal, war. He did not seek authorization from Congress, as required by the Constitution, before ordering the bombing of ISIS targets or sending in advisers on the ground. Nor did he seek authorization from Congress within sixty days of engaging the military in hostilities, as required by the War Powers Act. That was a problem when Nixon invaded Cambodia back in 1970. It should've been a problem now.[57]

While volunteering that he would "welcome" any show of support from Congress, Obama insisted he had full authority to launch military action against ISIS under the Authorization for the Use of Military Force, or AUMF, passed by Congress shortly after September 11, 2001, and granting President Bush authority to take whatever military actions were necessary to retaliate against al Qaeda. Much as President Bush got his Justice Department to justify the use of torture under the AUMF, President Obama got his Justice Department to justify authority to go to war against al Qaeda as sufficient authority to go to war against ISIS, even though ISIS didn't even exist when the AUMF was enacted.[58]

Of course, Obama was able to get away with his end run around the law because most members of Congress, focused on their own re-election, didn't want to vote on starting a new war, anyway. Even though Republicans frequently complained about what they considered his abuse of executive power, both Republicans and Democrats were more than happy to let Obama launch a new war on his own, without any congressional authorization. They never even brought his request for a new AUMF up for debate or vote.

And Obama was more than willing to act on his own. Once again, he sent troops into war without consulting Congress—something candidate Obama had promised us he would never do. If George W. Bush had done that, progressives would be accusing him of waging an illegal war. As on civil liberties, Barack Obama should be treated no differently, just because he's a Democrat.

Today, like the first Iraq War, the second Iraq War—against ISIS—drags on, with no end in sight and, apparently, with no strategic plan to win. ISIS, meanwhile, has demonstrated its ability to strike far beyond its caliphate, with deadly terrorist attacks in the Sinai Peninsula, Beirut, and Paris.

Success on Two Fronts

There's something magical about the last two years of a two-term presidency. Heading into the home stretch, with their legacy very much in mind, presidents often hit their stride and rack up lasting accomplishments. As, to his credit, President Obama's done on at least two foreign policy fronts: Cuba and Iran.

For over sixty years, American policy toward Cuba was a total disaster, based not on what was best for the United States, or Cuba, but on what was considered best for the anti-Castro Cuban population of Miami. Under every president from Dwight Eisenhower to George W. Bush, foreign policy toward every other country in the world was made at the State Department, while foreign policy toward Cuba was made in Miami. The embarrassing results included the Bay of Pigs, the Mariel Boatlift, attempts to assassinate Fidel Castro, the Elian Gonzalez saga, and the "wet foot, dry foot" policy, whereby Cuban refugees who made it to land were treated completely differently than those just offshore. It also resulted in deeply stupid constraints on travelers, unable to enjoy the beauty of the largest island in the Caribbean, just ninety miles from Key West, and on American business leaders, unable to seize on business opportunities there.

On December 17, 2014, Obama finally and dramatically changed all that, to the benefit of both countries.

With some divine intervention. In the paperback edition of their solidly researched book, *Back Channel to Cuba: The Hidden History of Negotiations between Washington and Havana*, authors Peter Kornbluh and William LeoGrande tell the amazing story of the role Pope Francis played in the thawing of U.S.-Cuban relations. It was Pope Francis himself who raised this issue in a March 27 audience at the Vatican with President Obama. The pope then enlisted the help of Cuban cardinal Jaime Ortega. Secret negotiations got under way between representatives of the United States and Cuba, meeting first in Canada and then at the Vatican. By mid-December, a phone call between President Obama and Cuban president Raul Castro sealed the deal.[59]

Under this agreement, the United States and Cuba will gradually normalize relations between the two countries. As an important first step, on May 29, the United States removed Cuba from the list of countries that sponsor terrorism. For the first time in over fifty years, an American embassy has opened its doors in Havana; and a Cuban embassy, in Washington. Ferry service between the United States and Cuba has resumed. American Airlines and JetBlue are planning regularly scheduled flights to Havana. Travel restrictions for American tourists and Cuban citizens have been largely lifted. And many American businesses—including Google, Microsoft, MasterCard, and Coca-Cola—will soon start selling their wares in Cuba.[60]

In a sense, given our geographical proximity, and the many cultural and economic ties that link our two countries, restoring relations between the United States and Cuba was a no-brainer. But no president before Barack Obama had the political courage to do it. For that, a big high five.

As big a deal as it was to resume normal relations with Cuba, it was an even bigger deal to engage in any dialogue with Iran, with which we had severed relations in 1979 after the Iran hostage crisis. Yet Obama pulled off that miracle, too.

While there was no way short of military intervention to prevent Iran from meddling in Middle Eastern affairs—funding terrorist organizations Hezbollah and Hamas, as well as backing terrorist operations in Yemen, Saudi Arabia, Syria, Iraq, and Kenya—the one goal that the United States and our allies agreed on was that Iran should never be allowed to develop a nuclear weapon.

When it became obvious that Iran was, in fact, developing its nuclear capacity, the United States, the United Nations, and the European Union joined to impose against Iran the toughest sanctions ever imposed on any country. And they worked. Unable to sell its oil on world markets or secure loans from international banks, Iran was eventually on its knees, economically, and Iran's new, moderate president, Hassan Rouhani, finally agreed to talks with the United States and other world powers about abandoning its nuclear weapons program—after resisting calls for negotiations for over ten years.[61]

The first round of talks between Iran and the United States, France, Germany, Britain, Russia, and China—the so-called P5+1—got under way in Geneva in November 2013. The fact that Iran was even willing to sit down at the same table was surprising enough. Even more surprising was the fact that all parties reached agreement on the framework for a final deal—whereby Iran would agree to abandon its nuclear weapons buildup in return for relaxation of sanctions—close to their self-imposed deadline of the end of March 2015. On April 2, the outline of a preliminary agreement was announced.[62]

While President Obama successfully fought off efforts in Congress to impose even more sanctions on Iran, negotiators returned to the table in Vienna to begin work on the final nuclear deal. They gave themselves a new deadline of June 30, 2015. They reached agreement on July 16, close enough for government work. In announcing the historic successful completion of the talks, President Obama was able to reassure the nation: "I can say with confidence but, more importantly, nuclear experts can say with confidence that Iran will not be in a position to develop a nuclear bomb. We will have met our number-one priority."[63]

The 109-page Iran nuclear deal was then sent to Congress for a sixty-day review and a nonbinding up-or-down vote. After a tense two months, with both Republicans and the powerful lobbying group AIPAC working to drum up opposition, Obama still managed to hold the line in Congress. Twice in September 2015, Senate Democrats managed to block a vote of disapproval against it, and the Iran nuclear deal took effect. It is now up to Iran to fulfill the terms of the deal, up to the International Atomic Energy Agency (IAEA) to make sure they do, and up to the United States and our allies to respond by reimposing sanctions if they don't.

Summing Up

Which still leaves unanswered the difficult question of how to define the foreign policy of President Obama.

"The world has always been messy," Obama said in the middle of exploding foreign policy crises in Ukraine and Iraq. Indeed it has, but many wondered: Was he capable of cleaning up the mess? As the *New York Times* editorialized on May 4, 2014, "The world sometimes seems as if it is flying apart, with Mr. Obama unable to fix it." On foreign policy, the *Times* faulted him for "not articulating a strong, overarching blueprint for the exercise of American power."[64]

As shown above—in Iraq, Syria, Crimea, Ukraine, and other hot spots—doubts about Obama's command of foreign policy stemmed from the same source as his domestic problems: his seeming detachment from the issues. He was frustratingly cautious, to the point of appearing weak or tired. He was hesitant and vacillating to the point of appearing world-weary.

There have been foreign policy successes during his time: winding down the wars in Iraq and Afghanistan; a climate change deal with China; international coalitions against Libya and ISIS; bringing Iran to the negotiating table; normalizing relations with Cuba. But they have been few and far between, and even those achievements were marred by the impression that Obama was lurching from crisis to crisis, with no overall foreign policy strategy.

America remains the most powerful nation on earth. But there is no doubt that, while the damage was not nearly as bad as what happened under George W. Bush, and, overall, President Obama's record on foreign policy was not the unmitigated disaster his harshest critics contend, it was also not as strong or as consistent as either the times or the nation demanded.

FIVE

Immigration Reform

For progressives, disappointment in President Obama took several forms. There were things he promised but never delivered on, such as closing Guantanamo. There were things he promised but delivered just the opposite, such as reining in the security state. And then there were things he promised but took too long to get around to and, even then, didn't go as far as he should have, such as immigration reform—an issue with which his dithering helped Republicans engineer two midterm election triumphs in 2010 and 2014. Obama gets some credit for making any progress at all on immigration in the face of fierce congressional opposition, but whatever he accomplished still falls under the category of "too little, too late."

Even though he came around eventually, Obama's actions on immigration reform hardly tell a story of bold leadership. Instead we see the same pattern of promising and not delivering, stopping and starting and stopping again, bobbing and weaving, setting deadlines and delaying them, building up expectations and dashing them—all with little end result.

To be fair, not that many other recent presidents have a better track record. It's ironic, given the almost universal opposition among Republicans to any plan for immigration reform today, that Ronald Reagan is the only president who was able to break the political deadlock on immigration. In 1986, he convinced his fellow conservatives that granting legal status—or "amnesty," he wasn't afraid to call it that—was the only way to deal with roughly three million Latinos then living illegally in the United States.[1]

But that was before the Republican Party lopped off its own moderate wing and was subsequently captured by its extreme right fringe, the Tea Party. One thing is for sure, as both George W. Bush and Barack Obama discovered the hard way: Not even Reagan could make that sale today. Bush broke his pick on comprehensive immigration reform. Five years later, Barack Obama tried the same approach, with the same result.

Indeed, powerful House Republican Majority Leader Eric Cantor became a poster boy for the political perils of immigration reform in 2014, when he was trounced by unknown Tea Party challenger Dave Brat in his Republican primary because Cantor had committed the unforgivable sin of saying he was open to the possibility of discussing—not necessarily acting on, but only "discussing"—some legislation to deal with the status of young people brought to this country illegally by their parents.[2]

Cantor's fall illuminated the strong feelings on this issue. For decades, illegal immigration had been one of the most controversial issues in the Southwest, especially California, Arizona, and Texas. By the turn of the twenty-first century, showing any moderation on immigration, or empathy for new arrivals, was considered political poison by most conservatives nationwide, Jeb Bush and Lindsey Graham being the sole exceptions. By contrast, real estate tycoon and notably absurd candidate Donald Trump rocketed to the top of the Republican presidential primary in the summer of 2015, mainly by calling immigrants drug dealers, criminals, and "rapists" and promising to build a giant wall along the southern border.[3]

Here's the reality. Driven by harsh economic conditions and lack of opportunities in their own countries, millions of people from Central and South America took advantage of lax enforcement at the southern border to enter the United States illegally—where, many with fake IDs, they were able to find jobs, establish families, buy homes, get a driver's license, and put their kids in school. For all practical purposes, they became productive members of our society. Except, of course, for the fact that they were in this country illegally and therefore faced the possibility of being rounded up and deported by the Immigration and

Naturalization Service (INS) at any time. In the eighties, under President Reagan, the population "living in the shadows" was estimated at 3 million. By 2009, when President Obama took office, their numbers had swelled to somewhere between 11 and 13 million.[4]

But the politics remain the same: deeply divided. For progressives like me, immigration reform is a moral imperative. These "undocumented workers" from south of the border may have come here illegally, but they have long ago integrated themselves into their communities. Once here, they obey the laws. They pay taxes. Many of their sons and daughters serve in the military. They make up the majority of the workforce in several key industries: agricultural workers, child care, kitchen help in restaurants, housecleaning, maid service in hotels, and more. I've seen the great contribution they've made to their communities in California. Like generations of immigrants before them, they have become American citizens by choice, not by birth. They are, in effect, already citizens in every respect but one. It's now important to make it official, as Ronald Reagan did, and grant them citizenship—or at least a path to citizenship—in order to save families from the fear of being torn apart by federal agents.

Of course, most conservatives see it just the opposite. The law's the law. These "illegal immigrants" broke the law and they must be punished. Period. Besides, they're taking jobs from "real" Americans, using public services without paying for them, draining local economies, and dragging down standards in public schools. Not only that, they speak Spanish everywhere, when everybody knows English is our national language. And, worst of all, those who can vote mostly vote for Democrats. The best solution is to put them all on a bus and send them back to Mexico. (Never mind that we took much of California, Texas, and the Southwest from Mexico less than two centuries ago.) But under no circumstances should they be rewarded for breaking the law. Granting them anything approaching "amnesty" would only encourage millions more to come here.

With immigration such a hot political issue, most politicians do what politicians do best when confronted with a tough decision: run for the tall weeds. Even Republicans will talk a good game, acknowledging the need for some kind of legislation to deal with the problem of illegal immigration. But when it comes down to action—on anything other than building Donald Trump's longer and higher fence at the southern border—and especially when political pressure from anti-immigrant zealots builds up, most Republicans, and even a few Democrats, suddenly find a thousand excuses for delay or inaction.

President George W. Bush, in fact, put forth a fairly strong proposal for comprehensive immigration reform, which won the support of a number of Republican senators. But once right-wing talk radio hosts turned up the heat, accusing Republicans of abandoning their principles and rewarding lawbreakers, Bush dropped his plan like a hot potato.[5]

But not Barack Obama. He promised to be different. He would make immigration reform his top priority, starting on day one—and he'd never run away from it. "I don't know about you, but I think it's time for a president who won't walk away from something as important as comprehensive reform just because it becomes politically unpopular," candidate Obama told the National Council of La Raza in San Diego in July 2008. "That's the commitment I am making to you, and I will make it a priority in my first year as president."[6]

That may be the commitment he made, but that's not the commitment he kept. Not in his first year. Nor his second year. Nor his third or fourth years. During his entire first term, in fact, Obama often talked about the need for comprehensive immigration reform, but, convinced he could never round up enough votes in Congress, especially after Republicans took over the House in 2010, he put forth no new legislative proposal. He talked the talk, but never walked the walk. Given that he was never guaranteed a second term, this could count as a promise broken.[7]

As some pointed out, perhaps it should have come as no surprise that President Obama walked away from immigration during his first year in office. After all, he appointed as his chief of staff Illinois congressman Rahm Emanuel, who had warned Democrats running for Congress in 2008 that immigration was "the third rail of American politics" and urged them to stay away from it. No doubt, he gave Barack Obama the same advice once in the White House.[8]

For his part, Obama came up with a novel excuse. He couldn't fulfill his promise to tackle immigration reform during his first year in office for two reasons: because he was too busy dealing with the economy; and because Republicans, who once supported immigration reform, now opposed it. Who could have guessed?

His look backward came in an interview with famed Univision anchor Jorge Ramos on September 20, 2012. Reminding him of his 2008 campaign promise—"I can guarantee that we will have, in the first year, an immigration bill that I strongly support"—Ramos pressed Obama: "At the beginning of your governing, you had control of both chambers of Congress, and yet you did not introduce immigration reform. And before I continue, I want for you to acknowledge that you did not keep your promise."[9]

In response, Obama blamed everybody but himself:

> When we talked about immigration reform in the first year, that's before the economy was on the verge of collapse. . . .
>
> And so we had to take a whole series of emergency actions to make sure that we put people back to work—cutting taxes for middle-class families and small businesses so that they could stay open or pay the bills; making sure that states got assistance so they didn't have to lay off teachers and firefighters and police officers; saving an auto industry that was on the brink of collapse. And so that took up a huge amount of time in the first year.
>
> And what I confess I did not expect—and so I'm happy to take responsibility for being naïve here—is that Republicans who had previously supported comprehensive immigration reform—my opponent in 2008, who had been a champion of it and who attended these meetings—suddenly would walk away. That's what I did not anticipate.[10]

Was Obama leveling with the American people? The *Washington Post* didn't think so. For claiming that the economy took up too much of his time and Republicans double-crossed him, the *Post* awarded him "two Pinocchios." "A guarantee is a guarantee," they wrote. "Obama failed to deliver on a promise, and he blamed Republicans instead of acknowl-edging any real responsibility for that failure."[11]

As the *Post's* Josh Hicks also noted, Obama's argument that he couldn't handle both immigration reform and the economy in the same year doesn't hold water. After all, this was the candidate who said repeatedly in his 2008 campaign that "presidents are going to have to deal with more than one thing at a time." No excuses, in other words. They have to juggle. In fact, toward the end of the campaign, when John McCain proposed postponing a scheduled debate so the two campaigns could focus all their attention on the economy, Obama fa-mously rejected and ridiculed him: "It is going to be part of the presi-dent's job to deal with more than one thing at once."[12]

As for the economic workload: Yes, to start digging out of Bush's 2008 recession, Obama had to focus first on the $837 billion stimu-lus, or American Recovery and Reinvestment Act—but that was signed into law less than a month after he took office. He also hammered to-gether a plan to rescue America's auto industry, but that was wrapped up by July. And as early as March he launched his proposal for uni-versal health care, which evolved into the Affordable Care Act, or Obamacare.

There was plenty of time to add immigration reform to the mix, in other words. Ever heard of Franklin Roosevelt's "100 Days"? The truth of the matter is, once in the Oval Office, for whatever reason, Obama decided immigration reform just wasn't a top priority, after all.

Nor could the president blame it all on recalcitrant Republicans. Neither Democrats nor Republicans were excited about rushing into immigration reform. Like two kids playing "Not It," legislators from both parties said they were waiting for some "push" from the White House, while the White House insisted it wasn't going to act without some "pull" from Congress. As the *New York Times* reported on June 24, 2009, when neither side would take the initiative to champion im-migration reform, that was a clear sign nothing would get done: "Aides to Mr. Obama say he does not intend to get out in front of any proposal until there is a strong bipartisan commitment to pass it. That stance has the potential to paralyze the process, since lawmakers are looking to him to use his bully pulpit, and high approval ratings, to help them fend off any political backlash among their constituents."[13]

In the end, there was little appetite in Congress for dealing with immigration reform in 2009, and little or no leadership from President Obama on the issue. They were waiting for him to act, he was waiting for them to act. Speaking for the president, the statement of then–senior adviser David Axelrod would hardly merit a badge of courage. He told the *Times*: "Obviously work needs to be done, and not just from our end, but from the proponents in Congress, to bring it to the point where it can get passed."[14]

At this point, with no opposition from the White House, several Democrats and Republicans openly suggested it might be better to wait a year or so before taking up immigration reform—and delay, in fact, won the day. But New Jersey's Robert Menendez, the only Hispanic Senate Democrat, proved to be prophetic in disagreeing with that approach: "I think it is one of those issues that if you don't pass this year, it slips several years away." As, indeed, it did.[15]

Less than a year after a new president had taken office vowing to make the issue one of his top priorities, any momentum for immigration reform had stalled. Even for Obama himself, it seemed. In his 2010 State of the Union speech, he devoted only one ho-hum line to immigration: "We should continue the work of fixing our broken immigration system—to secure our borders and enforce our laws, and ensure that everyone who plays by the rules can contribute to our economy and enrich our nation." This nod to the laundry list—Immigration? Check!—was met with the tepid applause it deserved.[16]

Obama did score one partial victory on immigration in 2010. After the midterm elections, with Republicans about to take control of the House, he persuaded still-Speaker Nancy Pelosi and House Democrats to pass their version of the DREAM Act, which had been bouncing around Congress for almost a decade. Originally introduced by Senators Orrin Hatch (R-Utah) and Dick Durbin (D-Ill.) in 2001, the DREAM Act proposed that immigrants up to age thirty-five who had been brought to this country illegally, as children, by their parents be eligible for residency, so long as they were going to school or serving in the military and didn't have criminal records.[17]

The bill passed the House, but met defeat in the Senate, where it fell 55–41, five votes short of the sixty votes needed for cloture. Five Democrats defied Obama's personal lobbying and voted against it. That would not have happened if a stronger president were in the White House. When Lyndon Johnson fought for the Civil Rights Act of 1964, his hard-nosed personality offensive to influence individual members of Congress was legendary. "The president grabbed me by the shoulder," recalled one senator—his future vice president Hubert Humphrey—"and damn near broke my arm." But Obama's no LBJ.[18]

The DREAM Act would eventually resurface in 2012 as an executive order. Meanwhile, like other presidents before him, with no action on comprehensive immigration reform in 2009, President Obama focused instead on only one aspect of the problem: increasing security at the border. In Obama's first two years, under orders of Homeland Security Secretary Janet Napolitano (former governor of border state Arizona), the number of agents guarding the border increased to a record high of 21,444, and 649 miles of the border, out of a planned 652 miles, were protected by a fence. In 2010, Obama even dispatched 1,200 National Guard troops to help guard the border, but the cost/benefit ratio of their mission soon came under criticism. While they were credited with helping Border Patrol agents apprehend 25,514 people trying to enter the country illegally, the cost of their deployment hit $160 million—or $6,271 for each immigrant detained. It would have been cheaper to hire a corporate jet to fly them all home.[19]

By 2012, as a result of stepped-up border security, as well as a lagging U.S. economy and depressed job market, apprehensions at the southern border had actually fallen to the lowest level since 1970. Things changed so much that by 2013, estimates suggested that there may actually have been more people crossing the border going south than coming north.[20]

So what? Politically, for Obama, it didn't make any difference. He was, in effect, just wasting his time. Either opponents of immigration reform were unaware of changes at the border or, if they did notice, they never gave Obama any credit for it. Republicans continued to decry hordes of people crossing the border every day, as if we were still living in the heyday of illegal immigration, back in the nineties.

In the White House, Obama's advisers figured they could pick up a few Republican votes for immigration reform if the president showed he was tough on border security and on deportations. They were only kidding themselves—Charlie Brown and the football again. In the end, the preemptive compromising didn't work. Obama didn't pick up any Republican votes. In fact, he lost a few, such as that of Arizona's John McCain, who backed comprehensive immigration reform as long as it had George Bush's name on it, but wouldn't support the same plan when offered by a former political opponent named Barack Obama.

Deporter in Chief

What angered immigration activists most in his first year, however, was not President Obama's failure to fulfill his promise of enacting immigration reform legislation. It was his aggressive policy of deportation.

That was the one aspect of immigration reform where Obama did act without waiting for congressional authorization. Arguing that he had no choice but to enforce existing law—a mandate that somehow didn't hold when it came time to prosecute Wall Street bankers or CIA torturers—Obama dramatically increased the number of people deported to Latin America: 1.06 million already by September 2011 and more than 2 million by the end of 2013, compared to 1.57 million by George W. Bush over his entire eight years. Frustrated immigration activists pressured him to sign an executive order protecting from deportation millions of Latinos who had lived here at least five years and had no criminal record, but the president insisted he had no such authority under the Constitution.[21]

Even as a candidate, he had expressed his hesitancy about signing too many executive orders. "I take the Constitution very seriously," he told a Pennsylvania town hall in 2008. "The biggest problems that we're facing right now have to do with George Bush trying to bring more and more power into the Executive Branch and not go through Congress at all, and that's what I intend to reverse when I'm President of the United States of America."[22]

After two years of congressional inaction on immigration legislation, and facing increasing pressure from immigration activists to exercise his executive authority to limit deportations, Obama told a Univision town hall in 2011 that there "are enough laws on the books by Congress that are very clear in terms of how we have to enforce our immigration system." Ignoring those congressional mandates through executive order, insisted Obama, would "not conform with my appropriate role as president."[23]

Later that year, Obama expressed that same frustration when pushed on the subject of deportations during a roundtable with Latino reporters. "I just have to continue to say this notion that somehow I can just change the laws unilaterally is just not true," he told them. "We are doing everything we can administratively. But the fact of the matter is there are laws on the books that I have to enforce." Again, tell that to Dick Cheney and JPMorgan CEO Jamie Dimon.[24]

But that strategy suddenly changed, the closer Obama got to the 2012 elections. Accepting the fact that Congress would never act before the November vote, but realizing he could not face the American public again without having something to show for immigration, Obama decided to exercise his executive authority, after all.

On June 15, he announced a dramatic change in deportation policy as carried out by the Department of Homeland Security. Technically, it was not an executive order, but a presidential directive to a cabinet agency to do things differently. Under Obama's orders, about eight hundred thousand young people who had been brought to the United States illegally as children would henceforth be considered ineligible for deportation proceedings and eligible for two-year work permits, which could be renewed without limit. It was, in effect, the DREAM Act with another name—DACA (Deferred Action for Childhood Arrivals).[25]

Having entered the United States illegally through no fault of their own, these children, Obama correctly insisted, should not be punished for it. "These are young people who study in our schools and play on our playgrounds. They are Americans in every single way but one—on paper."[26]

To qualify under the new policy, individuals would have to be between the age of sixteen and thirty, been brought to the United States before they turned sixteen, and have resided in the country for at least five continuous years. They also had to be either currently in school or graduated from high school with a GED—or serving in, or honorably discharged from, the military. Anyone convicted of a felony offense or significant misdemeanor was automatically ineligible.

Announcing the new policy in the Rose Garden, President Obama acknowledged that his new directive was only a "stopgap" measure, not "amnesty," not a "path to citizenship," and not a "permanent fix." The answer was still congressional legislation. "I've said this time and again to Congress," Obama told reporters, "send me the DREAM Act, put it on my desk, and I'll sign it."[27]

Winning the Latino Vote

Obama's executive action on Dreamers won the praise of immigration activists and Democratic legislators. And with that, the stage was set for his re-election campaign—which pitted a man who talked a good game on immigration, but who had done little about it, against a man who didn't even bother to talk a good game.

The Latino community may have been disappointed that Barack Obama had not delivered more on immigration, but Mitt Romney offered them even less. He opposed comprehensive immigration reform, and he vowed to veto the DREAM Act unless it was limited to military service. Romney sealed his fate with Latino voters in a January 2012 debate among GOP candidates, when he insisted the ultimate solution was for people here illegally to "self-deport." "The answer is self-deportation," he said to audience snickers, "which is people decide they can do better by going home because they can't find work here because they don't have legal documentation to allow them to work here." He added: "And so we're not going to round people up."[28]

He didn't round up many votes that way, either. His disastrous showing among Latino voters was the worst among recent Republican candidates. Running for re-election in 2004, President George W. Bush won 44 percent of the Hispanic vote, which many said promised "Un Nuevo Dia" for the Republican Party among the fastest-growing segment of the voting population. But that promise was lost by 2008, when John McCain and Sarah Palin won only 31 percent of the Latino vote, compared to 67 percent for Barack Obama and Joe Biden. Mitt Romney sank Republican fortunes even lower. Forever known as the "self-deportation" candidate in immigration circles, Romney snared only 27 percent of the Latino vote, compared to 71 percent of Latinos who voted for Obama—which, Romney later insisted, digging his hole even deeper, was only because Obama promised them "gifts" like health care and Social Security.[29]

Romney's dismal returns from the Latino electorate did serve one useful purpose, however. They scared the hell out of some Republicans, who saw any chance of winning the White House slipping away, and thus gave new impetus to the drive for comprehensive immigration reform.

In fact, Senator Lindsey Graham of South Carolina declared that, given their pitiful performance among Latino voters in 2012, Republicans could give up any hope of ever winning the White House again unless they were seen as taking the lead on immigration reform. "The demographics race we're losing badly," Senator Graham said of his party as early as August 2012. "We're not generating enough angry white guys to stay in business for the long term."[30]

After his party's drubbing that year, Graham was even more emphatic on the need for the Republican Party to embrace immigration reform. "If we don't pass immigration reform, if we don't get it off the table in a reasonable, practical way, it doesn't matter who you run in 2016," he told Meet the Press in June 2013. "We're in a demographic death spiral as a party, and the only way we can get back in good graces with the Hispanic community, in my view, is pass comprehensive immigration reform. If you don't do that, it really doesn't matter who will run, in my view."[31]

Surprising, perhaps, coming from a southern conservative. But even more surprising was the conclusion of the Republican National Committee's own analysis of the November 2012 election returns, dubbed its "autopsy" report, which blamed Romney's loss in large part on his stand on immigration reform and concluded that the Republican Party must reverse its policy on immigration in order to stay alive politically. Facing the possibility of forever alienating the Latino community—which already numbered 50.5 million, 16.3 percent of the population and the fastest-growing segment of the American electorate—the party's hundred-page *Growth And Opportunity* report stated boldly:

"We are not a policy committee, but among the steps Republicans take in the Hispanic community and beyond, we must embrace and champion comprehensive immigration reform. If we do not, our Party's appeal will continue to shrink to its core constituencies only. We also believe that comprehensive immigration reform is consistent with Republican economic policies that promote job growth and opportunity for all."[32]

Even before his re-election, President Obama had predicted that the stars would align for immigration, once both parties moved into 2013. On October 24, he told editors of the *Des Moines Register*, in what he thought would remain an off-the-record phone conversation (the *Register* thought otherwise): "The second thing I'm confident we'll get done next year is immigration reform. And since this is off the record, I will just be very blunt. Should I win a second term, a big reason I will win a second term is because the Republican nominee and the Republican Party have so alienated the fastest-growing demographic group in the country, the Latino community. And this is a relatively new phenomenon. George Bush and Karl Rove were smart enough to understand the changing nature of America. And so I am fairly confident that they're going to have a deep interest in getting that done. And I want to get it done because it's the right thing to do and I've cared about this ever since I ran back in 2008."[33]

And once having secured his second term, President Obama re-

newed his commitment to immigration reform. He made it a highlight
of his second Inaugural Address in January 2013: "Our journey is not
complete until we find a better way to welcome the striving, hopeful
immigrants who still see America as a land of opportunity."[34]

Later that month, he issued a challenge to Congress in his State of
the Union Address: "Our economy is stronger when we harness the
talents and ingenuity of striving, hopeful immigrants. And right now,
leaders from the business, labor, law enforcement, faith communities—they all agree that the time has come to pass comprehensive immigration reform. Now is the time to do it. Now is the time to get it
done. Now is the time to get it done."[35]

They'd been working on it for a long time, Obama reminded lawmakers. Any plan, he insisted, would have to include measures to
strengthen border security, provide a responsible path to earned citizenship, and remove barriers to retaining highly skilled entrepreneurs
and engineers to help grow the American economy. The important
task was to get to work, Obama concluded: "We know what needs to be
done. And as we speak, bipartisan groups in both chambers are working diligently to draft a bill, and I applaud their efforts. So let's get this
done. Send me a comprehensive immigration reform bill in the next
few months, and I will sign it right away. And America will be better
for it. Let's get it done. Let's get it done."[36]

As Obama's repeated refrain illustrates, hope was in the air in early
2013. Leading Republicans were calling for immigration reform. President Obama had made it a priority. The stage was set for action. Expectations were high. The time is now! Let's get it done! *Si se puede!* But,
once again, Obama failed to deliver. Despite his passionate appeal for
immigration reform in his inaugural and State of the Union addresses,
there was no follow-through on the president's part.

Opportunity Lost

At least in the Senate, the promise of 2013 translated into some legislative action. There, the so-called gang of eight, four Republicans and

four Democrats, drafted a comprehensive immigration reform bill and brought it to the floor.

On June 27, the bill passed the Senate 68–32, with strong bipartisan support. Every Senate Democrat voted for the legislation, plus fourteen Republicans. President Obama promised to sign the bill into law once it reached his desk. Which it never did. House Republicans insisted they wanted to "do their own thing" on immigration. John Boehner, exercising his authority as Speaker, refused even to allow a vote on the Senate bill in the House (where it surely would have passed).[37]

President Obama spent the next six months cajoling House Republicans to act and convening occasional meetings at the White House with immigration activists. But, in the end, it amounted to one more year of Obama's presidency with no action on immigration reform. After languishing without a vote in the House for eighteen months, the Senate bill died in December 2014 with the end of the 113th Congress.

Of course, several factors contributed to that stalemate: the monumental distraction caused by problems with the official launch of the Obamacare website; strident opposition of Tea Party Republicans; John Boehner's refusal to challenge Tea Party members of his own caucus and schedule a House vote on the Senate bill; and the sense among some lawmakers that, because the border was now more secure and fewer people were getting across, immigration reform was no longer such a pressing issue.

But the primary factor for lack of action on immigration was Obama's failure to use the "bully pulpit," as Ronald Reagan had done, to rally the American people behind immigration reform. In speeches and news conferences, he called on Congress to act. He urged Boehner to schedule a vote on immigration reform. But he stopped there. He never used the immense personal or public powers of the presidency—from arm-twisting, to favor-denying, to barnstorming across the country—to build enough pressure to force Congress to act.

True, there's no guarantee Obama could have shaken Boehner loose. Maybe his efforts would have failed. But he didn't even try. The message from the White House came across as: We want the House to vote on the Senate bill on comprehensive immigration reform. If they do, the president will sign it. If they don't, well, there's nothing we can do about it.

Opportunity Delayed

Meanwhile, fairly or unfairly, response in the Latino community to the lack of progress on immigration reform took an unexpected turn. Instead of blaming John Boehner, they blamed Barack Obama. Why? Again, not so much for failing to persuade Congress to act on immigration reform—though that was irritating enough—but for actually making the plight of undocumented immigrants worse through his continued, aggressive policy of mass deportation.

As noted earlier, by this time, according to immigration officials, and despite his new policy on Dreamers, President Obama had deported close to 2 million foreigners, a record number and more than George W. Bush deported during two full terms. The administration continued to insist it focused on removing criminals and serious immigration offenders. But immigrant advocates pointed out the practice was far more widespread than that, and was having a devastating impact on communities by separating breadwinners from their families and parents from children.[38]

The *New York Times*, for example, reported on the case of businessman Enrique Morales of New Orleans. Years ago, he came here illegally from Honduras and built up a thriving floor business. In August 2013, while he was driving his girlfriend Karen Sandoval and her two daughters to the store to buy school supplies, police pulled him over for a routine traffic stop. Even though he'd committed no crime, once they discovered his illegal status, police turned Morales over to immigration authorities, who immediately deported him, leaving his live-in girlfriend and children to fend for themselves. As many as thirty thousand people faced the same fate every day.[39]

Once again, immigration leaders called on Obama to use his executive authority to halt wholesale deportations. In early February 2014, the National Day Laborer Organizing Network filed a formal petition, asking Obama to use his "extremely broad and virtually unreviewable discretion" to allow millions of undocumented immigrants to stay in the United States. They pointed out that he'd already exercised his executive authority in 2012—the famous "DACA"—to protect young people who'd been brought to America illegally as children. He could and should use that same authority today, they argued, to save from deportation those who would most likely be able to stay in the country legally should Congress ever reach a compromise on immigration reform.[40]

"It simply makes no sense, at a time when he says he's optimistic about immigration reform, to be hand-over-fist deporting the very people who would benefit from that reform," said Network attorney Peter Markowitz. "Yet, even though Obama already used his executive authority to help young people, the White House now mysteriously insists he has no authority to help any other group of immigrants, absent an act of Congress."[41]

Adding to the pressure, hecklers started showing up at almost every public presidential event, interrupting Obama and accusing him of not doing enough on immigration. Activists staged sit-ins in offices of Democratic lawmakers on Capitol Hill. Several hundred people staged a hunger strike outside the Northwest Detention Center in Tacoma, Washington, a facility used by the INS to house immigrants targeted for deportation. On my way to the daily press briefing, I saw anti-Obama immigration protesters every day in front of the White House chanting *"Si, se puede"*—an echo of Obama's 2008 campaign slogan, "Yes, we can," which of course he had borrowed from none other than Cesar Chavez.[42]

It wasn't long before protesters were clearly getting under Obama's skin. On November 25, 2013, in San Francisco, he turned around at the lectern and chastised one heckler: "If, in fact, I could solve all these problems without passing laws in Congress, then I would do so. But we're also a nation of laws. That's part of our tradition. So the easy way out is to try to yell and pretend like I can do something by violating our laws, and what I'm proposing is the harder path which is to use our democratic processes to achieve the same goal that you want to achieve."[43]

But that didn't silence the protests. (And, as we've seen, Obama can be much more flexible on laws when he wants to be, as on the war on terror and civil liberties fronts.) In March 2014, National Council of La Raza (NCLR) president Janet Murguía added fuel to the fire by calling Obama the "deporter in chief." Speaking in Washington to NCLR's annual conference, Murguía dismissed the notion that Obama had to wait for Congress before taking action himself: "We respectfully disagree with the president on his ability to stop unnecessary deportations. He can stop tearing families apart. He can stop throwing communities and businesses into chaos. He can stop turning a blind eye to the harm being done. He does have the power to stop this. Failure to act will be a shameful legacy for his presidency."[44]

Lorella Praeli, director of advocacy for United We Dream, an organization formed to represent Dreamers, warned that Obama's excuse of having to wait for Congress to act was wearing thin: "At this point anything short of an affirmative administrative relief program for parents of U.S. citizens and DREAMers is not enough. The clock on Obama has run out."[45]

Later that month, obviously stung by the criticism, Obama summoned immigration activists to a White House meeting, gently scolded them for focusing their ire on him and not on John Boehner—and asked them to give him ninety more days to address their concern. At the same time, he informed them that he'd asked Department of Homeland Security secretary Jeh Johnson to conduct a review of what actions he might unilaterally take, using his executive authority, to ease the problem.[46]

At which point, the situation at the border suddenly became more serious with news of a flood of unaccompanied children, some as young as three, crossing the border and being held in dismal detention facilities pending hearings before a deportation judge. By midsummer, they numbered some fifty-seven thousand children, most of them from El Salvador, Guatemala, and Honduras.[47]

Unlike other immigrants, these kids did not run to avoid Border Patrol agents. They willingly turned themselves in to the first agents they saw, under a misapprehension that had somehow spread through

Central America that minors who reached the United States would automatically be given a work permit—when, in fact, they were given instead a notice to appear in detention court. Images of thousands of innocent young faces pressed up against thick glass panes or huddled under aluminum-foil blankets on concrete floors behind chain-link fences and barbed wire shocked an entire nation.

Politicians from President Obama on down decried what they called a "humanitarian crisis, not an immigration crisis." But the plight of these children stepped up the pressure on the president to do something about immigration. When Speaker Boehner again informed him that he had no intention of scheduling a vote on the Senate bill, and as protests continued, Obama decided to wait no longer. Or so it seemed.[48]

Suddenly, on June 30, 2014, Obama summoned reporters to the Rose Garden for a major announcement on immigration reform. I was there with the regular White House beat reporters. With Vice President Joe Biden at his side, and showing more emotion than reporters had seen from him on any recent issue, Obama began by blasting Boehner and House Republicans for refusing to allow a vote on the bipartisan Senate bill, which had languished in the House for over a year. "Our country and our economy would be stronger today if House Republicans had allowed a simple yes-or-no vote on this bill or, for that matter, any bill," he stated. "They'd be following the will of the majority of the American people who support reform. Instead, they've proven again and again that they're unwilling to stand up to the tea party in order to do what's best for the country. And the worst part about it is a bunch of them know better."[49]

The president said he wasn't going to wait for Republicans any longer, because "the failure of House Republicans to pass a darn bill is bad for our security, it's bad for our economy, and it's bad for our future." They left him no choice, he insisted, but to take executive action, in two areas. First, he ordered Homeland Security Secretary Jeh Johnson and Attorney General Eric Holder to send extra resources to the border. Second, he said he had also instructed both men "to identify additional actions my administration can take on our own, within my existing legal authorities, to do what Congress refuses to do and fix as much of our immigration system as we can. If Congress will not do their job, at least we can do ours."[50]

Then Obama made another promise he would live to regret: "I expect their recommendations before the end of summer and I intend to adopt those recommendations without further delay."[51]

"Before the end of summer." That was the key phrase that everyone—members of Congress, immigration activists, and reporters—remembered out of that news conference. But it wasn't long before we also realized that "end of summer" did not necessarily have the same meaning for the White House that it did for everybody else. For President Obama, in fact, "end of summer" could actually mean "after the midterm elections in November."

At first, members of the Latino community rejoiced. This was the Obama they had believed in and counted on. Two years earlier, he had used his executive authority to save the Dreamers in the middle of his re-election campaign. Now, heading into the 2014 midterm elections, he was willing to upset the apple cart by bypassing Congress and taking strong action on immigration—"before the end of summer."

But supporters grew wary as June turned to July, and July turned to August, without any sign of action from the White House. Was Obama falling back on his word? Was he giving in to pressure from some Democratic candidates to postpone any moves on immigration until after the midterm elections?

Obama himself, appearing on *Meet the Press*, denied that his delay had anything to do with political calculations. He insisted he was taking his time only in order to make "sure that the t's are crossed and the i's are dotted" and to get "all our ducks in a row." He also said he needed more time to explain what actions he planned to the American people.[52]

Which some people may have believed until the other shoe dropped on Saturday, September 6. Then, an anonymous White House official let the cat out of the bag, telling reporters: "Because of the Republicans' extreme politicization of this issue, the president believes it would be harmful to the policy itself and to the long-term prospects for comprehensive immigration reform to announce administrative action before the elections."[53] Suddenly, "before the end of summer" had morphed into "before the end of the year."

Obama didn't decide that on his own. Reports indicate he was talked into yet another delay by overly cautious political advisers, on the dubious theory it would help protect moderate, red state Democrats running for re-election. But, as we will soon see, it didn't.

For many immigration activists, this was the final straw. If Obama was tired of waiting on Congress, they were tired of waiting on him. Some even publicly complained they'd made a big mistake in putting their trust in Obama and the Democratic Party. Frank Sharry, president of America's Voice, one of the largest immigrant rights organizations, spoke of their frustration: "We advocates didn't make the reform promise; we just made the mistake of believing it. The President and Senate Democrats have chosen politics over people; the status quo over solving real problems."[54]

Sharry pointed out the latest delay would badly damage relations between the Latino community and the Democratic Party, which depended more and more on the growing Latino vote in border states. "What is the relationship between the Democratic Party and the fastest-growing group of voters in the country?" he asked. "What's galling to us is the implication of 'Oh, we'd love to help the brown people, but we might lose some white votes in doing it, so you're expendable.'" Sharry said the comment he now heard most often on the street among young Hispanics was: "He's a liar. We elected him, and he's given us nothing but deportations."[55]

La Raza's Janet Murguía slammed Obama for even temporarily letting partisan politics triumph over basic human rights: "When candidate Obama asked our community for support in 2008 and 2012, he urged us all to vote based on our hopes, not our fears," she lamented. But now, she pointed out, Obama had given in to a different kind of fear: "the fears of Democratic political operatives, crushing the hopes of millions of hard-working people living under the constant threat of deportation and family separation."[56]

Even Neera Tanden, head of the progressive, pro-Obama Center for American Progress, called Obama's change of plans "a disappointment with real consequences." California congresswoman Loretta Sanchez, who had worked closely with the White House on formulating its immigration strategy, complained that Obama had given members of the Hispanic Caucus no "heads-up" that he was going to punt until after the midterms. "So when President Obama said to us—in particular the Hispanic Caucus—'I'm going to get something done and you'll know by August,' it is a disappointment, it is a frustration. . . . We should be getting it done now instead of after the election, so, yes, of course we're disappointed in the president."[57]

Hispanic Caucus leader Luis Gutierrez also expressed his frustration. Obama, he argued, was paying far less attention to Latino voters than he did to other elements of the Democratic Party's traditional base. "We would not wait until after November if it was an issue affecting the gay and lesbian community," he told reporters. "If this was about women's reproductive rights, if this was about the minimum wage, if this was about a series of other issues, the Democratic Party would come together."[58]

Adding to the frustration of Latino leaders was the realization that there was no guarantee Obama's politically inspired delay would achieve its goal of helping beleaguered Democrats. Charles Chamberlain, executive director of Howard Dean's Democracy for America, warned: "Slow-walking justice for millions will not prevent Republicans from using nativist animosity to get their base to the polls and does even less to inspire Democrats' grassroots progressive base at a critical political moment."[59]

Chamberlain's warning was no sooner issued than it proved to be true. On October 1, barely a month after the White House announced its delay, the *Washington Post* reported: "Activists in key states say it is increasingly difficult to register would-be Latino voters who would vote for Democrats because of unhappiness over the decision. Poll numbers for Obama and Democrats have also dropped further among Hispanics than the population at large."

"The president has not helped us," activist Leo Murrieta, twenty-eight, who was working to register Latino voters in Colorado for *Mi*

Familia Vota, told the *Post*. "People are disappointed. They wanted action, they wanted activity, they wanted movement."

Obama's on-again, off-again approach to immigration reform had already hurt his own standing among Latinos. In a July 2014 *Washington Post–ABC News* poll, Obama had a 68 percent approval rating among Hispanics for his handling of immigration. By early October, that number had dropped to 42 percent. "The president's ongoing broken promises have certainly depressed the engagement in the Latino community," Arturo Carmona, executive director of Presente Action, told *The Hill* just before the election. "There's no question it's going to affect Democrats in this midterm. There's no one to blame but Democrats themselves."[60]

And, sure enough, when all the votes were counted, the president's delay did not help those Democrats considered most vulnerable: Mary Landrieu of Louisiana, Mark Pryor of Arkansas, Kay Hagan of North Carolina, and Mark Begich of Alaska. All four lost. "Hey Dems—how's ignoring Latinos working for you today?" the executive director of the National Association of Latino Independent Producers tweeted on Election Night. In at least one state and likely more, waiting to act until after the midterms may, in fact, have backfired. Several political analysts attributed Mark Udall's loss in Colorado to lower-than-expected turnout among Latino voters, disappointed in Obama's failure to deliver. "Tonight you lost your job, but you will still go back to your family," one immigration activist wrote of Kay Hagan. "However, because of the inaction and ineptitude of your party, many parents will not get that chance . . . if you ask me, you got what you deserve."[61]

Obama's waffling was a monumental mistake on several fronts. It simply continued the hardship of many Latino families facing the threat of deportation. Meanwhile, Democrats still lost control of the Senate. Four Democratic senators who were presumed to benefit from the delay lost anyway, and they were definitely not helped by lower Latino turnout. Hispanics began to lose confidence that Obama was on their side, after all. And when he finally did take action, he disappointed them yet again by not going far enough.

Opportunity Missed

After he and his fellow Democrats were roundly drubbed by Republicans (again) on November 4, losing control of the Senate and thirteen more seats in the House, President Obama did what any smart politician would do: He blew town for a while—a nine-day trip to China, Myanmar, and Australia. But he didn't wait long after his return to try to atone for his errors on immigration reform.

In a prime-time address to the nation from the White House on Thursday evening, November 20 (which the major networks refused to cover), President Obama announced he was finally taking action and outlined the most sweeping steps on immigration reform since President Reagan's executive order of 1986.[62]

His plan had two major components. First, out of an estimated 11 million undocumented immigrants in the United States, some 4.4 million immigrants, who are parents of U.S. citizens and legal permanent residents, and who had lived in the United States for at least five years, would be allowed to remain in the country temporarily, without the threat of deportation. They could legally apply for jobs under a three-year, renewable work permit. And they could, in effect, openly join American society in all ways but two. They are not allowed to vote and they do not qualify for coverage under the Affordable Care Act.[63]

Second, Obama also expanded his 2012 DACA action to cover an additional 270,000 young Latinos who had been brought to the United States illegally as children by their parents.

Anticipating the inevitable angry reaction from Republicans in Congress, the president defended his actions and issued them a pointed challenge: "The actions I'm taking are not only lawful, they're the kinds of actions taken by every single Republican president and every Democratic president for the past half century," he said. "And to those members of Congress who question my authority to make our immigration system work better, or question the wisdom of me acting where Congress has failed, I have one answer: Pass a bill."[64]

Republicans reacted as expected. Speaker John Boehner sniffed: "The president has said before that 'he's not king' and he's 'not an em-

peror,' but he sure is acting like one." And Congressman Michael Mc-
Caul, chair of the House Committee on Homeland Security, warned that
Obama's actions would open the floodgates: "We will see a wave of ille-
gal immigration because of the president's action, and in no way is the
Department of Homeland Security prepared to handle such a surge."[65]

McCaul and other Republicans pledged to use every tool at their
disposal to block the president's executive order. They threatened everything from defunding the program to impeaching the president.
But, in the real world, there was little they could do. Immigration programs were independently funded by fees, thus not part of the federal
budget Congress could cut. And nobody had the stomach for another
round of Clinton-style impeachment hearings. In the end, all Republicans managed to do was cut the Department of Homeland Security,
responsible for carrying out immigration policies, out of the Omnibus 2015 spending bill—and fund the agency for just three months at
a time. But Republicans, afraid of being accused of leaving America
vulnerable to a terrorist attack without a fully operational DHS, soon
caved and provided funding for DHS as well.[66]

But even among immigration reformers, response to the president's
executive order was lukewarm. Most organizations hailed it as a step in
the right direction, but still "too little, too late." They believed Obama
should have protected more people from his "deportation machine,"
which had averaged 400,000 annual deportations since 2009. A record
number of immigrants, 438,421, were sent home during 2013—and
they were not all hardened criminals, as the president often insisted.
Families were still being ripped apart after a mother or father was deported for a routine traffic stop.[67]

And, of course, no matter how well-intentioned, limited action
by the president fell far short of comprehensive immigration reform,
which many Latinos blamed as much on President Obama's lack of
leadership as they did on solid opposition by Republicans.

At this late date, nothing Obama did could entirely erase the anger
generated among Hispanics by the bobbing and weaving he did before
issuing his executive order. Many felt, quite legitimately, that he had
treated the issue—and the Latino community—as a pawn to be played

only when necessary for political gain. The executive order did not compensate for his many delays. When they finally saw what was contained in the order, people still kept asking why he had to wait so long, and why he couldn't have acted earlier, as promised.

"This could have happened in the summer," said Juan Escalante, an online activist and blogger. "We essentially wasted three or four months waiting for this for no reason whatsoever. And it's not just time in terms of this Congress, it's time in people's lives. . . . What is going to happen to all those people that have been deported whose children are now in foster care, whose families have been torn apart and who have no option but to watch their families grow up from afar?"[68]

For Escalante, what Obama delivered was not enough. "This is something that the president has continuously promised us since he took office," he said. "People will blow this out of proportion and use this in their fundraising emails and try to say 'yeah we did it' but it doesn't do anybody any favors."[69]

So immigration reform, which at one time held the promise of being one of the major achievements of the Obama administration, ended up as another unfinished chapter, with Obama caught in the cross fire. Red state attorneys general filed a lawsuit claiming the president had exceeded his legal authority in issuing the executive order, and a federal district court and the Fifth Circuit Court of Appeals agreed with them. The Obama administration has asked the Supreme Court to decide the case. Latino activists argued the president could and should do even more to provide deportation relief, while the White House insisted he'd already done all he could legally do without an act of Congress.

The reality is there will be no comprehensive immigration reform under the Obama presidency. At the end of his administration, despite Obama's soaring rhetoric and good intentions, the promise of immigration reform today will remain unfulfilled, another failure of leadership, and yet another blown opportunity—which could have a profound impact on the 2016 elections, and the future of the Democratic Party.

The only thing saving the Democratic Party is the fact that the Republican Party remains so hidebound on the issue—refusing to consider even the most modest of immigration reforms, stubbornly trying to repeal the DREAM Act, and practically declaring war on the Latino community. But Democrats shouldn't have to rely on the dismal behavior of Donald Trump Republicans. President Obama should've done the right thing and worked harder to deliver the comprehensive immigration reform he promised.

SIX

Guns

Gun violence prevention is one of the issues on which President Obama's heart is definitely in the right place. He cares about the issue. And he speaks passionately about it. Once again, he just didn't do enough to make it happen.

Indeed, for the first two years of his presidency, he did almost nothing—which stunned both his supporters and White House reporters. After all, given his campaign statements on gun control, and his criticism of President Bush on the issue, we expected gun safety to be one of his top priorities.

In a debate against Alan Keyes in his 2004 Senate campaign, Obama went on record in support of a ban on assault weapons. "They have only one purpose," he said, "to kill people." He called it "a scandal that this president [George W. Bush] did not authorize a renewal of the assault weapons ban."[1]

Running for president in 2008, he again talked about the need for sensible gun safety measures, while rebutting the NRA's absurd claim that he wanted to go house-to-house, confiscating all firearms: "I just want to be absolutely clear, all right. So I don't want any misunderstanding. When y'all go home and you're talking to your buddies, and they say, 'Ah, he wants to take my gun away,' you've heard it here—I'm on television so everybody knows it—I believe in the Second Amendment. I believe in people's lawful right to bear arms. I will not take your shotgun away. I will not take your rifle away. I won't take your handgun away. . . . So, there are some common-sense gun safety laws that I believe in. But I am not going to take your guns away. So if you want to find an excuse not to vote for me, don't use that one. Cause that just ain't true."[2]

But Obama's voice fell silent once he arrived in the White House, even on the already-resolved (for him) issue of the assault weapons ban. At least once a week, one of us reporters would badger then–press secretary Robert Gibbs on what the president was doing about renewing the assault weapons ban, which President Bush had allowed to expire in 2004. Remember, candidate Obama had called Bush's inaction a "scandal." But, like a broken record, Gibbs would only repeat that President Obama "strongly supported" a ban on assault weapons, but it was up to Congress to act. And how much effort was the president expending to prompt Congress to take action? No answer. Because the answer, as on so many other issues, was: nothing.[3]

The gun issue took on much more urgency on January 8, 2011, when a mad gunman shot Congresswoman Gabby Giffords in the head as she met with constituents outside a supermarket in Tucson, Arizona. Six people at the outdoor meeting were killed; thirteen were wounded. Giffords suffered major brain damage, but has recovered remarkably, retired from Congress, and, together with her astronaut-husband Mark Kelly, made ending gun violence her life's passion.[4]

Four days after the shooting, Obama appeared at a rally at McKale Center on the University of Arizona campus. In a stirring, emotional address, he electrified the crowd by revealing that Congresswoman Giffords had opened her eyes for the first time that afternoon, while he was visiting her in the hospital. He then went on to salute in very personal tones every one of the twenty people wounded or killed that day, from congressional aide Gabe Zimmerman, murdered as he lunged to stop the shooting, to Christina-Taylor Green, just nine years old. Obama then made an impassioned plea for healing and national unity in the wake of this tragedy and, without mentioning any specific measure, called for a "national conversation" on firearm safety.[5]

Many presidential observers called it the best speech of his presidency. "I thought it was one of the best speeches he's ever given," said historian Michael Beschloss. Calling it "Obama's Finest Hour," Garry Wills even compared it to Lincoln at Gettysburg and Henry V at Agincourt. "It was his most important speech so far," argued presidential historian Douglas Brinkley, "one that history is going to reflect on. There was a bit of Dr. King to him. That's simply been missing in his presidency so far. I was sitting there and I realized, 'This guy might be a great man.' I had forgotten about that."[6]

But, once again, there was little follow-up. At Obama's direction, Vice President Biden did convene several meetings to seek consensus on gun safety measures. But Congress still didn't act, and Obama didn't really pressure them to. What would it take to wake America up to the need for some sensible new restrictions on gun ownership? The massacre of innocent first-graders?

Of course, that's exactly what happened. At Sandy Hook Elementary School in Newtown, Connecticut, on December 14, 2012, when twenty-year-old Adam Lanza slaughtered twenty first-graders and six adults with an assault weapon. Two days later, Obama again gave another powerful testimony to those senselessly murdered, and spoke of the need to prevent the repetition of these mass shootings. "We can't tolerate this anymore," he said. "These tragedies must end, and to end them, we must change."[7]

And this time, it looked as if the president was actually going to deliver. "In the coming weeks," he told the crowd of parents and community leaders in Newtown, "I'll use whatever power this office holds to engage my fellow citizens, from law enforcement to mental health professionals to parents and educators, in an effort to prevent more tragedies like this. Because—what choice do we have?"[8]

A few weeks later, on January 16, 2013, President Obama announced a series of measures aimed at controlling gun violence. About half of these the president could accomplish by executive order, the rest required congressional action. New executive policies included requiring federal agencies to make relevant data available to the federal background check system; publishing a letter from the Bureau of Alcohol, Tobacco, Firearms, and Explosives to federally licensed gun dealers providing guidance on how to run background checks for private sellers; and starting a national dialogue on mental health led by then–HHS secretary Kathleen Sebelius and Education Secretary

Arne Duncan. Action on those items, to the president's credit, began immediately.[9]

"I will put everything I've got into this," Obama promised us, "and so will Joe." The problem was, the most critical measures on the president's list—criminal background checks on all gun sales, reinstating the ban on assault weapons, limiting ammunition magazines to ten rounds—depended on passage of legislation by Congress, which is always slow to act, if it does anything at all. And pushing Congress to act has never been President Obama's strong suit.[10]

Nonetheless, Senator Dianne Feinstein immediately introduced legislation to renew the ban on assault weapons—which the president quickly endorsed. Democrat Joe Manchin and Republican Patrick Toomey forged a bipartisan plan to require background checks on all gun sales, supported by 90 percent of Americans—legislation also quickly endorsed by Obama. Parents of the victims of Sandy Hook came to Washington and dramatically walked the halls of Congress, pleading with senators and members of Congress to pass both measures. But, once again, the NRA proved too powerful. With Speaker Boehner afraid of, and controlled by, his Tea Party members, the House of Representatives sat on its hands. The Senate failed to find sixty votes for Manchin-Toomey. Four Senate Democrats actually joined the NRA in killing the bill. And despite promising "everything I've got," President Obama either did not know how, or chose not, to use the persuasive powers of the presidency, à la Lyndon Baines Johnson, to force them to act.[11]

Tragically, the same scenario repeated itself over and over again. On April 2, 2014, a troubled former army psychiatrist killed three soldiers and injured sixteen more at Fort Hood, Texas, before shooting himself in the head, echoing a similar tragedy there five years earlier that left thirteen dead. In Lafayette, Louisiana, on July 23, 2015, a disturbed gunman opened fire on a showing of the movie *Trainwreck*, killing two and injuring nine. (This, too, conjured grim reminders of an earlier Obama-era mass shooting. At a 2012 showing of *The Dark Knight Rises* in Aurora, Colorado, James Holmes murdered twelve and injured seventy midnight moviegoers.) On the morning of August 26, 2015, two young journalists in Virginia—Alison Parker and Adam Ward—were shot and killed while on the air by a coworker, who later committed suicide.[12]

In total, as of this writing in October 2015, there have been 972 mass shootings since the Sandy Hook murders, resulting in at least 1,217 people dead and 3,509 wounded. At the very moment I was writing this, news broke of another ten Americans killed by a gunman at Umpqua Community College in Roseburg, Oregon. And those are just the mass shootings. In a column soon after the Parker-Ward slayings, Nick Kristof pointed out that more Americans are killed by guns every six months than died in all the wars and terror attacks of the last twenty-five years combined. In total, more Americans have perished from shootings since 1968 than died in all the wars in our history.[13]

Yet another such shooting took place on June 17, 2015, when a lone twenty-one-year-old white gunman walked into a Bible study group in Charleston, South Carolina's historic Emanuel AME Church. After sitting with the group for about an hour, he suddenly stood up, pulled out a pistol, and aimed it at the parishioners. He was there "to shoot black people," he explained. "I have to do it. You rape our women, and you're taking over our country. And you have to go." He then killed nine African-American church members, reloading five times.[14]

It was the fourteenth time in his presidency that a mass murder involving guns was sufficiently shocking that President Obama had to respond. (Although, as noted earlier, there have been many, many more such murders, terrifying in their everyday mundanity.) Angered and saddened by yet another senseless attack, this one clearly motivated by hatred of black people, an emotional President Obama appeared in the White House the next morning to lament the latest outbreak of racial turmoil: "This is not the first time that black churches have been attacked, and we know that hatred across races and faiths poses a particular threat to our democracy and our ideals."[15]

The Associated Press described Obama as "visibly infuriated." But, unlike his attitude after similar mass shootings, this time the president seemed resigned to the fact that nothing would happen as a result of it: "At some point, we as a country will have to reckon with the fact that this type of mass violence does not happen in other advanced countries. It is in our power to do something about it. I say that recognizing the politics in this town foreclose a lot of the avenues right now. But it would be wrong for us not to acknowledge it. And at some point it's going to be important for the American people to come to grips with it."[16]

No call to action. No angry attack on the gun lobby. No challenge to Congress. No "fierce urgency of now." Just "at some point," we're going to have to do something. It sounded as if he'd already given up. In the *Washington Post*, columnist Chris Cillizza featured Obama's statement under the headline: "President Obama Waves the White Flag on Gun Control." But his new restraint on gun safety, Cillizza argued, had even deeper meaning: "In many ways, Obama's progression on gun control—from optimism to anger to acceptance—is the story of his presidency. From the economic stimulus to Obamacare to immigration and, of course, gun control, he has watched as the politics of Washington have proven too much for him (or anyone else) to overcome."[17]

Reflecting Obama's hesitancy to re-engage on guns, members of Congress maintained their own radio silence. From even the most outspoken proponents of sensible gun control—Senators Chuck Schumer, Dianne Feinstein, Joe Manchin, Pat Toomey—barely a peep about new legislation. When asked about it separately, Senators Manchin and Toomey said they would like to get a bill passed, but nothing was imminent. Harry Reid made a speech in favor of background checks and then ceded the field. The NRA had won again; this time, without even trying.[18]

In October 2014, CNN asked then–outgoing attorney general Eric Holder what he saw as the failures of his time in office. "I think the inability to pass reasonable gun safety laws after the Newtown massacre is something that weighs heavily on my mind," Holder replied, "and the thought that we could not translate that horror into reasonable—I mean, really reasonable—gun safety measures that were supported by the vast majority of the American people is something that I take personally as a failure, and something that I think we as a society should take as a failure, a glaring failure, that I hope will ultimately be rectified."[19]

He's right. It was a tremendous failure. Not one of Obama's proposals became law. In the end, his efforts on gun safety consisted only of a handful of executive orders requiring federal agencies to do a better job of sharing information. In response to the massacre at Sandy Hook, the federal government did almost nothing. And, despite the Gabby Giffords shooting, the Aurora, Colorado, theater murders, Sandy Hook, Charleston, and other mass murders on his watch, Obama will leave office having done almost nothing substantial about the growing problem of gun violence. As candidate Obama told us in 2008, that is a scandal.

Nuclear Arms

Obama's surprising failure to act on guns extends to nuclear weapons as well. Given his brief record in the Senate, progressives had also been confident that Barack Obama would exhibit strong leadership on nuclear arms reduction. As senator, he'd cosponsored the bipartisan Obama-Lugar bill to help lock down nuclear weapons around the world. And campaigning for president in 2008, he famously vowed to make nuclear disarmament the centerpiece of his national defense strategy. Early on in his presidency, he seemed determined to deliver on that promise.[20]

Speaking in Prague's historic Hradcanske Square in April 2009, Obama declared that "the existence of thousands of nuclear weapons is the most dangerous legacy of the Cold War." Keeping nuclear weapons ready to launch on a moment's notice, he said, only increases "the risk of catastrophic accidents or miscalculation." He then reaffirmed "America's commitment to seek the peace and security of a world without nuclear weapons."[21]

"A world without nuclear weapons." Powerful stuff! Obama was pledging to deliver the long-held dream of peace activists. Indeed, later that same month, the Nobel Committee cited the promise he made in Prague in awarding Obama the 2009 Peace Prize.[22]

Alas, that dream was not to be. Six years later, as reported by William J. Broad in the *New York Times*, the same doves "who once cheered

President Obama for his antinuclear crusades and later fell silent as he backpedaled are now lining up to denounce him." In October 2014, the Federation of American Scientists blasted Obama, despite his flowery rhetoric, for in fact reducing the size of the nation's nuclear stockpile far less than did any of his three predecessors, including both presidents Bush.[23]

In its 2014 report, the federation, which tracks the record of all presidents who have served in the nuclear age, reported that Obama had reduced the size of America's nuclear arsenal by 507 warheads, or about 10 percent of the stockpile, since taking office—which, according to Hans M. Kristensen, the report's author, is the lowest number of weapons destroyed (in numbers, not percentages) of "any administration ever."[24]

Surprisingly, the most aggressive nuclear disarmament president was George W. Bush. During his two terms, he's credited with cutting the nation's nuclear arsenal in half. His father came close, with a 41 percent reduction. Together, the two presidents Bush ordered destruction of a staggering 14,801 warheads. Obama? Not so much.[25]

What disturbs activists even more is the fact that, while lagging behind previous presidents in cutting warheads, President Obama has also spent more than previous administrations in modernizing our remaining nuclear weapons and in authorizing a new generation of weapon carriers. As reported in *The Nation* in December 2014, the administration's far-reaching "modernization" program "aims to overhaul the entire U.S. nuclear-weapons arsenal, with a particular focus on improving the fusing systems and accuracy of long-range land- and sea-based ballistic missile warheads and on increasing the killing power of other nuclear warheads."[26]

Obama's plan calls for new multibillion-dollar facilities for plutonium components at Los Alamos, New Mexico, and highly enriched uranium at Oak Ridge, Tennessee. It also includes a new Kansas City, Missouri, plant to build the thousands of non-nuclear components needed to make nuclear weapons deliverable. All these new production plants are planned to manufacture nuclear weapons until 2075.[27]

Estimated price tag: $1 trillion. To help pay for which, Obama proposed in fiscal year 2015 to cut funding for dismantling of nuclear weapons by 45 percent and cut nonproliferation programs by 20 percent. In other words, moving us in the wrong direction.[28]

In effect, Obama's nuclear critics charge him with a double double cross. Not only did he not destroy as many warheads as he promised, he actually began "engaging in extensive atomic rebuilding," as a September 2014 *Times* report put it. "Supporters of arms control, as well as some of President Obama's closest advisers, say their hopes for the president's vision have turned to baffled disappointment as the modernization of nuclear capabilities has become an end unto itself."[29]

The Alliance for Nuclear Accountability condemned the administration's plans as "the largest expansion of funding on nuclear weapons since the fall of the Soviet Union." Joe Cirincione, president of the Ploughshares Fund and a longtime Obama supporter, urged him to "suspend plans to develop a new arsenal." Writing in the *Los Angeles Times*, Cirincione warned: "Unless something is done soon, we will buy thousands of new hydrogen bombs and mount them on hundreds of new missiles and planes." Other critics warned that modernization of the arsenal would only enable future presidents to even more rapidly expand the nation's atomic forces.[30]

How to explain or defend such an abrupt reversal of course from where Barack Obama was supposed to be heading on nuclear disarmament? The White House insists it's really nothing new, merely a necessary exercise to update our national defense system, increase the "reliability" of U.S. nuclear forces, and prevent existing weapons from becoming obsolete. They also contend they had no choice, because Senate Republicans demanded the upgrade as their price for ratifying the 2010 arms treaty with Moscow.[31]

That argument is convincingly shot down by MIT professor of science, technology, and international security Theodore A. Postol in *The Nation*. He points out that, rather than a routine, harmless "modernization" program, upgrading our nuclear weapons capacity carries within it two inherent dangers. First, it will be seen by many, especially the Kremlin, as an attempt to prepare U.S. nuclear forces for a direct confrontation with Russia. The Cold War all over again: triggering God only knows what response from a jittery and unpredictable Vladimir Putin, not to mention rogue states like North Korea.

Second, and perhaps more seriously, it perpetuates the disastrously wrongheaded notion, which still exists among many leaders of the military, that the United States can initiate, limit, and win a nuclear war. Warns Postol: "In the end, the U.S. modernization program reveals a fundamental misunderstanding of the most basic characteristics of nuclear weapons. The scale and character of these weapons' effects are so large and so deadly that any notion of using them in a controlled or limited way is completely disconnected from reality."[32]

Postol concludes: "In a world that is fundamentally unpredictable, the pursuit of an unchallenged capacity to fight and win a nuclear war is a dangerous folly." Which is exactly what Barack Obama used to say—before he became president.[33]

On nuclear disarmament, the net effect of President Obama's actions will be to leave the United States with slightly fewer warheads, perhaps, but still a large and even more powerful and deadly nuclear arsenal. Whatever his excuses for doing so, and despite his success in blocking Iran from building a nuclear weapon, he does not leave the world a safer place.

Asked about Obama's retreat on the nuclear issue, Senator Sam Nunn, another longtime supporter of disarmament, summed up the Obama era just as succinctly as Chris Cillizza did when talking about gun control. "A lot of it is hard to explain," he said. "The president's vision was a significant change in direction. But the process has preserved the status quo."[34]

SEVEN

Climate Change

For progressives, climate change may be the classic Obama frustration: Even though he actually took many positive and decisive steps forward, he still fell far short of what scientists and environmentalists believed was necessary. Not desirable, but necessary. After all, this is the future of our planet at stake.

Yes, Obama did more to address the issue of global warming than any other president before him, yet he failed in so many ways to use the powers of the presidency to take ownership of the issue.

For starters, Barack Obama is no climate change denier. He's a true believer. As a senator, he studied and talked about the problem. As a candidate for president, he left no doubt that he saw dealing with global warming as one of the great challenges of our time and one on which his presidency would be judged. On June 3, 2008, the night he clinched the Democratic nomination for president, he spoke about climate change in almost messianic tones: "I am absolutely certain that generations from now, we will be able to look back and tell our children . . . that this was the moment when the rise of the oceans began to slow and our planet began to heal."[1]

Once in the White House, in news conferences and speeches, Obama spoke often of the need to act on climate change because, as he said in his second inaugural address, "the failure to do so would betray our children and future generations." And on a hot, sultry June 25, 2013, President Obama went to nearby Georgetown University to give what many environmentalists still consider the best speech of any American politician on climate change. "As the world's largest economy and second-largest carbon emitter, as a country with unsurpassed ability to drive innovation and scientific breakthroughs, as the country that people around the world continue to look to in times of crisis, we've got a vital role to play," he told the students. "We can't stand on the sidelines. We've got a unique responsibility."[2]

And Obama took upon himself responsibility for leading the charge: "I refuse to condemn your generation and future generations to a planet that's beyond fixing. We will be judged as a people, and as a society, and as a country on where we go from here."[3]

On climate change, then, President Obama said all the right things, as usual—and in this case he actually took some important actions, too. So why do environmentalists remain disappointed in his leadership on the issue? It boils down to what he dared do, stacked up against what he dared not do. Given the demands of our times, did he take full advantage of the opportunities he had as president?

Let's examine what was accomplished—and what was left undone.

Among the strong, positive steps taken by President Obama to save the planet from the threat of global warming:

- He believes in the science of climate change, and talked about the importance of the issue. It's sad that acknowledging overwhelming evidence has to be considered a positive step, but some presidents—like his predecessor—haven't even met this basic requirement.
- He dedicated roughly $30 billion of the 2009 stimulus package to energy efficiency and renewable energy projects: from new investments in wind and solar, to development of advanced batteries for electric cars, to making homes more energy-efficient, to biofuel research.[4]
- He persuaded auto manufacturers to adopt tough, new CAFE standards—not once, but twice. In 2009, with Detroit's support, Obama announced a goal of 35.5 mpg by 2016. Two years later, again with support of the Big Three, Obama announced the even more ambitious goal of 54.5 mpg by 2025. It is, by far, the largest mandatory fuel economy increase in history.[5]
- At the end of his first year in office, in December 2009, Presi-

dent Obama flew to Copenhagen and the United Nations Climate Change Conference. The conference turned out to be something of a train wreck, falling far short of expectations and what was needed to get serious about the climate crisis. Nonetheless, Obama managed to broker a weak nonbinding accord with several other nations and committed the United States to achieving a 17 percent reduction in greenhouse gases by 2020. Legislation to create a "cap and trade" system had already passed the Democratic-controlled House by then, but it died in the Senate.[6]

- In January 2014, buoyed by a 2007 Supreme Court ruling that the EPA was required by law to regulate greenhouse gases, the Obama administration proposed a rule limiting the carbon dioxide released by new coal-fired power plants. It required that all new coal-powered plants capture some of the carbon they release and bury it underground.[7]

- In June 2014, the EPA also proposed new rules for existing power plants—requiring states to come up with a plan to cut carbon dioxide emissions from existing plants, the nation's largest source of carbon emissions, by as much as 30 percent by 2030. After these were temporarily blocked by the Court in a 5–4 decision the following year, the Obama administration released even-stronger emissions rules, calling for a 32 percent cut, two months later, as part of its "Clean Power Plan." There is hope that this marks the beginning of the end for coal-powered power plants.[8]

- In November 2014, President Obama traveled to China and announced a major new agreement on climate change with the Chinese government. Under terms of the accord, the United States agreed to cut net greenhouse gas emissions at least 26 percent by 2025, doubling its current pace of carbon reduction. At the same time, China announced a stepped-up time frame for its carbon reduction and for increasing China's investments in nuclear, wind, and solar energy. And in September 2015, President Xi Jinping came to the White House and announced that China was adopting its own cap and trade program.[9]

- That same month, while in Asia, the president pledged $3 billion to

the United Nations Green Climate Fund, to help developing countries prepare for and slow the effects of climate change. Created in
2011, the UN fund asks industrialized countries that pump most of
the greenhouse gases into the atmosphere to provide aid to developing countries so they can shift to low-carbon fuel and adapt to
the effects of climate change.[10]

• As a dramatic sign of his commitment, President Obama led the
United States delegation to the all-important United Nations Summit on Climate Change in Paris in December 2015 and pledged
that the United States, the world's second-worst source of greenhouse gases, would adopt strict new limits on emissions.

That's a good record, as far as it goes. The problem is, according to
many concerned about climate change, it just doesn't rise to address
the level of catastrophe we face. Not even close.

Obama gets a bad rap, first, for not making climate change his flat-
out, number-one priority—which, environmentalists believe, the issue
deserves, and needs, if we are ever going to turn the corner toward a
fossil-free energy policy. Obama, in other words, has been hit-and-
miss: speaking out strongly on global warming, then ignoring it for
months; eking out a promise in Copenhagen, then not delivering on
this promise. No focused, concentrated attention.

Early on, former vice president Al Gore, who's made climate change
his life's passion, with a book and documentary to show for it, faulted
Obama for not making the same commitment. Writing in the June
2011 issue of *Rolling Stone*, Gore complained: "President Obama has
never presented to the American people the magnitude of the climate
crisis. He has simply not made the case for action. He has not defended
the science against the ongoing, withering and dishonest attacks."[11]

Obama almost admitted as much in November 2012, in his first
post-reelection news conference. In response to a question about
whether climate change would assume added importance in his second
term, Obama gave a classic Obama wandering-around-the-barn answer in which he acknowledged that yes, climate change is real; yes, we
have an obligation to do something about it; and yes, doing something

about it will require tough political choices; but—I'm not sure this is the right time to make those choices, or I'm even prepared to make them.[12]

Here's how he put it: "There's no doubt that for us to take on climate change in a serious way would involve making some tough political choices, and you know, understandably, I think the American people right now have been so focused and will continue to be focused on our economy and jobs and growth that, you know, if the message is somehow we're going to ignore jobs and growth simply to address climate change, I don't think anybody's going to go for that."[13]

But, he added, if he could push climate change without rocking the economic boat, he might actually go for it: "If, on the other hand, we can shape an agenda that says we can create jobs, advance growth and make a serious dent in climate change and be an international leader, I think that's something that the American people would support."[14]

Suffice to say, it was not the kind of wholehearted commitment environmentalists were looking for.

Obama also gets a well-deserved bad rap for balancing his actions on climate change, no matter how laudable, with unprecedented growth in domestic production of fossil fuels. It's all part of his "all of the above" strategy on energy: a little bit of energy conservation, a little bit of offshore drilling, a dash of nuclear power. Everything is part of the mix. Once again, Obama is trying to have it all ways—but when it comes to climate change, that's just not going to work.

Knowing full well that expanding fossil fuel production only traps more heat in the atmosphere and accelerates the climate crisis, frustrated environmentalists watched as Obama seemed to approve one new drilling plan for every alternative energy move he made. In January 2015, shortly after he declared 1.2 million acres of the Arctic National Wildlife Refuge, or ANWR, as a wilderness area, off-limits for oil exploration, he opened up portions of Alaska's Beaufort Sea for more drilling. At the same time, he also opened up the Atlantic Coast, from Virginia to Georgia, for offshore oil and gas exploration. He reopened the Gulf of Mexico for deep-water drilling, shortly after the BP oil spill. And the Bureau of Land Management agreed to auction off 316 million tons of publicly owned coal in Wyoming's Powder River Basin.[15]

Bill McKibben, cofounder of the climate change organization 350 .org and perhaps America's leading environmentalist, summed it up in *Rolling Stone*'s edition of December 17, 2013: "By the time Obama leaves office, the U.S. will pass Saudi Arabia as the planet's biggest oil producer and Russia as the world's biggest producer of oil and gas combined. In the same years, even as we've begun to burn less coal at home, our coal exports have climbed to record highs. We are, despite slight declines in our domestic emissions, a global-warming machine: At the moment when physics tell us we should be jamming on the carbon brakes, America is revving the engine."[16]

Like any good oil producer, President Obama even bragged about his record in Cushing, Oklahoma, on March 22, 2012, when he gave his blessing to the first, or southern, leg of the controversial Keystone XL pipeline. "Over the last three years, I've directed my administration to open up millions of acres for gas and oil exploration across 23 different states," he told the crowd of pipeline supporters. "We're opening up more than 75 percent of our potential oil resources offshore. We've quadrupled the number of operating rigs to a record high. We've added enough new oil and gas pipeline to encircle the Earth, and then some. . . . In fact, the problem is that we're actually producing so much oil and gas . . . that we don't have enough pipeline capacity to transport all of it where it needs to go."[17]

Not so. As McKibben points out in *Rolling Stone*, the real problem is that climate change becomes a more serious crisis by the day. The evidence is all around us in melting glaciers, strange new weather patterns, more devastating storms, wildfires, hurricanes, tornadoes, rising sea levels, changes in crops and animal migrations. Climate change is here. It's real. And the more we try to "balance" action on climate change with continued development of fossil fuels, the less likely we are to move in a new direction. McKibben says it best: "In any event, building more renewable energy is not a useful task if you're also digging more carbon energy—it's like eating a pan of Weight Watchers brownies after you've already gobbled a quart of Ben and Jerry's."[18]

Speaking of the Keystone XL pipeline, that particular project ultimately became much more than another tar sands pipeline. It became the symbol of whether the United States would really turn the corner from a fossil-fuel-driven economy to a renewable energy policy. From a climate-change perspective, forgoing the Keystone pipeline should have been a no-brainer. So, of course, it became the locus of another extended Hamlet routine from the president. As of October 2015, a full seven years after the permit was first applied for, a decision had still not been made. (When Republicans in Congress tried to force his hand earlier that year, President Obama vetoed the legislation, a veto the Senate could not override.)[19]

Ironically—or perhaps this was his intent—the longer Obama delayed his decision on Keystone, the weaker the arguments in support of the pipeline. By early 2015, the United States was producing more oil than we were importing. Keystone was not needed for energy independence. The price of gas had fallen to under three dollars per gallon. Keystone would not help lower gas prices. Oil prices had fallen to a low of forty dollars a barrel. Nobody needed expensive tar sands oil from Canada. Keystone would not produce that many jobs either. Even its backers admitted that perhaps ten thousand short-term construction jobs would soon dwindle to fewer than fifty permanent jobs.[20]

Then, finally, on November 6, 2015, President Obama lowered the boom on Keystone and announced his decision to deny the project, because, he said, "the pipeline would not make a meaningful long-term contribution to our economy," and because it would impede the move toward climate change. "America's now a global leader when it comes to serious action to fight climate change," he told reporters in the Roosevelt Room. "And frankly, approving this project would have undercut that global leadership."

While not unexpected, Obama's rejection of the Keystone XL pipeline was rather anticlimactic, because just three days earlier, TransCanada Corp., sponsor of the project, perhaps anticipating bad news, had asked the State Department to suspend its review of the project for at least two years.

Even while the Keystone pipeline was being considered, however, Obama continued drilling deeper in other arenas. In May 2015, he approved more deep-water offshore drilling in the Arctic, granting permission to Shell to drill for oil in the remote Chukchi Sea, again frustrating and infuriating environmentalists. Bill McKibben immediately condemned the decision: "Shell helped melt the Arctic and now they want to drill in the thawing waters; it beggars belief that the Obama administration is willing to abet what amounts to one of the greatest acts of corporate irresponsibility in the planet's history. Arctic oil, like tar sands, is exactly the sort of carbon we need to leave underground if we're going to have any chance of avoiding catastrophe."

Fortunately, in this case, the environment was saved from serious damage and Obama was saved from embarrassment when, in late September 2015, Shell Oil abruptly announced that, after having spent $7 billion in exploration, it was abandoning its entire Arctic drilling project. Why? Because there were not enough oil deposits to merit the cost. On October 17, the Interior Department canceled any new drilling permits in the Arctic over the next two years.

So the polar bears are still safe . . . for now—but no thanks to President Obama.

And that's the trick when it comes to Barack Obama and climate change. Too often, he talked a good game when giving a "climate change" speech, but then turned around and exacerbated the crisis with his fossil fuel and drilling policy. The *New Yorker's* Elizabeth Kolbert charitably called this tendency "self-sabotaging," while *Slate's* Eric Holthaus simply deemed the president a "climate change hypocrite." Either way, it was not the leadership we needed on this critical issue. As McKibben put it of the president's "catastrophic climate change denial" in a scathing May 2015 op-ed: "This is not climate denial of the Republican sort, where people simply pretend the science isn't real. This is climate denial of the status quo sort, where people accept the science, and indeed make long speeches about the immorality of passing on a ruined world to our children. They just deny the meaning of the science, which is that we must keep carbon in the ground."[21]

From his public statements, we know that Barack Obama wanted his leadership on climate change to be one of the major positive planks of his legacy. Unfortunately, this record, like his record on so many other issues, is a mixed bag. He blew hot and cold. He took some bold actions, yet he always seemed to stop short of doing what he could accomplish, if only he applied the full, persuasive powers of the presidency. And he could never quite get himself to let loose of the old appetite for fossil fuels, or make climate change his top priority.

Indeed, in terms of legacy, Obama may have chosen the wrong horse to ride. In the perspective of McKibben, "When the world looks back at the Obama years half a century from now, one doubts they'll remember the health care website; one imagines they'll study how the most powerful government on Earth reacted to the sudden, clear onset of climate change."[22]

EIGHT

Race Relations

One key area where progressives expected to encounter little to no difficulty with President Obama was on the issue of racial justice. But here, too, such was not to be, especially during his first term. He's our first African-American president, a living symbol of the immense progress we've made in this country in burying the ugly and official racism of the past. Yet at times, Obama thoroughly frustrated African-Americans by his reluctance to speak out more strongly on racial issues.

In truth, race has always been an issue for Obama—how could it not be?—but never the central issue as it is, for example, for Reverend Jesse Jackson or Reverend Al Sharpton. In his book *Dreams from My Father*, Obama talks openly and eloquently about his continuing struggle—as the son of a white woman and black man, raised by white grandparents—to learn his identity as a young black man. However, once involved in politics, Obama's goal was never to be the first black whatever. It was to be the best at whatever he tried. And while I'm sure he's proud to go down in history as America's first black president, his real goal, it seems, was to be remembered as America's first postracial president, introducing that magic time when Martin Luther King, Jr.'s own dream would finally come true: that day—sadly, still not yet arrived—when little children "will not be judged by the color of their skin, but by the content of their character."[1]

That helps explain Obama's initial awkwardness in dealing with unfortunate remarks made by his longtime Chicago friend and pastor, the Reverend Jeremiah Wright. For too long, Obama tried to ignore the mounting controversy over allegedly anti-American comments—"Not

God Bless America. God Damn America!"—made during some of
his Sunday sermons, which Obama claimed never to have been present for. He disassociated himself from Wright, but refused to condemn
him. The point was, Obama didn't want race to become a big issue in
the campaign. He was running as the Democratic candidate for president, not the "black" candidate for president.[2]

But Wright wouldn't shut up, and the controversy wouldn't die
down. So Obama finally stepped up, went to the National Constitution
Center in Philadelphia in 2008, and, in a speech titled "A More Perfect Union," outlined his views on racism in America for the first time.
He noted the great progress made on race relations, while pointing
out that the struggle for equality was still going on. Indeed, he identified his own campaign as an extension of the civil rights movement
"to continue the long march of those who came before us, a march for
a more just, more equal, more free, more caring and more prosperous
America."[3]

Obama then directly rejected Reverend Wright's stated views as
"not only wrong but divisive . . . at a time when we need unity." He
couldn't disown his pastor, he said—"no more than my white grand-
mother"—but he condemned him for presenting "a profoundly dis-
torted view of this country—a view that sees white racism as endemic,
and that elevates what is wrong with America above all that we know is
right with America."[4]

It was a powerful speech, which generated wide media coverage.
The Pew Research Center reported that 85 percent of Americans said
they had seen or heard about parts of the speech. But, almost in de-
fiance of Obama, the Reverend Jeremiah Wright followed with fiery,
racist speeches before the NAACP and the National Press Club—after
which Obama finally and formally cut all ties with him.[5]

The stage was thus set for the Obama presidency. Barack Obama,
who proclaimed in his famous keynote address to the 2004 Democratic
Convention that "there is not a black America and a white America,"
decided not to make race relations a core issue of his presidency. He certainly didn't want to be perceived as an angry black man. When he met
early on with members of the Congressional Black Caucus, he rejected

their plea that he specifically target black joblessness, even though the unemployment rate among black men has stubbornly remained twice what it is among whites. As he phrased his position in an interview later that year, "I can't pass laws that say I'm just helping black folks."[6]

July 17, 2009, brought the possibility of a truly historic occasion: the first African-American president helping the NAACP celebrate its hundredth anniversary. Obama recognized the great accomplishments of the civil rights movement—"I believe that overall, there probably has never been less discrimination in America than there is today"—while recognizing the many imbalances that still exist today, particularly in jobs, health care, and education. But again, he disappointed many by putting forth no specific policies or programs to narrow the gap, other than a general promise to "lay a new foundation for growth and prosperity that will put opportunity within the reach of not just African Americans, but *all Americans* [emphasis added]. All Americans. Of every race. Of every creed. From every region of the country. We want everybody to participate in the American Dream. That's what the NAACP is all about."[7]

Nobody could accuse the first black president of using his power just to help black people. Clearly, Obama wasn't even going to address the issue of race, unless forced to by events. "He doesn't want to be the black president," former NAACP chairman Julian Bond later argued. "He wants to be the president, and that constrains him a great deal. I don't think he'll ever overcome that."[8]

But just five days after the NAACP speech, events did force Obama's hand. In one of his first news conferences, on July 22, President Obama had spent most of an hour taking questions about his plans for health-care reform when he offered the opportunity for a last question to crack reporter Lynn Sweet, Washington bureau chief for one of Obama's hometown newspapers, the *Chicago Sun-Times*. Lynn dramatically shifted gears, asking him for his reaction to the arrest by a Cambridge, Massachusetts, police officer of Harvard professor Henry Louis Gates, Jr., for allegedly breaking into his own home. Gates accused Sergeant James Crowley of automatically assuming he was a burglar just because he was a black man in a white residential neighborhood.

Obama surprised us all by responding with unusual candor:

"Now, I don't know, not having been there and not seeing all the facts what role race played in that, but I think it's fair to say, number one, any of us would be pretty angry. Number two, that the Cambridge police acted stupidly in arresting somebody when there was already proof that they were in their own home and, number three, what I think we know separate and apart from this incident is that there is a long history in this country of African-Americans and Latinos being stopped by law enforcement disproportionately. And that's just a fact."[9]

Even more than the Philadelphia speech, it was the first window into what Obama felt about the state of race relations in America today, and especially the issue of racial profiling. But he proposed no plan to deal with it, other than to invite Professor Gates and Sergeant Crowley to the White House for a "beer summit" and apologize to the latter for calling him stupid. Indeed, there was no mention of race or race relations from the White House, until almost three years later.

That second window opened on February 26, 2012, with the killing of unarmed teenager Trayvon Martin as he was walking home from a convenience store to his father's girlfriend's home in Miami Gardens, Florida. At first, there was no official comment from the White House on Martin's death at the hands of vigilante George Zimmerman, the local police department's bungling of the case, or the applicability of Florida's so-called Stand Your Ground law. When he did finally react to Martin's death, at a news conference on March 23, President Obama surprised reporters with a personal response: "If I had a son he would look like Trayvon and I think they [his parents] are right to expect that all of us as Americans are going to take this with the seriousness it deserves."[10]

Off and on, for over a year, we reporters tried to get some further reaction out of the White House, but Press Secretary Jay Carney steadfastly declined to comment on a matter that was still before the courts. It was not until July 19, 2013, three days after a Florida jury found Zimmerman not guilty, that Obama interrupted Carney's daily briefing, took over the podium, and for the first time offered his own reaction to the Trayvon Martin verdict, again referencing his own experience with racial profiling.

"You know, when Trayvon Martin was first shot I said that this could have been my son. Another way of saying that is Trayvon Martin could have been me 35 years ago. And when you think about why, in the African American community at least, there's a lot of pain around what happened here, I think it's important to recognize that the African American community is looking at this issue through a set of experiences and a history that doesn't go away."[11]

He continued: "There are very few African American men in this country who haven't had the experience of being followed when they were shopping in a department store. That includes me. There are very few African American men who haven't had the experience of walking across the street and hearing the locks click on the doors of cars. That happened to me—at least before I was a Senator. There are very few African Americans who haven't had the experience of getting on an elevator and a woman clutching her purse nervously and holding her breath until she had a chance to get off. That happens often.[12]

"And I don't want to exaggerate this, but those sets of experiences inform how the African American community interprets what happened one night in Florida."[13]

After these powerful words, many African-American leaders were hoping Obama would follow these remarks with a comprehensive agenda to address racism and economic injustice. "The president is now in his second term," argued Marc Morial, president of the National Urban League. "I think that the table is set for the president to think about how he can address these issues not just in words, but renew some of the issues that he's championed." "As far as I'm concerned, he does not have to put a dashiki on, wave a red-black-and-green flag, put up a black power fist," said Congresswoman Gwen Moore. "What I need him to do is try to level the playing field to make sure that African-Americans have the same opportunities." But no such luck—it was radio silence on race all over again.[14]

Until three similar, explosive days in 2014: the killings of Michael Brown, Eric Garner, and Tamir Rice—two unarmed black men, and one black twelve-year-old with a toy gun—all three by white police officers. Protests against racial profiling and excessive use of force by police officers began in August in Ferguson, Missouri, with the shooting of eighteen-year-old Brown on August 9—and soon spread nationwide. Brown's apparently senseless murder also prompted the media to re-examine the case of forty-three-year-old Eric Garner, killed by a police officer's chokehold on Staten Island on July 17. Facts surrounding his death had been largely ignored until an amateur video appeared, showing Garner thrown to the ground by several policemen, placed in a chokehold, and held down by one officer until he succumbed—after pleading "I can't breathe" eleven times. On August 1, the New York City medical examiner ruled Garner's death a homicide by chokehold. Use of the chokehold is prohibited under NYPD rules.[15]

For the next few months, sporadic protests continued and tension remained high—until it broke wide open after three more related events. On November 25, a Ferguson grand jury announced its decision not to file charges against Officer Darren Wilson in the death of Michael Brown. On December 3, a Staten Island grand jury announced that no charges would be filed against Officer Daniel Pantaleo, despite the shocking video of Eric Garner's murder, which had gone viral on the Internet. And in Cleveland, on November 22, police officer Timothy Loehmann responded to reports of a man carrying a gun—which the caller admitted was probably a fake gun. Arriving at the scene, Loehmann jumped out of his squad car and within two seconds had shot and killed twelve-year-old, toy-gun-wielding Tamir Rice. Loehmann and his partner then stood by, doing nothing to help Rice. Meanwhile they handcuffed his fourteen-year-old sister and blocked her from approaching little Tamir as he lay on the ground.[16] The boy received no help until a third law enforcement officer arrived within four minutes and administered CPR until paramedics arrived almost ten minutes later.

And during all that time and turmoil, where was President Obama? Nowhere to be seen or heard. Aides said he was deeply troubled by the latest examples of racial profiling and police brutality, but publicly he said and did nothing beyond a few token gestures. He sent Attorney General Holder to Ferguson to meet with local officials. He sent three low-level White House officials to Michael Brown's funeral. He called New York mayor Bill de Blasio to congratulate him on peaceful protests held in the wake of the Staten Island grand jury decision, even as the NYPD embarrassed themselves with wrongheaded protests of the mayor at police funerals.[17]

The day after the Ferguson grand jury decision, as I was walking into the Northwest Gate of the White House, I was surprised to encounter Reverend Al Sharpton and a small group of civil rights leaders walking out. Sharpton told me they'd just come from an Oval Office meeting with the president, where they pressured him to be more visible and vocal in demanding reforms in police conduct. That was a secret meeting. It was not posted on the president's official daily schedule.

What did appear prominently on the president's schedule was a meeting of forty-seven activists he convened at the White House to discuss community/police issues on Monday, December 1: twelve civil rights leaders, eight youth group leaders, seven police officials, five mayors, four ministers, two academics, and nine administration officials, including Vice President Biden and Attorney General Holder.[18]

Afterward, he came into the briefing room to announce his plan of action. It was far from the robust push for reform civil rights leaders had hoped for in the wake of the recent tragedies. As the *National Journal's* George Condon reported, "His response was Obama at his most thoughtful and his most cautious." And, to many, his most frustrating.[19]

Obama outlined four timid next steps: (1) The administration would not stop the Pentagon practice of supplying local police departments with military equipment, but a government task force would study the program and make sure local cops got better training on how and when to use it. (2) The administration would not require police officers to wear body cameras, but would work with Congress to provide funding for communities that wanted to adopt them. (3) The attorney general would "convene a series of these meetings all across the country." (4) The president would name a task force to further study the situation, leading a "national conversation on race."[20]

The "national conversation on race" thereby joined the continuing "national conversation on gun safety" Obama had called for after Tucson. Neither one went anywhere. There was a lot of talking about the issues of gun and police violence, but no action.

Even here, responding to national outrage over the needless killing of young African-Americans, in Ferguson, Staten Island, Cleveland, and elsewhere, President Obama went out of his way to argue the problem was larger than race: "When anybody in this country is not being treated equally under the law, that's a problem. It's incumbent on all of us as Americans . . . that we recognize that this is an American problem and not just a black problem. It is an American problem when anybody in this country is not being treated equally under the law." That's true. It's also true, of course, that African-Americans are far more likely to be abused by police.[21]

For President Obama, this was another one of those times when the train of opportunity stopped at his station—and he failed to jump on board. A few days after the White House meeting, the *New York Times* reported: "Mr. Obama has not been the kind of champion for racial justice that many African-Americans say this moment demands." The *Washington Post* featured an article on disaffected blacks in Jacksonville, Florida, whose disappointment in Obama had led to a frustration with politics in general. Asked if she was going to vote in the next presidential election, twenty-three-year-old Regenia Motley told the *Post*: "What's the point? We made history, but I don't see change." Obama was the first black president, faced with very important issues facing the black community, yet he seemed to feel more constrained by the presidency than empowered by it.[22]

One person not surprised by the president's tepid response was Congressman Elijah Cummings. The Maryland congressman and former chair of the Congressional Black Caucus says he was amazed how many African-Americans felt that, after his re-election in 2012, the "real" Obama would emerge, now "liberated" to speak out more about race. By "real," Cummings told the *National Journal*, "they mean, I guess, he's going to show up in a dashiki." Cummings said he tried to tell them to lower their expectations: "The president is who he was in the first term. And it would be foolish for me . . . to give them the impression that the nation and the world will see some kind of reincarnation of Eldridge Cleaver and Huey Newton." Obama was cautious in his first term and started out cautious in his second.[23]

While disappointed with his leadership, most black leaders—with the notable exceptions of professor Cornel West and talk show host Tavis Smiley—hesitated to criticize Obama publicly. Tanya Clay House, director of public policy for the Lawyers' Committee for Civil Rights Under Law, couched her criticism in the mildest possible terms. "People appreciate the fact that he heightened the public awareness of this by making statements and making sure that the attorney general has been present," she told the *Times*. "But there's a desire to push the administration further."[24]

But that wasn't the end of it. In a way, what happened in Ferguson, Staten Island, and Cleveland merely set the stage for Baltimore. Yet another unarmed black man killed at the hands of police, in a city with a long, sad history of police brutality.

On April 19, 2015, just as everyone thought things were quieting down and maybe even some progress was being made in police/community relations nationwide, twenty-five-year-old Freddy Gray died in police custody from serious neck and spine injuries. A video showed him being dragged and thrown into the back of a police van a week earlier, after being arrested for no apparent reason.[25]

Several days of remarkably peaceful protests erupted into widespread violence and looting on April 27, the day of Gray's funeral. A state of emergency was declared. The National Guard was called in. Within two days, order was restored and residents of Baltimore began to rebuild. And, unlike in Ferguson, Staten Island, or Cleveland, action was soon taken against police officers responsible for Gray's death. On May 1, based on her own investigation and a report from the Baltimore Police Department, Maryland State's attorney for Baltimore, Marilyn Mosby, declared Freddy Gray's death to be a homicide and filed charges against six officers involved in the incident, including one charge of second-degree murder.[26]

On April 28, the day after the Baltimore riots began, President Obama strongly condemned the violence at a White House news conference: "There's no excuse for the kind of violence that we saw yesterday. It is counterproductive. . . . When individuals get crowbars and start prying open doors to loot, they're not protesting. They're not making a statement. They're stealing. When they burn down a building, they're committing arson. And they're destroying and undermining businesses and opportunities in their own communities."[27]

Obama also again called on Americans to take meaningful action to solve poverty and law enforcement issues fueling what he described as a national crisis. But, as in similar cases, other than condemning the violence and urging collective action to heal police/community relations, he took no action and announced no new programs—giving rise to the charge that he was once again standing on the sidelines.

By that time, America's continuing racial divide had yawned open once again. According to a CBS/*New York Times* poll taken April 30 through May 3, 2015, 61 percent of Americans rated race relations as "bad"—the worst reading since it reached 68 percent when race riots exploded in Los Angeles in 1992, following the acquittal of police officers in the beating of Rodney King. On race, the world had turned upside down. In April 2009, shortly after Barack Obama took office, 66 percent of Americans had ranked race relations as "good."[28]

And then there was Charleston, South Carolina, where, as mentioned earlier, racist gunman Dylann Roof murdered nine black parishioners in cold blood at a Bible study group. Unable to hold back any longer, Obama responded with passion, frustration, and anger.

The president himself went to Charleston's Emanuel AME Church to deliver a remarkable, soul-stirring eulogy for Pastor Pinckney, in which he not only praised the civic and religious leader, but traced the powerful history of black churches and spoke openly about the lingering and very real problem of racism in this country. Maybe Charleston would be the trigger, said the president, for us finally to take the effects of racism seriously. "Perhaps this tragedy causes us to ask some tough questions about how we can permit so many of our children to languish in poverty . . . or attend dilapidated schools or grow up without prospects for a job or for a career. Perhaps it causes us to examine what we're doing to cause some of our children to hate. Perhaps it softens hearts towards those lost young men, tens and tens of thousands caught up in the criminal-justice system and lead us to make sure that that system's not infected with bias . . . that we embrace changes in how we train and equip our police so that the bonds of trust between law enforcement and the communities they serve make us all safer and more secure."[29]

Obama concluded his remarks with a call for change. "We don't need more talk," he said. Now was the time for action. After initial outrage over every such tragedy, he pointed out, the tendency is to fall back to "business as usual." Not this time, pleaded Obama: "But it would be a betrayal of everything Reverend Pinckney stood for, I believe, if we allow ourselves to slip into a comfortable silence again. . . . To settle for symbolic gestures without following up with the hard work of more lasting change, that's how we lose our way again."[30]

But, of course, that's exactly what happened. South Carolina and other states took down the Confederate flag. But after Charleston there were no new initiatives announced by the White House on race relations, gun safety, chronic unemployment among young blacks, or police/community relations. It was, in effect, back to business as usual.

Responding to the criticism that Obama hasn't done enough for the African-American community, the White House offers a multilayered response. First, it notes that African-Americans, like all Americans, have benefited from the president's initiatives on health care, jobs, raising the minimum wage for federal contractors, and improving the economy in general. Second, it points to the Federal Sentencing Act, which mitigated (but did not completely end) the hundred-to-one mandatory sentencing disparity for simple possession of crack versus powder cocaine—thus contributing to the disproportionate percentage of African-Americans incarcerated for drug abuse.[31]

Most of all, it swells with pride over "My Brother's Keeper," a public/private initiative Obama launched in the East Room of the White House on February 27, 2014. Its goal, accomplished through an interagency task force, is "creating and expanding ladders of opportunity for boys and young men of color." Obama said he was motivated to design a program aimed exclusively at young African-Americans because of the "persistent gaps in employment, education outcomes and career skills" that divided young black men from their white peers. In September 2014, he issued a challenge to towns and cities across the country to become "MBK Communities" and come up with plans to improve life outcomes for all their citizens, although it remains to be seen if this call is effective and how many cities actually develop such programs.[32]

Notably, "My Brother's Keeper," as good a program as it may be, is the only directly race-related program of the Obama presidency. While it and the new sentencing guidelines are universally applauded, they are far from addressing the whole range of issues affecting the black community—from racial profiling, to voting rights, to black joblessness, urban schools, affirmative action, criminal and penal reform, and "stop and frisk" practices—that African-American leaders, perhaps naïvely, were counting on Obama to tackle directly.

Harvard professor Randall Kennedy summed up their frustration in the July/August 2014 edition of *Politico* magazine, in an article titled "Did Obama fail Black America?": "For many African-Americans," Kennedy writes, "he has been a hero—but also a disappointment. On critical matters of racial justice, he has posited no agenda, unveiled no vision, set forth no overarching mission to be accomplished."[33]

It's one thing for Obama to praise leaders like Congressman John Lewis for his courage in fighting for change. But, Kennedy asks: "Why can't Obama muster some passion of his own?" Why indeed?[34]

NINE

Labor and Trade

What is it about recent Democratic presidents? They lean on labor unions to get elected. They couldn't get elected without them. Then, once in the White House, they turn around and stab them in the back.

In Bill Clinton's case, he stuck us with the North American Free Trade Agreement, or NAFTA—the mega-free-trade agreement with the United States, Mexico, and Canada signed into law in 1994. Back then, it was promised that NAFTA would net us two hundred thousand jobs a year. Instead, it has proved as harmful to the U.S. economy as labor leaders predicted.[1]

As Matt Stoller, writing in *Salon* magazine, reported: "Today, the U.S. has lost one out of every four manufacturing jobs that existed before NAFTA—over 5 million, with 42,000 factories closed. A modest trade surplus with Mexico was replaced with a large, persistent deficit. . . . NAFTA's new investor protections dramatically increased the ability of corporations to outsource entire factories to Mexico"—resulting in the "giant sucking sound" presidential candidate Ross Perot warned us about. All of which resulted, not just in job loss, but also in lower wages and smaller pensions for millions of American workers—and less bargaining leverage for labor unions.[2]

Twenty years later, we've seen the damage NAFTA caused. So how does our new progressive president learn from this history? He pushes for an even bigger trade deal.

The Trans-Pacific Partnership

If corporations liked NAFTA, they will *love* TPP—and American workers hate the prospect of it. As some Democratic members of Congress succinctly put it, TPP is "NAFTA on steroids."

First unveiled by the Obama administration in 2009 as the centerpiece of the new president's "pivot to Asia," TPP is the largest free-trade agreement ever adopted, setting new partnership rules for trading between the United States and eleven Asian markets: Australia, Brunei, Canada, Chile, Japan, Malaysia, Mexico, New Zealand, Peru, Singapore, and Vietnam. These countries make up 40 percent of the global economy. China was deliberately left off the list.

The administration sold TPP as a critical step in opening Asian markets to American companies, yet every single labor union, public and private, denounced it as another giant, corporate power grab that would endanger food safety and access to medicines and national security, and destroy millions more American jobs. A study by the Center for Economic and Policy Research predicted that a whopping 90 percent of workers in the United States would see a decrease in real wages because of TPP.[3]

The proposed agreement was also opposed by the vast majority of congressional Democrats. In 2012, twenty-four senators sent a letter asking the White House to make workers' rights a top priority in treaty negotiations. And on April 21, 2014, three Democratic leaders in the House—Rosa DeLauro of Connecticut, George Miller of California, and Louise Slaughter of New York—blasted the draft proposal in an op-ed in the *Los Angeles Times*: "This agreement would force Americans to compete against workers from nations such as Vietnam, where the minimum wage is $2.75 a day. It threatens to roll back financial regulation, environmental standards and U.S. laws that protect the safety of drugs we take, food we eat and toys we give our children. It would create binding policies on countless subjects, so that Congress and state legislatures would be thwarted from mitigating the pact's damage."[4]

There were two other big problems with TPP: the blank check Obama wanted in order to negotiate the deal on his own, so-called fast-track authority, and the total secrecy surrounding negotiations. Both were deal-breakers for congressional Democrats.[5]

For TPP, Obama sought the same unbridled power to make a deal, or that fast-track authority that President Clinton was once awarded for NAFTA. Under its terms, the president alone could negotiate a new free-trade agreement—with the role of Congress reduced to giving a quick thumbs-up or thumbs-down vote, after the deal was completed. No other options. Congress, whose oversight of trade deals is explicitly outlined in Article 1, Section 8 of the Constitution, would be stripped of that authority, with no power to amend the deal.[6]

For most Democrats, once burned by Clinton and NAFTA, fast-track authority was a nonstarter, a total abdication of their congressional responsibilities. "Fast track would be yet another insult to the American worker," Congresswoman DeLauro told reporters at the beginning of the 114th Congress. And she predicted Obama's request would be denied: "It will not happen. We are not going to do it."[7]

From the beginning, Obama's request for fast-track ran into roadblocks in Congress. While most Republicans supported the concept of TPP, many were reluctant to yield Obama unlimited executive authority on trade, after having slammed him repeatedly for, they believed, abusing his presidential powers by issuing executive orders on health care and immigration reform. In fact, they had sued him for doing so. Among Democrats, the problem wasn't just the president but the underlying deal. In fact, when legislation to create fast-track authority was first introduced in 2014, the bill failed to attract one single Democratic sponsor.

If Obama was concerned about opposition within his own party, however, he didn't show it. During a ten-day trip to Asia in November 2014, the president dismissed TPP's critics as conspiracy theorists. "My point is you shouldn't be surprised if there are going to be objections, protests, rumors, conspiracy theories, political aggravation around a trade deal," he told NBC's Chuck Todd. "That reflects a lack of knowledge of what is going on in the negotiations." Of course, the reason this lack of knowledge existed is that Obama's administration had been working overtime to keep the deliberations top-secret.[8]

Ironically, it was only after Republicans had seized control of both houses of Congress in 2015 that Obama had the opportunity to win fast-track authority for TPP—and he was able to do so only by turning his back on fellow Democrats and making a deal with Republicans.

For Obama, after six years of hanging progressives in his own party out to dry time and again, asking Congress to give him a blank check on trade was when Democrats finally rebelled.

Seldom has anything like what happened with TPP been seen before in Congress. It was Obama and Republicans v. Democrats. In the Senate, Republican Leader Mitch McConnell and most Senate Republicans sided with Obama. Lined up solidly against him were 30 out of 44 Democrats.

In the House, Obama faced an equally embarrassing scorecard. On his side were Speaker John Boehner, the entire Republican leadership, and a majority of House Republicans. Opposition was led by Democratic Leader Nancy Pelosi and 160 out of 188 Democrats.[9]

Also lined up against the president were 100 percent of America's labor unions. Veteran labor leaders I spoke to said they could never remember a time when every single labor union, both public and private, both large and small, were united on one single issue. But they all stood solidly against fast-track.[10]

How'd a Democratic president end up opposed by a majority of his own party? He brought it on himself—by trying to push another dubious trade deal onto a group of Democratic lawmakers who still regretted voting in 1992 for NAFTA.

The Obama White House didn't help matters by its secretive behavior. Drafts of the long, complicated treaty were shared with representatives of the twelve countries and six hundred corporations that had a stake in TPP, but not with the public or members of Congress. While the White House denounced those who complained about this secrecy, insisting that any members of Congress could read the trade deal any time they wanted, in reality it was not that easy. Yes, members of Congress could read the entire near-thousand-page document, but they could do so only in a special, secured room, all alone, with no staff or advisers, no cell phone, no pen or paper, no notes—and, of course, they couldn't take a copy with them.

And Obama had another big problem as well. For six years, congressional Democrats hadn't felt much love coming from the president. On any number of progressive-minded issues—many of which we have gone over in this book—Obama had refused to make a big push in Congress, even when the power of the bully pulpit could have made all the difference. Democrats also blamed him, in part, for losing control of the House in 2010. In May 2015, when I asked California congresswoman Jackie Speier whether, this far into his presidency, Obama had a reservoir of goodwill among House Democrats he could count on to line up a few votes for TPP, she responded candidly: "I can't say that he does."[11]

What little goodwill did exist was lost when Obama stooped to personal attacks against his progressive critics, dismissing Senator Elizabeth Warren, for example, as just another "politician, like everybody else."

In the end, with near-unanimous support of House and Senate Republicans, Obama won fast-track approval, but only after turning his back on labor unions and betraying the vast majority of his own party. For many progressive Democrats, it was the final blow in a long string of disappointments from Barack Obama.

Workers' Rights

Frankly, labor leaders might not have resented Obama's fighting *against* them on TPP so much—if only he had fought *for* them on other important issues. But he never seemed to have the time or inclination to do so, and that was clear from the very beginning.

Case in point: the Employee Free Choice Act, or EFCA. In 2008, that was the number-one issue for labor unions. I know this particularly well. My radio/TV program is strongly supported by many of our great labor unions: the Laborers, Machinists, Teamsters, AFSCME,

Ironworkers, SMART Union, Steelworkers, AFT, NEA, Ironworkers, and AFGE. In interviews during the 2008 campaign, the presidents of every one of those unions told me their top priority was EFCA—which Barack Obama supported and promised to make one of his top priorities as president.[12]

EFCA wasn't complicated. It simply said that workers could organize a union, and have that union certified to bargain with the employer, simply by collecting the signatures of a majority of employees on cards. Employers could no longer demand an additional secret ballot vote, as they could in the past, and use that opportunity to browbeat, threaten, or fire pro-union workers.[13]

"The current process for forming unions is badly broken," Congressman George Miller of California had argued when he first introduced the bill in 2007, "and so skewed in favor of those who oppose unions, that workers must literally risk their jobs in order to form a union. Although it is illegal, one quarter of employers facing an organizing drive have been found to fire at least one worker who supports a union. In fact, employees who are active union supporters have a one-in-five chance of being fired for legal union activities. Sadly, many employers resort to spying, threats, intimidation, harassment and other illegal activity in their campaigns to oppose unions." EFCA would fix that. So Miller reintroduced the bill on March 10, 2009, alongside Senator Ted Kennedy of Massachusetts, with every expectation that the new Democratic president would help them push it over the top.[14]

Labor leaders knew they had their work cut out for them in the Senate. Democrats never quite achieved a sixty-vote veto-proof majority, especially after they lost Kennedy's seat to Scott Brown. And even some Democrats, like Arkansas's Blanche Lincoln and Delaware's Tom Carper, refused to support the bill. Complicating things further: As a Republican, the late Arlen Specter of Pennsylvania voted for EFCA; when he switched parties to become a Democrat, he opposed it. Go figure.[15]

What surprised union leaders the most, however, was not their troubles in the Senate, it was the silence from the White House. Where was Barack Obama when they needed him? Nowhere to be seen or heard.

Several times during that period, I asked Press Secretary Robert Gibbs what President Obama was doing to help secure passage of EFCA. The response was always the same: "He strongly supports the legislation." Yes, but what is he doing to help make it happen? Is he twisting arms? What senators has he talked to? Again, all we could get out of Gibbs was: The president has told everybody he supports the bill. As if all a president has to do is snap his fingers and Congress snaps to attention. As we've seen on countless issues now, it doesn't work that way, and never will.

Clearly, Obama was not lifting a finger or phone to help round up votes for EFCA, despite his campaign promises to union supporters. No speeches. No statements of support. No EFCA rallies. Nothing.

But we later discovered it was even worse than that. Unbeknownst to labor leaders, White House chief of staff Rahm Emanuel, with Obama's blessing, had put out the word to Democratic leaders in Congress that there would be no vote on EFCA until after Obamacare had passed and been signed into law. By that time, it was too late. Scott Brown was in office, more Democrats had defected, and EFCA disappeared without ever even being brought up for a vote.[16]

For President Obama and organized labor, it was a clear case of: promise made, promise broken.

Another blow to organized labor came on February 15, 2012, when President Obama signed the Federal Reauthorization Act, a seemingly innocuous refunding measure that contained a poison pill for labor unions—which strongly opposed it.

For Obama, signing that bill destroyed all the goodwill he had gained with unions three years earlier, in naming new progressive members to the National Mediation Board. In 2010, the NMB adopted a new rule governing elections for railroad and airline workers seeking to unionize. Before then, those workers had been covered by the 1935 Railway Labor Act, rather than the National Labor Relations Act that covers most American workers.[17]

Under the old NLRA rule, in order to organize a union, workers had to obtain a majority of all potential voters in a bargaining unit, not just a majority of those who voted. (Note: If that same rule applied in

electoral politics, most members of Congress could never get elected.)
Under the new rule, the outcome of an election was determined the
same way it is for other unions, or for president of the United States:
Whoever gets the most votes, wins.[18]

Everybody was happy with the new arrangement—except big corporations and Republicans in Congress, who introduced legislation to
override the NMB rule, which President Obama vowed to veto. After
Republicans forced a thirteen-day shutdown of the FAA over the issue,
Senate Leader Harry Reid announced a compromise: The override
language would be dropped from the bill, which meant the new NMB
rule remained in place. But, and here was the big problem—BUT—
a whole new demand would be added to the process. Rather than having to gather signatures of 35 percent of workers to hold an organizing
election, unions would have to submit signatures from a majority of all
workers—just for a vote to be held.[19]

As unions pointed out, that unnecessary extra step would give management an opportunity to derail or delay any election, despite majority support of actual workers, by packing an employee list with retired
workers, challenging voter eligibility, hiring temporary promanage-
ment shills, or otherwise monkeying around with the core electorate.
And, remember, this compromise was forced through when Democrats still controlled the Senate.[20]

Led by CWA president Larry Cohen, union leaders blasted Democrats, who had always refused past requests to attach pro-union provisions to funding bills, for now agreeing to an anti-union amendment to
an FAA appropriations bill. "The leadership in the Senate didn't even
see fit to include [the pro-labor NMB rule] in this gutting of the statute,"
Cohen protested. "Our little crumb of an advancement is left as a rule, so
the day that there's ever a Republican president elected . . . they're going
to strip the rule. The statute will remain. It's worse than it's ever been."[21]

If unions thought they could count on their friends, they were mis-
taken. Democrats passed the bill, a Democratic president signed it,
and millions of union members were left asking themselves: Why did
we spend so much money and energy electing Democrats who turn
around and stab us in the back?

Yet another "Et tu, Brute?" knife wound occurred during the fight for the Affordable Care Act. Without labor unions, there would be no Obamacare. It's as simple as that. For decades, unions were the ones that made universal health care a top priority of the Democratic Party. Unions convinced Americans of the need for it. Unions built the constituency for it. Unions negotiated health-insurance protection for their own members—and wanted to extend it to all American families. Unions were the major force in rounding up the votes for Obamacare in Congress, even after the president disappointed them by dropping the public plan option.

Without labor unions, there would be no Obamacare. Barack Obama knows it. And labor leaders know he knows it. So imagine the shock felt by some union presidents, then, when it turned out that Obamacare, as signed into law, would actually undermine some long-held union health plans. They were only further shocked when they appealed to the White House for relief—and Obama turned them down.[22]

At issue were so-called Taft-Hartley, or multiemployer plans, which cover workers, such as construction workers, who might work for more than one company in a year. Unions claimed that Obamacare as written would drive up the costs of such plans to the point where employers would drop them. To save the Taft-Hartley plans, they asked the White House to support an amendment to Obamacare that would make their low-income workers eligible for the same type of federal subsidies other low-income Americans received through the new health exchanges.[23]

Unions figured they had a good shot at it. After all, they had delivered for Barack Obama. Now it was his turn to deliver for them. During this period, I ran into a group of labor leaders—including Teamster president James Hoffa, UFCW president Joe Hansen, and AFL-CIO president Richard Trumka—who had just left a meeting in the West Wing. They told me they were confident White House officials understood their dilemma and would grant the necessary relief.

A couple of months later at its convention in Los Angeles, as a sign of how important this issue was to organized labor, the AFL-CIO

passed a strongly worded resolution reaffirming its continued support for the Affordable Care Act, but warning that without relief on the
Taft-Hartley provision, they would support the repeal of Obamacare.

But Obama didn't need them any longer. Obamacare was already
the law of the land, and Obama would veto any legislation to repeal
it. On September 13, 2013, the administration summoned a group of
labor leaders to the White House and told them their request had been
denied. With friends like these . . .[24]

No one has ever accused President Obama of being a champion of
organized labor. Reviewing the first term in November 2012 in *The
Nation,* reporter Josh Eidelson noted that, at best, "his record was
mixed. . . . He appointed National Mediation Board members who
made it easier for airline and railroad workers to form a union, then
signed a law making it harder. His stimulus kept teachers on the job,
but his [Department of Education's] 'Race to the Top' program rewarded states that made it easier to fire them." He supported labor-
backed reforms on Wall Street, but did nothing to realize the Employee
Free Choice Act. He stepped up trade cases against China, while pushing the antilabor Trans-Pacific Partnership, or TPP. He came as close
as any president to passing universal health care, but he undermined
some of the best union health plans.[25]

That left unions in somewhat of a bind, going into the president's
re-election in 2012 and the midterm elections of 2014. Many of their
members, who volunteered in record numbers in 2008, felt betrayed
by the Democrats they had worked so hard to elect, starting with President Obama. What ended up motivating union members in both
2012 and 2014 was less excitement about all the support they were getting from Democrats—and more how much worse it would be under
Republicans.

For example, Lee Saunders—president of the mighty AFSCME,
the largest health-care and public workers union in the country—
reminded his members how Mitt Romney had supported anti-union
Republican governors such as Scott Walker of Wisconsin and John Ka-
sich of Ohio. ATU president Larry Hanley says transit workers understand that "the right wing is completely engaged in a full frontal attack

to eliminate our rights to even bargain contracts," and that "the way you fight back is to deny the White House, the Senate and hopefully the Congress to the Republicans."[26]

They may not get the support they were counting on from Democrats, union members concluded, but that was better than getting wiped out by Republicans. Hanley summed up their attitude in 2012: "We do not see this as an election that will, if we're successful, bring in a whole new wave of pro-labor legislation." But, he said, we have "worked hard to make sure our people understand that if Republicans are successful at taking over the federal government, there will be no such thing as a labor movement."[27]

Let down by Obama, labor unions were forced to play defense, not offense. Which doesn't work as well, as a winning political strategy, as being enthusiastic about the team you're playing for. And for all their efforts on behalf of Obama in 2012, they were rewarded with . . . the TPP.

It was sometime during Obama's second year in office that Press Secretary Robert Gibbs, as part of his daily briefing, announced that President Obama would hold a big meeting at the White House the next day on jobs, and proceeded to read a long list of business executives who would attend. I raised my hand and asked, since they were going to talk about jobs, what labor leaders had been invited. Gibbs looked down the list. Answer: none. Which shows you what kind of priority organized labor was for Barack Obama.

The Minimum Wage

There's no doubt that President Obama supports an increase in the federal minimum wage. If he had the power, he'd raise it himself, in a New York minute, without waiting for Congress to act.

There's also no doubt that Republicans are sometimes willing to vote to increase the minimum wage, depending on who's in the White House. The last time they did so was in 2007, when 82 out of 202 House Republicans voted to support President George W. Bush in raising the minimum wage to $7.25. But they weren't about to extend that same favor to a Democratic president.[28]

Obama missed his best opportunity to raise the minimum wage, making no effort to do so during his first two years in office—when Democrats controlled both the House and Senate, and he was preoccupied with health care. After that, he did little but exhort Congress to act.

In his 2013 State of the Union address, he proposed raising the minimum wage as a way of lifting people out of poverty: "We know our economy is stronger when we reward an honest day's work with honest wages. But today, a full-time worker making the minimum wage earns $14,500 a year. Even with the tax relief we put in place, a family with two kids that earns the minimum wage still lives below the poverty line. That's wrong. . . . Tonight, let's declare that in the wealthiest nation on Earth, no one who works full-time should have to live in poverty, and raise the federal minimum wage to $9.00 a hour."[29]

On my show the next morning, Senator Tom Harkin, then-chair of the Health, Education, Labor & Pensions Committee, blasted President Obama for proposing so small a hike. At $9.00 per hour, people are still living in poverty, Harkin argued. It should be raised to at least $10.10 an hour. By a year later, Obama had agreed.[30]

In his 2014 State of the Union address, Obama saluted business leaders, mayors, governors, and state legislators who had acted on their own to raise the minimum wage, proving you didn't need an act of Congress to get things done.

At the same time, he challenged Congress to get on board. "Today the federal minimum wage is worth about twenty percent less than it was when Ronald Reagan first stood here. And Tom Harkin and George Miller have a bill to fix that by lifting the minimum wage to $10.10. It's easy to remember: 10.10. This will help families. It will give businesses customers with more money to spend. It does not involve any new bureaucratic program. So join the rest of the country. Say yes. Give America a raise."[31]

But, true to form, Republicans in Congress refused to do so. Leaving Obama no choice but to act on his own, with two minimum-wage-related actions. First, immediately following his State of the Union address, on February 12, 2014, he signed an executive order requiring all federal contractors to pay their employees at least $10.10 an hour. "If you cook our troops' meals or wash their dishes," he argued, "you should not have to live in poverty."[32]

The following year, in June 2015, he directed the Labor Department to radically revise its regulations on overtime pay. Under the old rules, salaried workers had to earn less than $23,660 per year in order to qualify for time-and-a-half overtime pay when they work more than forty hours per week. Under the new proposal, workers would be guaranteed overtime if they earned up to $50,400 per year. Labor Secretary Tom Perez estimated that action alone represented a pay increase of $1.2 billion for over 5 million American workers.[33]

In April 2015, Democrats in Congress raised their proposed minimum wage from $10.10 to $12.00 per hour, but that legislation also went nowhere.[34]

And that's where it stands. As of July 2015, twenty-nine states and the District of Columbia had adopted a minimum wage higher than the federal level of $7.25. So had many cities, and many big companies, including Gap, Aetna, and Walmart. Seattle, San Francisco, and Los Angeles raised their minimum wage to $15.00 per hour. Even McDonald's raised the minimum wage, but only for a fraction of its employees.[35]

Yet, despite his best efforts and intentions, Barack Obama, unlike George W. Bush, will leave office without having found a way to persuade Congress to raise the minimum wage for all workers nationwide. Thus, as of this writing, the federal minimum wage remains $7.25— which, in terms of purchasing power, is lower than it was in 1968. Little wonder that so many working Americans are struggling.[36]

TEN

The Democrat in Chief

It's not an official part of the president's job. It's not even mentioned in the Constitution. And, in fact, had it been suggested at the Constitutional Convention in Philadelphia, the Founding Fathers, so opposed to the idea of "factions," would have roundly rejected it.

Yet, in addition to all the formal duties of the office, every president does have one other important role: As long as he is in office, the president of the United States is also the undisputed leader of his own political party. George W. Bush was the top Republican. Barack Obama's the top Democrat.

And that's a huge responsibility. It means, first of all, shaping and delivering the party's message. Nobody else can do that except the president. The president can't go in one direction, and the party in another. The president's agenda is de facto the party's agenda. His priorities are the party's priorities. His policies become the policies of his party. Whether all Democrats agree or not, under President Obama, the policies and priorities of the Democratic Party have been Obamacare, immigration reform, ending the wars in Iraq and Afghanistan, same-sex marriage, energy independence—and whatever else Barack Obama decided to tackle.

But leading the party involves more than just the lofty work of setting the tone. It also entails getting down and dirty, doing the nitty-gritty work of helping other Democrats get elected: raising money for them, appearing at rallies, campaigning with them, defending them, even—as in the case of Barack Obama in 2014—staying away from them if they think that will help more than showing up. By spending so much time on pure party politics, presidents often get dubbed as "the Fund-Raiser in Chief," or "the Campaigner in Chief." But they do it anyway because that's an important part of their job. It comes with the territory.

And it's important to any president. Not because he owes his party anything, even though he does. After all, it helped get him elected. It's important because the success of his party provides the president a unique benefit. It's the only way the president knows that his policies and programs will last longer than the brief time he spent in the White House.

No president wants his priorities to disappear the moment he leaves the scene. He wants them to be carried on, and even expanded, by those who follow him. He wants his legacy to live on. And the only way he can be sure of that is to make sure more Democrats are elected to the House, to the Senate, to the governor's office, to state legislatures—and, ultimately, to the White House.

A big part of the president's job, in other words, is to leave his party in stronger shape than it was when he took the oath of office as president. In that respect, the numbers don't lie: President Obama has been a dismal failure.

It's not that he hasn't tried. He campaigned for House and Senate candidates, although perhaps not nearly as much as House and Senate Democratic leaders asked him to. In 2014, he even agreed *not* to campaign for several Democrats running for re-election in red states.

Charged with raising what legendary California Assembly Speaker Jesse Unruh called the "mother's milk" of politics, Obama became the biggest political fund-raiser of all time. According to CBS Radio White House correspondent Mark Knoller, unofficial keeper of presidential records, Obama led and attended thirty-eight party fund-raisers in 2013, and another whopping sixty-five events in 2014. He not only raised more money for his own re-election than any other presidential candidate ever, he set new fund-raising records for all party committees: the Democratic National Committee, the Democratic Congressional Campaign Committee, the Democratic Senate Campaign Committee, and the Democratic Governors Association.[1]

Running for re-election in 2012, he raised $730 million, easily dwarfing Mitt Romney's $473 million and just $20 million shy of the three-quarters of a billion raised in 2008. Obama's combined total haul for all party committees in 2012 was $1.24 billion.[2]

Without the big-tent attraction of the White House, midterm elections generate less campaign cash. But, still, with Obama's help, according to reports filed with the Federal Elections Commission in April 2015, Democratic Party committees and candidates raised almost a billion dollars in campaign contributions in 2014, dwarfing the combined Republican Party total, $854.9 million to $665.5 million.

And what did Democrats get for all that cash? They got wiped out.

In the Senate, twenty-one seats held by Democrats were up for election or re-election. Republicans won nine of them, thereby taking control of the Senate for the first time since January 2007. Before the midterm elections of 2014, the Senate breakdown was 53 Democrats and 45 Republicans, with 2 Independents, Bernie Sanders and Angus King, who caucused with the Democratic Party. The new lineup is 54 Republicans, 44 Democrats, and 2 Independents.[3]

In January 2009, when President Obama took office, there were 57 Democrats in the Senate, and only 41 Republicans.

It didn't take long after the midterms for Democrats to point the finger of blame at President Obama for losing the Senate, even though he was persona non grata in most senatorial and gubernatorial campaigns.

David Krone, chief of staff for then–majority leader Harry Reid, told the *Washington Post* publicly what a couple of Democratic senators told me privately: that, in several cases, Obama hurt more than he helped. Democrats had the right issues, Krone insisted, but not the right leader: "It doesn't mean that the message was bad, but sometimes the messenger isn't good." Citing the problems with Obamacare, for example, Krone said: "No member of the Democratic caucus screwed up the rollout of that health-care website, yet they paid the price—every one of them."[4]

Krone also accused White House staffers of caring more about

Obama's personal political fate than the party's in general. "I don't think that the political team at the White House truly was up to speed and up to par doing what needed to get done," he complained. Nobody in official Washington believed Krone would have made such a damning charge to the *Washington Post* had he not first cleared it with his boss, Leader Reid.[5]

In the House of Representatives, things went no better for Democrats. Republicans had won control of the House in November 2010 after picking up 62 Democratic seats. That meant they started out 2011 with a margin of 242 Republicans to 193 Democrats. After 2012, they still held on to a 234-to-201 lead over Democrats. But the midterm elections of 2014 were a big setback for Democrats. They lost 13 seats, giving Republicans a 247-to-188 margin in the House.

In January 2009, when President Obama took office, there were 257 Democrats in the House, and only 178 Republicans.[6]

The same debacle happened among state governors. After Election Night 2008, there were twenty-nine states with Democratic governors. As of January 2015, there were eighteen. With the election of Matt Bevin as governor of Kentucky on November 3, 2015, there are now only seventeen.

And among state legislatures. Across the country, more than nine hundred Democratic seats have been lost since Obama took office—which means Republicans could redistrict the House of Representatives in 2010 to cement their majority for the next ten years.[7]

All of which leaves the Democratic Party in worse shape today than it's been in decades. There are many factors involved in elections: weather, voter turnout, how good the candidates are, effectiveness of TV ads, breaking news events, and so on. You can't blame it all on President Obama. But he is the leader of his party. And under his leadership, the Democratic Party has been on a constant downslide. Since 2009, when he first took over as president:

- Democrats have lost 13 seats and control of the Senate.
- Democrats have lost 69 seats and control of the House.
- Democrats have lost 12 state governors.

- Democrats have lost control of 30 state legislature chambers and are now the minority in over two-thirds of those chambers, their worst showing in history.[8]

Nobody can look at those numbers and conclude anything other than that, for the national Democratic Party, President Obama's leadership has been a disaster. The party actually fared better under George W. Bush.

Conclusion

Looking Back at the Obama Presidency

A funny thing happened on the way to finishing the final pages of this book. President Obama came out of the closet—as a progressive! Or almost.

He signed executive orders, left and right. He re-established normal relations with Cuba. He made a deal with Iran. He reduced sentences of many criminals in prison for nonviolent drug offenses. He talked openly about problems with race relations in America. He created new national monuments. He won two big cases in the Supreme Court. He went after his Republican critics—by name.

Suddenly commentators were talking about the new, liberated Obama, squeezing every opportunity out of the few months he had left in office. As Vermont congressman Peter Welch said on my show: "Where's this guy been all this time?"

Strangely enough, Obama's political pivot came after Democrats got wiped out—again!—in the November 2014 midterm elections. But instead of being down and depressed, the president seemed set free. He drew new life and energy from the defeat—and started to show the backbone we'd been longing for for six years.

First he went off to Asia and signed a far-reaching deal with China on climate change. Then on to Australia, where he pledged $3 billion to the United Nations Green Climate Fund to help developing nations prepare for and slow down the effects of climate change.

Returning to the United States, as we saw in Chapter Five, he at last delivered on his promise to act on immigration reform if Congress did not.

Then President Obama delivered a 2015 State of the Union address, most of which could have been written by Bernie Sanders or Elizabeth Warren. There were no more office-team-building-seminar platitudes like "Win the Future." Instead, he identified income inequality as the most important challenge facing the nation and Congress, rebranding it "middle-class economics." And he presented Congress with a set of priorities to help the middle class, which included:

- Two years of free community college for every high school graduate
- Six weeks of paid maternity leave and seven days of paid sick leave for every worker
- Raising the minimum wage
- Paying women the same as men for the same work
- Rebuilding the nation's broken-down infrastructure
- Raising taxes on the 1 percent in order to pay for tax breaks for the 99 percent
- Reforming the criminal justice system to end lengthy sentences for nonviolent drug crimes
- Shutting down Gitmo at last
- Ending the embargo and normalizing relations with Cuba[1]

If that's not a progressive agenda, I don't know what is.

There's just one problem—all this came too little, too late. If he'd made this speech in January 2009, and then taken concrete steps to put this agenda in place, just think of what he could have accomplished. This burst of progressivism at the end of his term just could not erase the failed leadership and missed opportunities of his first six years—as documented in these pages.

And there are countless other examples we have not delved into. Civil liberties reformers wonder why he has been so slow to dismantle the War on Drugs. Many teachers and education reform advocates take issue with his Race to the Top and Common Core standards. Campaign finance activists deplore his many broken promises to fix the political process and get the big money out of campaigns. In these and other areas he also let his progressive supporters down.

Besides, by January 2015, we all knew the score. How many times had we seen Barack Obama deliver an amazing speech, and then cede the field back to the Republicans? Even if this president was inclined to follow up his words with real, concrete action this time, since Republicans now controlled both the House and the Senate, there was little likelihood he could get any of his progressive proposals through Congress. Just disasters like the TPP, where, as documented in Chapter Nine, Obama proceeded to hand progressives one of their worst defeats ever.

Obama Looks Back

Oddly enough, while progressives look back on the Obama presidency as a string of "what might have beens," President Obama himself doesn't seem to regret not accomplishing more. Blaming everyone but himself yet again, he chalks up his own shortcomings as a reflection on the nature of the political process and the limitations on the powers of the presidency.

In June 2015, he gave a very revealing interview to podcast host Marc Maron in which he discussed how he responds to those who complain about his failure to deliver more and bigger things. "[W]hat I have to explain to them is that, progress in a democracy is never instantaneous," Obama explained, "and it's always partial, and you can't get cynical or frustrated because you didn't get all the way there immediately."[2]

Relaxing in the environment of Maron's Los Angeles garage/studio, Obama offered revealing insights into how he approaches the task of governing. "Sometimes your job is just to make stuff work," he said. "Sometimes the task of government is to make incremental improvements or try to steer the ocean liner 2 degrees north or south so that 10 years from now, suddenly, we're in a very different place than we were.... At the moment, people may feel like we need a 50-degree turn, we don't need a 2-degree turn. Well, if I turn 50 degrees, the whole ship turns over." And there's your Obama presidency in a nutshell—from "Yes, we can" to "If we do, the whole ship turns over."[3]

Those who want more, those who demand bigger change, Obama

concluded, just don't understand how government works. "And it's not just because of you know, corporate lobbyists, it's not just because of big money. It's because societies don't turn 50 degrees. Democracies certainly don't turn 50 degrees, and that's been true on issues of race. That's been true on issues of the environment, that's true on issues of discrimination. As long as we're turning in the right direction, and we're making progress, then government is working the way it's supposed to."[4]

In other words, in Barack Obama's world, incrementalism is good enough. Fortunately, nobody ever told that to FDR or Teddy Roosevelt, or Lyndon Johnson. Only days after the murder of JFK, an aide advised now-president Johnson not to expend his political goodwill working to pass a civil rights law over the opposition of the South. "Well, what the hell's the presidency for?" Johnson angrily replied. That's a question Obama should've asked himself, earlier and more often.[5]

Moving Forward

Even as an incrementalist, President Obama can still take credit for some notable achievements. He rescued the nation from fiscal collapse and slowly, albeit too slowly, brought the economy back. He saved and gave new life to the American auto industry. He ended George Bush's wars in Iraq and Afghanistan (yet started a new one of his own). He did more than any president to develop renewable sources of energy and achieve energy independence. He's the first president to support same-sex marriage, and he ended the military's discriminatory policy of "Don't Ask, Don't Tell." With the Affordable Care Act, he brought the nation closer than we've ever been to the goal of universal health care.

Even more impressive, everything Obama accomplished was achieved against incredible headwinds. From day one, he faced a stone wall of opposition from congressional Republicans. Having failed to prevent his re-election, they then determined to kill every legislative proposal he sent to Congress, even ones they had previously crafted or supported. Given that kind of blind opposition, perhaps we should be thankful that Obama achieved anything at all.

And yet, notwithstanding the implacable opposition of congressional Republicans and the difficult challenges he inherited from his predecessor, the record of what President Obama failed to accomplish—or, in some cases, failed even to fight for—is a much longer list of missed opportunities and neglected priorities.

As I said at the beginning, the overwhelming response of progressives to the Obama presidency can still be summed up in one word: disappointment.

But while we're disappointed, we do not despair.

That's the crazy thing about us: No matter how many times we've been let down, we never give up hope. If Barack Obama ultimately failed to embrace and deliver the progressive agenda, we'll just work harder to make sure the next president does.

And there's every reason to believe she, or he, will. And must. Because the country today is even more attuned to and hungry for progressive ideals than it was before Obama took office.

Consider:

- Income inequality is recognized as a serious economic problem by politicians of both parties.
- Marriage equality is the law of the land.
- Latinos, young people, and women are growing as powerful political forces.
- Renewable energy sources are fast outpacing fossil fuels.
- There's overwhelming support for a fifteen-dollar minimum wage.
- Many states are moving to decriminalize or legalize marijuana.
- The vast majority of Americans support action to combat climate change.
- A majority of Republicans and Democrats believe there is too much big money in politics and support new limits on campaign contributions.

The time is ripe, then, for America's next president to seize the full progressive agenda and run with it.

So I close with a few words of advice for the forty-fifth president of the United States—full of hope that I will never have to write a book like this one again.

Postscript

"To the Next President"

Presidential campaigns start too early and drag on too long. As of this writing, late in 2015, we've been at it for a year already, and we still have a long way to go.

That means anything could happen. Who knows? The next president could even end up being a Republican with terrible hair. But, for many reasons, and despite the losses the party absorbed under Obama, the odds still favor the Democrats, and the smart betting is that either Hillary Clinton or Bernie Sanders will be the Democratic nominee in 2016 and the next president of the United States.

Which could be trouble, no matter who wins. Because either will be surrounded by some of the same old Washington insiders, who will give them the same old stale advice: Sure, it's okay to say all those progressive things while campaigning for president, but now that they're in office, they need to head to the middle, reach out and be all things to all people, seek common ground with Republicans, and be prepared to compromise, temporize, triangulate.

Wrong, wrong, wrong. That's not what the times demand. And that's not what the American people want or deserve.

And so, without being asked, and based on the lessons drawn from this book, I hereby offer my own best advice to the next president of the United States.

Letter to Hillary Clinton

Dear Madam President:

Congratulations!

You have already made history. As First Lady of the United States. As the first First Lady to run for office after leaving the White House. As United States senator from New York. As secretary of state. As a candidate for president.

And now you make history again as the first woman to serve as president of the United States.

We progressives are very excited. Yes, many of us supported Bernie Sanders in the primary, because he had a stronger progressive platform. But, once you became our nominee, we worked hard to help you get elected, because we also believe in you. And now we have only one request: Be bold!

You may have a reputation for being a moderate, but we know you're a real progressive at heart. As First Lady, you championed paid family leave and universal health care—and were denounced for your efforts as a wild-eyed liberal. As early as May 2007, you described yourself as a "modern progressive" who was out to "curb the excesses of the market-place" and reduce the alarming increase in income inequality. In fact, you were talking about income inequality before income inequality was cool.

We also remember that in 2008 you ran for president on a platform that was to the left of Barack Obama on many issues. As secretary of state, you warned Arab nations about the consequences of rewarding only those people at the top and failing "to invest in their own people." In a May 2014 speech to the New America Foundation, you indirectly criticized President Obama by lamenting government policies that have made "the dream of upward mobility . . . further and further out of reach." "Forget about getting rich," you stated, "I'm just talking about getting into the middle class and staying there."

In the video announcing your candidacy for president in 2016, you struck a populist tone by lamenting that "the deck is still stacked in favor of those at the top and there is something wrong with that." And, in words that surely did Elizabeth Warren proud, you told the crowd at the first public rally of your campaign, on Roosevelt Island, June 13, 2015: "Prosperity can't be just for CEOs and hedge fund managers. Democracy can't be just for billionaires and corporations. . . . Prosperity and democracy are part of your basic bargain, too. You brought our country back. Now it's time, your time, to secure the gains and move ahead. And you know what? America can't succeed unless you succeed."

So, again, our one request is: Be true to yourself, Madam President. Be bold. Don't do what too many Democrats do, once elected, and rush to the middle. We didn't elect you to govern from the middle. We worked hard for you so you could lead from the left.

Be bold. Don't shrink from your progressive ideals. The top 1 percent have had more than their share of special favors from the federal government. Make your fight a fight for the middle class, instead. And use your bully pulpit to help Americans understand that a progressive, pro–middle-class agenda is just what America needs to get our economy back on track and make sure all Americans share in our economic recovery.

Be bold on climate change. Make history by being the president to lead America away from a fossil-fuel economy to a total renewable energy economy. Change America's status from one of the top greenhouse gas polluters to the world leader in fighting global warming.

Be bold on immigration reform. Don't let a handful of xenophobes or racists continue to deny the dreams of millions of immigrants who may have crossed the border illegally, but who have lived here for many years, have homes, jobs, and families here, got their education here, pay taxes, and serve in the military. They're helping build a better America. They've earned a path to citizenship.

Be bold on behalf of working-class families. Don't settle for a minimum wage. Insist on a living wage. Stand in solidarity with labor unions. Create millions of new jobs. Put Americans back to work rebuilding our broken-down infrastructure and building a high-speed rail system that can compete with China, Japan, and Western Europe. And, once and for all, reaffirm Social Security as a solid, fully funded earned benefit that all American workers can count on in their retirement years.

Be bold on health care. Obamacare's a good start. Now add a public plan option, "Medicare for Everybody," so consumers are no longer beholden to private insurance companies for health insurance for themselves and their families. Meanwhile, pressure governors to expand Medicaid in every state and encourage progressive governors to take advantage of the opportunity to transition their state to a proven, effective single-payer system of health care.

Be bold in protecting civil liberties, especially the right of privacy. Stand up to the intelligence agencies when they try to undermine the Constitution in the name of fighting terror. We don't have to surrender our rights of free speech and privacy in order to remain secure. Remind the heads of the NSA and the CIA: They work for you, you don't work for them.

And be bold in resisting any more wars, in the Middle East or anywhere else. After Iraq and Afghanistan, the longest and least productive wars in our history, Americans are war-weary. We must maintain a strong military to protect our nation. But the days of a long ground war are over. The very idea of nuclear warfare is obsolete. Strong international partnerships, economic sanctions, and diplomacy are the new paths to a peaceful world.

We're counting on you, Madam President. We don't want to be disappointed again. Don't let us down.

Be bold. Be yourself. Be the champion of the middle class America needs today and Americans are yearning for. Madam President, be the proud progressive Barack Obama so often didn't dare to be.

Letter to Bernie Sanders

Dear Senator Sanders:

Congratulations!
You defied the odds. You made it to the White House.
Now, be yourself, Bernie. That's all we ask.

ACKNOWLEDGMENTS

I recently had the opportunity to interview Paul Theroux, long one of my favorite, and one of America's most prolific, authors. We appeared before an adoring audience at the vibrant Hill Center on Capitol Hill to discuss *Deep South*, his delightful and insightful new book, and his first account of travels within the United States.

While it was an honor to meet and interview Theroux, I also felt somewhat intimidated. *Deep South* is his fifty-first book. For me, *Buyer's Remorse* is only number seven. We're almost the same age. What have I been doing all my life? But, no matter how far behind Paul Theroux I may be in books published, he and I are in the same place on this point: No author succeeds alone. Every book is a team effort.

My team starts with Carol, who helped develop the idea of this book over many conversations at the dinner table—and then suffered through the many evenings and weekends I chained myself to the word processor. It includes, perhaps unwittingly, my colleagues in the White House press corps, whose tough questions at the daily press briefings helped me appreciate both where President Obama has delivered and where he has fallen short.

For this book, I was lucky to reassemble the same team I've worked with before: research associate Kevin Murphy and friend and agent Ronald Goldfarb. Kevin's flatout the best, fastest, and most reliable researcher and editor there is. Ron's one of the most respected and successful agents in the book world. Both contributed as much to the ideas and substance of this book as its named author.

As captain of our team, we couldn't have done better than Mitchell Ivers, who steered me through publication of *Spin This*, my first book, in 2001. How great to work with Mitchell again, and the dedicated, hardworking team at Threshold Editions of Simon & Schuster, including President Louise Burke; Associate Editor Natasha Simons; Director of Publicity Jean Anne Rose; cover designer James Perales; copy editor Sean Devlin; production editor Al Madocs; and many more.

To one and all, a heartfelt thank-you.

NOTES

Introduction

1 Lisa Lerer, "Obamamania verges on obsession," *Politico*, February 2, 2008, http://www.politico.com/story/2008/02/obamamania-verges-on -obsession-008605. Caroline Kennedy, "A President like my father," *New York Times*, January 27, 2008, http://www.nytimes.com/2008/01 /27/opinion/27kennedy.html. Tom McGeveran, "Toni Morrison's letter to Barack Obama," *The Observer*, January 28, 2008, http://observer.com /2008/01/toni-morrisons-letter-to-barack-obama/. Thomas Schaller, "The Oprah Winfrey Show," *Salon*, December 10, 2007, http://www .salon.com/2007/12/10/obama_oprah/.

2 Andy Barr, "2008 turnout shatters all records," *Politico*, November 5, 2008, http://www.politico.com/news/stories/1108/15306.html.

3 Lorraine C. Minnite, "First time voters in the 2008 election," Project Vote, April 2011, http://www.projectvote.org/wp-content/uploads/2011 /04/FINAL-First-Time-Voters-in-2008-Election.pdf.

4 "Transcript: Illinois Senator Barack Obama," *Washington Post*, July 7, 2004, http://www.washingtonpost.com/wp-dyn/articles/A19751 -2004Jul27.html. Marlene Targ Brill, *Barack Obama: President for a New Era* (Minneapolis: Lerner, 2009), 39. David Alexander, "Mc-Cain's epiphany: Obama thinks he's a political messiah," Reuters, August 1, 2008, http://blogs.reuters.com/talesfromthetrail/2008/08/01 /mccains-epiphany-obama-thinks-hes-a-political-messiah/.

5 "Chris Matthews: 'I felt this thrill going up my leg' as Obama spoke," *Huffington Post*, March 28, 2008, http://www.huffingtonpost.com/2008 /02/13/chris-matthews-i-felt-thi_n_86449.html. "Transcript: Barack Obama's South Carolina Primary Speech," *New York Times*, January 26, 2008, http://www.nytimes.com/2008/01/26/us/politics/26text-obama .html.

6 "Obama's nomination victory speech in St. Paul," *Huffington Post*, June 3, 2008, http://www.huffingtonpost.com/2008/06/03/obamas-nomination -victory_n_105028.html.

7 "Transcript: 'This is your victory,' says Obama," CNN, November 4, 2008, http://edition.cnn.com/2008/POLITICS/11/04/obama.transcript/.

8 Sam Stein, "Conyers Rips Obama, Emanuel For 'Bowing Down' To GOP On Health Care," *Huffington Post*, November 19, 2009, http:// www.huffingtonpost.com/2009/11/19/conyers-rips-obama-emanue_n _363702.html."Dem Conyers: 'I'm getting tired of saving Obama's can,'" *RealClearPolitics*, November 19, 2009, http://www.realclearpolitics.com /video/2009/11/19/dem_conyers_im_getting_tired_of_saving_obamas _can.html.

9 Ibid. Molly K. Hooper, "President Obama told me to stop 'demeaning' him, says Rep. Conyers," *The Hill*, December 8, 2009, http://thehill.com /homenews/administration/71075-conyers-obama-told-me-to-stop -demeaning-him.

10 Don Gonyea, " 'How's That Hopey, Changey Stuff?' Palin Asks," NPR, February 7, 2010, http://www.npr.org/templates/story/story.php?storyId =123462728.

11 Les Daly, "Legendary cartoonist Pat Oliphant: 'We are in a forest fire of ignorance,'" *The Atlantic*, September 3, 2014, http://www.theatlantic .com/politics/archive/2014/09/legendary-cartoonist-pat-oliphant-we -are-in-a-forest-fire-of-ignorance/379524/.

12 Ibid.

13 Richard Wolffe, *Revival: The Struggle for Survival Inside the Obama White House* (New York: Broadway Press, 2011), 25.

14 Edward-Isaac Dovere, "Left revokes Obama's liberal card," *Politico*, September 13, 2013, http://www.politico.com/story/2013/09/barack -obama-liberals-096746.

15 "Michael Moore slams Obama: History will only remember you were a black president," *Hollywood Reporter*, September 9, 2014, http://www .hollywoodreporter.com/news/michael-moore-slams-obama-history -731563.

16 Nick Allen, "Matt Damon: 'Barack Obama broke up with me,'" *The Tele-graph*, August 10, 2013, http://www.telegraph.co.uk/news/worldnews /northamerica/usa/10234837/Matt-Damon-Barack-Obama-broke-up -with-me.html.

17 Thomas Frank, "Cornel West: 'He posed as a progressive and turned out to be counterfeit. We ended up with a Wall Street presidency, a drone

presidency,'" *Salon*, August 24, 2014, http://www.salon.com/2014/08
/24/cornel_west_he_posed_as_a_progressive_and_turned_out_to_be
_counterfeit_we_ended_up_with_a_wall_street_presidency_a_drone
_presidency/.

18 Dovere, "Left revokes Obama's liberal card."

19 Matt Patches, "Shepard Fairey on the Future of Political Art and
Whether Obama Lived Up to His 'Hope' Poster," *Esquire*, May 28, 2015,
http://www.esquire.com/news-politics/interviews/a35288/shepard
-fairey-street-art-obama-hope-poster/.

20 Hunter S. Thompson, *Fear and Loathing in Las Vegas: A Savage Journey
to the Heart of the American Dream* (New York: Random House, 1971),
68.

21 Sam Youngman, "White House unloads anger over criticism from 'professional left,'" *The Hill*, August 10, 2010, http://thehill.com/homenews
/administration/113431-white-house-unloads-on-professional-left.
Joan Walsh, "More taunts to the Democratic base," *Salon*, September 2, 2010, http://www.salon.com/2010/09/03/more_taunts_to_the
_democratic_base/.

22 Kevin C. Murphy, *Uphill all the Way: The Fortunes of Progressivism, 1919–
1929*, http://www.kevincmurphy.com/uatw-tragedy-american.html#10.
John Maynard Keynes. "When the Big Four Met," *New Republic*, December 24, 1919, 105.

23 Dovere, "Left revokes Obama's liberal card."

24 Scott J. Anderson "Obama's surveillance vote spurs blogging backlash,"
CNN, July 11, 2008, http://www.cnn.com/2008/POLITICS/07/11/obama
.netroots/index.html. Suzanne Goldenberg and Elana Schor, "Obama
supports supreme court reversal of gun ban," *The Guardian*, June 27,
2008, http://www.theguardian.com/world/2008/jun/27/barackobama
.usa.

25 "Transcript: Obama's speech against the war, October 2, 2002," NPR,
January 20, 2009, http://www.npr.org/templates/story/story.php?storyId
=99591469.

26 "Obama's Speech at Woodrow Wilson Center," Council on Foreign Relations, August 1, 2007, http://www.cfr.org/elections/obamas-speech
-woodrow-wilson-center/p13974.

27 Maureen Dowd, "Who Do You Trust?" *New York Times*, September 10,
2013, http://www.nytimes.co. m/2013/09/11/opinion/dowd-who-do
-you-trust.html.

28 Alexandra Jaffe, "Sanders: Obama should use bully pulpit more," *The*

Hill, September 14, 2014, http://thehill.com/blogs/blog-briefing-room
/news/217668-sanders-obama-should-use-bully-pulpit-more.

29 Doris Kearns Goodwin, *The Bully Pulpit: Theodore Roosevelt, William
Howard Taft, and the Golden Age of Journalism* (New York: Simon &
Schuster, 2013), xi.

30 Drew Westen, "Leadership, Obama Style, and the Looming Losses in
2010: Pretty Speeches, Compromised Values, and the Quest for the Lowest Common Denominator," *Huffington Post,* March 18, 2010, http://
www.huffingtonpost.com/drew-westen/leadership-obama-style-an_b
_398813.html.

31 Carl Hulse, Jeremy W. Peters, and Michael D. Shear, "Obama Is Seen as
Frustrating His Own Party," *New York Times,* August 18, 2014, http://
www.nytimes.com/2014/08/19/us/aloof-obama-is-frustrating-his-own
-party.html.

32 Michael A. Memoli, "For Obama, golf is an escape, even when he brings
along members of Congress," *Los Angeles Times,* August 20, 2015,
http://www.latimes.com/nation/politics/la-na-obama-golf-lawmakers
-20150820-story.html.

33 Ibid. Ana Radelat, "Obama-Courtney golf game not about Iran pact, aide
says," *Connecticut Mirror,* August 20, 2015, http://ctmirror.org/2015/07
/20/obama-courtney-golf-game-chat-not-about-iran-pact-aide-says/.

34 Matt Bai, "Obama vs. Boehner: Who Killed the Debt Deal?," *New York
Times Magazine,* April 1, 2012, http://www.nytimes.com/2012/04/01
/magazine/obama-vs-boehner-who-killed-the-debt-deal.html.

35 Faiz Shakir, "Mitch McConnell: I Want To Be Senate Majority Leader
In Order To Make Obama A One-Term President," *ThinkProgress,* October 25, 2010, http://thinkprogress.org/politics/2010/10/25/126242
/mcconnell-obama-one-term/. Jaffe, "Sanders: Obama should use bully
pulpit more."

36 "Obama on Romney's 'Extreme Views': AP Interview," Associated Press,
August 25, 2012, http://www.cbsnews.com/news/obama-on-romneys
-extreme-views-ap-interview/. Amy Chozick, "Obama Is an Avid
Reader, and Critic, of the News," *New York Times,* August 7, 2012, http://
www.nytimes.com/2012/08/08/us/politics/obama-is-an-avid-reader
-and-critic-of-news-media-coverage.html.

37 E. J. Dionne, Jr., "Obama's risky compromises," *Washington Post,*
December 2, 2010, http://www.washingtonpost.com/wp-dyn/content
/article/2010/12/01/AR2010120106291.html. Westen, "Leadership, Obama
Style, and the Looming Losses in 2010."

38 Hulse, Peters, and Shear, "Obama Is Seen as Frustrating His Own Party."

39 Sari Horwitz and Juliet Eilperin, "Obama commutes sentences of 46 nonviolent drug offenders," *Washington Post,* July 13, 2015, https:// www.washingtonpost.com/world/national-security/obama-commutes -sentences-of-46-non-violent-drug-offenders/2015/07/13/b533f61e -2974-11e5-a250-42bd812efc09_story.html.

40 Adam Hartung, "Obama outperforms Reagan on jobs, growth, and investing," *Forbes,* September 5, 2014, http://www.forbes.com/sites /adamhartung/2014/09/05/obama-outperforms-reagan-on-jobs -growth-and-investing/. Floyd Norris, "S&P More than Doubled Under Obama," *New York Times,* March 25, 2013, http://www.nytimes.com /2013/05/25/business/economy/sp-has-more-than-doubled-under -obama.html. Floyd Norris, "Corporate Profits Grow Ever Larger as Slice of Economy as Wages Slide," *New York Times,* April 5, 2014, http:// www.nytimes.com/2014/04/05/business/economy/corporate-profits -grow-ever-larger-as-slice-of-economy-as-wages-slide.html.

41 "Secretary Burwell previews third open enrollment," HHS.gov, September 22, 2015, http://www.hhs.gov/news/press/2015pres/09/20150922a .html. Caroline Humer, "U.S. says 17.6 million Americans gained health insurance through law," Reuters, September 22, 2015, http:// www.reuters.com/article/2015/09/22/us-usa-healthcare-uninsured -idUSKCN0RM1QC20150922.

42 "About Poverty-Highlights," Census.gov, September 16, 2015, https:// www.census.gov/hhes/www/poverty/about/overview/.

43 David Dayen, "There's no crying in the Oval Office," *Firedoglake,* June 15, 2010, http://shadowproof.com/2010/07/15/theres-no-crying-in-the -oval-office/.

44 John Greenleaf Whittier, "Maud Muller" (1856), http://www.poetry -archive.com/w/maud_muller.html.

Chapter One: Budget Battles and the Obama Economy

1 "Obama: 'We Saved the Country from a Great Depression,'" CNN, May 11, 2011, http://whitehouse.blogs.cnn.com/2011/05/11/obama -%E2%80%98we-saved-the-country-from-a-great-depression%E2%80 %99.

2 Heidi Shierholz, "Six Years from Its Beginning, the Great Recession's Shadow Looms Over the Labor Market," *Economic Policy Insti-*

tute, January 9, 2014, http://www.epi.org/publication/years-beginning
-great-recessions-shadow/.

3 Katy Barnato, "Risk of Triple-Dip Recession in Euro-Zone: S&P,"
CNBC, November 18, 2014, http://www.cnbc.com/2014/11/18/risk-of
-triple-dip-recession-in-euro-zone-sp.html.

4 Rob Garver, "The Pain the Job Numbers Don't Show," *Fiscal Times,*
May 8, 2015, http://www.thefiscaltimes.com/2015/05/08/Beyond-Jobs
-Report-US-Workforce-Hasn-t-Really-Recovered. Melinda Hennenberger, "Poverty is finally having its day as an issue in American politics," *Bloomberg,* May 13, 2015, http://www.bloomberg.com/politics
/articles/2015-05-13/poverty-is-finally-having-its-day-as-an-issue-in
-american-politics.

5 Erika Eichelberger, "6 More Reasons Larry Summers Should Not Be
Fed Chair," *Mother Jones,* July 30, 2013, http://www.motherjones.com
/politics/2013/07/lawrence-summers-federal-reserve-chair-financial
-regulation.

6 Felix Salmon, "How Larry Summers lost Harvard 1.8 billion," Reuters,
November 29, 2009, http://blogs.reuters.com/felix-salmon/2009/11/29
/how-larry-summers-lost-harvard-18-billion/.

7 Wolffe, *Revival,* 168.

8 Juliana Goldman and Phil Mattingly, "Yellen said to top Obama's fed
list after Summers' exit," *Bloomberg,* September 17, 2013, http://www
.bloomberg.com/news/articles/2013-09-17/yellen-said-to-top-obama-s
-fed-list-after-summers-s-exit.

9 Wolffe, *Revival,* 168.

10 Matt Stoller, "Wait. So THAT's what the bailouts were about?," *Medium,*
October 7, 2014, https://medium.com/@matthewstoller/hell-hath-no
-fury-like-a-bankster-scorned-8993ec09c8b7. "Ruling in A.I.G. Bailout Lawsuit," *New York Times,* June 15, 2015, http://www.nytimes.com
/interactive/2015/06/15/business/dealbook/document-ruling-in-aig
-bailout-lawsuit.html.

11 Ian Katz, "Failed nominee Weiss morphs into key debt official at Treasury," *Bloomberg,* February 24, 2015, http://www.bloomberg.com/news
/articles/2015-02-24/failed-nominee-weiss-morphs-into-key-debt
-official-at-treasury.

12 Noam Scheiber, *The Escape Artists: How Obama's Team Fumbled the Recovery* (New York: Simon & Schuster, 2012), 271–74.

13 Dean Baker, "Peter Orszag and the Drive to Cut Social Security," *Beat
the Press,* November 4, 2010, http://www.cepr.net/blogs/beat-the-press

/peter-orszag-and-the-drive-to-cut-social-security. Peter Orszag, "One Nation, Two Deficits," *New York Times,* September 6, 2010, http://www.nytimes.com/2010/09/07/opinion/07orszag.html.

14 Tobin Marshaw, "Obama's Endangered Economists," *New York Times,* August 6, 2010, http://opinionator.blogs.nytimes.com/2010/08/06/obamas-endangered-economists/. Noam Scheiber, "The Memo that Larry Summers Didn't Want Obama to See," *New Republic,* February 22, 2012, http://www.newrepublic.com/article/politics/100961/memo-Larry-Summers-Obama1.

15 Wolffe, *Revival,* 167. Thomas Frank, "Exclusive: Elizabeth Warren on Barack Obama: 'They Protected Wall Street, Not Families Losing Their Homes, Not People Who Lost Their Jobs, And It Happened Over and Over,'" *Salon,* October 12, 2014, http://www.salon.com/2014/10/12/exclusive_elizabeth_warren_on_barack_obama_they_protected_wall_street_not_families_who_were_losing_their_homes_not_people_who_lost_their_jobs_and_it_happened_over_and_over_and_over/.

16 Paul Steinhauser, "Poll: TARP not working; don't spend more, Americans say," CNN, January 16, 2009, http://politicalticker.blogs.cnn.com/2009/01/16/poll-tarp-not-working-dont-spend-more-americans-say/.

17 Martin Feldstein, "The Current Stimulus Plan: An $800 Billion Mistake," *Washington Post,* January 29, 2009, http://www.washingtonpost.com/wp-dyn/content/article/2009/01/28/AR2009012802938.html. "Nobel Laureate Krugman: Too Little Stimulus in Stimulus Plan," *Knowledge@Wharton,* February 19, 2009, http://knowledge.wharton.upenn.edu/article/nobel-laureate-paul-krugman-too-little-stimulus-in-stimulus-plan/.

18 Scheiber, "The Memo that Larry Summers Didn't Want Obama to See."

19 Ibid.

20 Jonathan Cohn, "Let's Play Counterfactual: What If Stimulus Had Been Bigger?" *New Republic,* September 1, 2010, http://www.newrepublic.com/blog/jonathan-cohn/77386/counterfactual-game-what-if-stimulus-had-been-bigger.

21 Martin Wolf, "Davos Man Waiting for Obama to Save Him," *Financial Times,* February 4, 2009, http://www.ft.com/intl/cms/s/0/4a44f222-f221-11dd-9678-0000779fd2ac.html. Martin Wolf, "Obama was too cautious in fearful times", *Financial Times,* August 31, 2010, http://www.ft.com/intl/cms/s/0/5799a774-b534-11df-9af8-00144feabdc0.html.

22 Scheiber, "The Memo that Larry Summers Didn't Want Obama to See."

23 "The Making Work Pay Tax Credit," Internal Revenue Service, March 25, 2015 http://www.irs.gov/uac/The-Making-Work-Pay-Tax-Credit.

24 Michael Cooper, "The Tax Cut Nobody Heard Of," *New York Times*, October 19, 2010, http://www.nytimes.com/2010/10/19/us/politics /19taxes.html. Derek Thompson, "10 Percent of America Knows that 95 Percent of America Got a Tax Cut," *The Atlantic*, October 10, 2010, http://www.theatlantic.com/business/archive/2010/10/10-percent-of -america-knows-that-95-percent-of-america-got-a-tax-cut/64820/

25 Scheiber, *The Escape Artists*, 136.

26 Ibid., 150–52, 162–65.

27 Christina Romer, "The Fiscal Stimulus: Flawed But Valuable," *New York Times*, October 21, 2012, http://www.nytimes.com/2012/10/21/business /how-the-fiscal-stimulus-helped-and-could-have-done-more.html.

28 The Editors, "What the Stimulus Accomplished," *New York Times*, February 23, 2014, http://www.nytimes.com/2014/02/23/opinion/sunday /what-the-stimulus-accomplished.html.

29 Robert Penn Warren, *All the King's Men* (New York: Harcourt, 1946), 26.

30 Paul Krugman, "Why weren't alarm bells ringing?," *New York Review of Books*, October 23, 2014, http://www.nybooks.com/articles/archives /2014/oct/23/why-werent-alarm-bells-ringing/.

31 "Which United States Presidents Have Run the Largest Budget Deficits," *Investopedia*, March 5, 2015, http://www.investopedia.com/ask /answers/030515/which-united-states-presidents-have-run-largest -budget-deficits.asp.

32 Jared Bernstein, "Lessons from the Recovery Act," *New York Times*, October 24, 2014, http://economix.blogs.nytimes.com/2014/02/24/lessons -from-the-recovery-act/.

33 Ibid.

34 Paul Krugman, "Barack Herbert Hoover Obama," *New York Times*, July 2, 2011, http://krugman.blogs.nytimes.com/2011/07/02/barack-herbert -hoover-obama/.

35 Ibid.

36 FiscalCommission.gov, https://www.fiscalcommission.gov/.

37 "The Moment of Truth: Report of the National Commission on Fiscal Responsibility and Reform," December 2010, http://www.fiscalcommission .gov/sites/fiscalcommission.gov/files/documents/TheMomentofTruth 12_1_2010.pdf. "In a 11-7 Tally, the Fiscal Commission Falls Short on Votes," *New York Times*, December 3, 2010, http://www.nytimes.com /interactive/2010/12/03/us/politics/deficit-commission-vote.html. Kevin Robillard, "Report: New Simpson-Bowles Plan," *Politico*, Feb-

ruary 19, 2013, http://www.politico.com/story/2013/02/report-new -simpson-bowles-plan-087769.

38 Jackie Calmes, "Debt Commission Seeks Social Security Cuts and Higher Taxes," *New York Times*, November 11, 2010, http://www.nytimes.com /2010/11/11/us/politics/11fiscal.html. "The Bowles-Simpson 'Chairmen's Mark' Deficit Reduction Plan," Tax Policy Center, http://www.taxpolicy center.org/taxtopics/Bowles_Simpson_Brief.cfm. Kevin Baker, "Whose Sacrifice Is It Anyway? The So-Called Grand Bargain Would Fleece the Middle Class," *New York Observer*, November 13, 2012, http://observer .com/2012/11/whose-sacrifice-is-it-anyway-the-so-called-grand-bargain -would-fleece-the-middle-class/.

39 "Some Fiscal Reality," *New York Times*, December 11, 2010, http://www .nytimes.com/2010/11/11/opinion/11thu1.html. Robert Kuttner, "What planet are deficit hawks living on?," *Huffington Post*, November 14, 2010, http://www.huffingtonpost.com/robert-kuttner/what-planet-are- deficit-h_b_783308.html.

40 Jan Schakowsky, "The Sham of Simpson-Bowles," Reuters, October 24, 2012, http://blogs.reuters.com/great-debate/2012/10/24/the-sham-of-simpson -bowles/. Baker, "Whose Sacrifice Is It Anyway?"

41 Dean Baker, "On Deficit Commission Proposals," *Monthly Review*, No- vember 11, 2010, http://mrzine.monthlyreview.org/2010/baker111110 .html. Kuttner, "What planet are deficit hawks living on?"

42 Paul Krugman, "A Public Service Reminder: Simpson-Bowles is Terrible," *New York Times*, September 30, 2012, http://krugman.blogs.nytimes.com /2012/09/30/a-public-service-reminder-simpson-bowles-is-terrible/

43 Baker, "Whose Sacrifice Is It Anyway?"

44 Andrew Taylor, "Simpson-Bowles Plan Rejected By House," AP, March 29, 2012, http://www.huffingtonpost.com/2012/03/29/simpson-bowles -plan-rejected-house-vote_n_1387601.html. John Bresnahan and Ste- ven Sloan, "How Ryan Spurned Deficit Panel," *Politico*, August 15, 2012, http://www.politico.com/story/2012/08/how-ryan-spurned-deficit -panel-079724.

45 Ed Henry, "Obama Wants to Freeze Discretionary Spending for Three Years," CNN, January 26, 2010, http://www.cnn.com/2010/POLITICS /01/25/obama.spending.freeze/. Peter Baker and Jackie Calmes, "Amid Deficit Fears, Obama Freezes Pay, *New York Times*, November 30, 2010, http://www.nytimes.com/2010/11/30/us/politics/30freeze.html. Steven Ohlemacher, "Federal government made $100 billion in improper payments last year," *PBS Newshour*, July 9, 2014, http://www.pbs.org

/newshour/rundown/federal-government-made-100-billion-improper
-payments-last-year/.

46 Baker and Calmes, "Amid Deficit Fears."

47 David Leonhardt, "What Does $60 Billion Buy?" *New York Times*, December 5, 2010, http://economix.blogs.nytimes.com/2010/12/05/what
-does-60-billion-buy/.

48 Ari Berman, "Obama Caves on Tax Cuts, Endorses 'Bush-McCain Philosophy,'" *The Nation*, December 6, 2010, http://www.thenation.com
/article/obama-caves-tax-cuts-endorses-bush-mccain-philosophy/.

49 Matt Bai, "Obama vs. Boehner: Who Killed the Debt Deal?" *New York Times Magazine*, April 1, 2012, http://www.nytimes.com/2012/04/01
/magazine/obama-vs-boehner-who-killed-the-debt-deal.html.

50 "Who Raised the Debt Ceiling?" *Washington Post*, July 14, 2011, http://
www.washingtonpost.com/business/economy/who-raised-the-debt
-ceiling/2011/07/14/gIQA7TIvEI_graphic.html. *BillMoyers.com*, John
Light, "The Partisan History of the Debt Ceiling," January 11, 2013, http://
billmoyers.com/2013/01/11/the-partisan-history-of-the-debt-ceiling/.

51 Bai, "Obama vs. Boehner."

52 Ibid.

53 Ibid.

54 Ibid. "Chained CPI Fact Sheet," *Social Security Works*, February 2013,
http://strengthensocialsecurity.org/sites/default/files/Chained_CPI
_Fact_Sheet_FINAL_Feb-2013_0.pdf.

55 Bai, "Obama vs. Boehner."

56 Ibid.

57 Ezra Klein, "Why Liberals Should Thank Eric Cantor," *Washington Post*, July
12, 2011, http://www.washingtonpost.com/blogs/wonkblog/post/wonkbook
-why-liberals-should-thank-eric-cantor/2011/07/12/gIQAiV4RAI_blog
.html. "Chained CPI Fact Sheet," *Social Security Works*.

58 Klein, "Why Liberals Should Thank Eric Cantor."

59 "White House Grand Bargain Offer to Speaker Boehner Obtained By
Bob Woodward," *NBC News*, November 11, 2012, http://presspass.nbc
news.com/_news/2012/11/11/15089281-white-house-grand-bargain
-offer-to-speaker-boehner-obtained-by-bob-woodward.

60 James K. Galbraith, "Hawk Nation: A Guide to the Catastrophic Debt
Ceiling Debate," July 11, 2011, http://www.nextnewdeal.net/hawk
-nation-guide-catastrophic-debt-ceiling-debate.

61 Speaker John Boehner, "CBO Confirms Spending Cuts Exceed Debt
Limit Hike in Budget Control Act," August 1, 2011, http://www.speaker

.gov/general/cbo-confirms-spending-cuts-exceed-debt-limit-hike
-budget-control-act. "To Escape Chaos, a Terrible Debt Deal," *New York Times*, August 1, 2011, http://www.nytimes.com/2011/08/01/opinion/to
-escape-chaos-a-terrible-debt-deal.html.

62 Noam Scheiber, "Obama's Worst Year," *New Republic*, February 10, 2012, http://www.newrepublic.com/article/politics/100595/obama-escape
-artist-excerpt.

63 Ted Barrett, Kate Bolduan, and Deirdre Walsh, "Super-Committee Fails to Reach Agreement," November 21, 2011, http://www.cnn.com/2011
/11/21/politics/super-committee/. Grace Wyler, "Obama: Sequestration will not happen," *Business Insider*, October 22, 2012, http://www.business insider.com/obama-sequestration-debate-foreign-policy-2012-10.

64 Chye-Ching Huang, "Budget Deal Makes Permanent 82 Percent of President Bush's Tax Cuts," Center for Budget Policy and Priorities, January 3, 2013, http://www.cbpp.org/cms/?fa=view&id=3880.

65 Jennifer Steinhauer, "Divided House Passes Tax Deal In End to Latest Fiscal Standoff," *New York Times*, January 2, 2013, http://www.nytimes
.com/2013/01/02/us/politics/house-takes-on-fiscal-cliff.html.

66 Agustino Fontevecchia, "Obama: I will veto attempts to get rid of automatic spending cuts," *Forbes*, November 21, 2011, http://www.forbes
.com/sites/afontevecchia/2011/11/21/obama-i-will-veto-attempts-to
-get-rid-of-automatic-spending-cuts/.

67 "How is the sequester affecting federal agencies?," *Washington Post*, February 26, 2013, http://www.washingtonpost.com/wp-srv/special
/politics/sequestration-federal-agency-impact/. Brad Plumer, "More Americans are feeling the effects of the sequester," *Washington Post*, May 29, 2013, http://www.washingtonpost.com/news/wonkblog/wp
/2013/05/29/more-americans-are-feeling-the-effects-of-the-sequester/.

68 Rosa DeLauro, "DeLauro, Miller release report detailing harsh impact of Republican budget cuts, sequestration, on children and families," October 10, 2013, http://delauro.house.gov/index.php?option=com_content
&view=article&id=1427:delauro-miller-release-report-detailing-harsh
-impact-of-republican-budget-cuts-sequestration-on-children-and
-families&catid=37&Itemid=148. L. Rafael Reif, "Remarks at the Greater Boston Chamber of Commerce," September 19, 2013, http://president.mit
.edu/speeches-writing/remarks-greater-boston-chamber-commerce.

69 David Dayen, "You thought the government shutdown was over. You were wrong," *New Republic*, October 18, 2013, http://www.newrepublic.com
/article/115256/government-shutdown-has-not-ended-and-wont-years.

70 John Cassidy, "The Crumbling Case for Austerity Economics," *New Yorker,* April 17, 2013, http://www.newyorker.com/rational-irrationality /the-crumbling-case-for-austerity-economics. Carmen Reinhart and Kenneth Rogoff, "Why we should expect low growth amid debt," *Financial Times,* January 2010, http://www.ft.com/intl/cms/s/0/f4630910 -0b7a-11df-8232-00144feabdc0.html.

71 Annie Lowrey, "A study that set the tone for austerity is challenged," *Economix,* April 16, 2013, http://economix.blogs.nytimes.com/2013/04 /16/flaws-are-cited-in-a-landmark-study-on-debt-and-growth/. Mike Konczal, "Researchers finally replicated Reinhart-Rogoff and there are serious problems," April 16, 2013, http://www.nextnewdeal.net/rorty bomb/researchers-finally-replicated-reinhart-rogoff-and-there-are -serious-problems. Dean Baker, "How much unemployment was caused by Reinhart and Rogoff's arithmetic mistake?" April 16, 2013, http:// www.cepr.net/blogs/beat-the-press/how-much-unemployment-was -caused-by-reinhart-and-rogoffs-arithmetic-mistake.

72 Thomas Herndon, Michael Ash, and Robert Pollin, "Does High Public Debt Consistently Stifle Economic Growth? A Critique of Reinhart and Rogoff," University of Massachusetts–Amherst, April 15, 2013, http://www.peri.umass.edu/fileadmin/pdf/working_papers/working _papers_301-350/WP322.pdf. Konczal, "Researchers finally replicated Reinhart-Rogoff." Paul Krugman, "The Excel Depression," *New York Times,* April 18, 2013, http://www.nytimes.com/2013/04/19/opinion /krugman-the-excel-depression.html.

73 Herndon, Ash, and Pollin, "Does High Public Debt Consistently Stifle Economic Growth?" Mark Gongloff, "Austerity fanatics refuse to admit they've been completely discredited," *Huffington Post,* April 22, 2013, http://www .huffingtonpost.com/2013/04/22/austerity-fanatics-discredited_n_3131391 .html. Eric Wasson, "Bowles dismisses flaws in favorite debt study," *The Hill,* April 19, 2013, http://thehill.com/policy/finance/295017-bowles-dismisses -flaws-in-favorite-debt-study. Jonathan Chait, "Remembering when Paul Ryan worried the debt was too small," April 15, 2011, http://www.new republic.com/blog/jonathan-chait/86893/remembering-when-paul-ryan -worried-the-debt-was-too-small.

74 Richard Eskow, "Why the spreadsheet scandal kills the last argument for Obama's Social Security cut," Campaign for America's Future, April 18, 2013, http://ourfuture.org/20130418/the-spreadsheet-scandal-kills-the -last-argument-for-obamas-social-security-cut."

75 Dayen, "You thought the government shutdown was over."

76 Mark Blumenthal, "Government shutdown: Polls showed voters blamed GOP for 1995 crisis," *Huffington Post,* May 30, 2011, http://www.huff ingtonpost.com/2011/03/30/voters-blamed-gop-for-1995-shutdown_n _842769.html.

77 Laura Meckler and Rebecca Ballhaus, "More than 800,000 Workers are Furloughed," *Wall Street Journal,* October 1, 2013, http://www.wsj.com /articles/SB10001424052702304373104579107480729687014. Matt-Lee Ashley, "Government Shutdown Cost National Parks Nearly 8 Million Lost Visitors Last Year," *ThinkProgress,* March 3, 2014, http://thinkprog ress.org/climate/2014/03/03/3353681/government-shutdown-national -parks/. Josh Hicks, "How much did the shutdown cost the economy?" *Washington Post,* October 18, 2013, http://www.washingtonpost.com /blogs/federal-eye/wp/2013/10/18/how-much-did-the-shutdown-cost -the-economy.

78 Jackie Calmes and Jeremy W. Peters, "Obama tells Republicans to 'Re-open the Government,'" *New York Times,* October 1, 2013, http://www .nytimes.com/2013/10/02/us/politics/shutdown-debate-congress.html.

79 Darla Cameron and Wilson Andrews, "Votes to End the Government Shutdown," *Washington Post,* October 16, 2013, http://www.washing tonpost.com/wp-srv/special/politics/congress-votes-to-end-shutdown /house.html.

80 Melanie Hicken, "Shutdown took $24 billion bite out of economy," CNN, October 16, 2013, http://money.cnn.com/2013/10/16/news/economy /shutdown-economic-impact/.

81 Mark Murray, "NBC/WSJ Poll: Shutdown debate damages GOP," *NBC News,* October 10, 2013, http://www.nbcnews.com/news/other/nbc-wsj -poll-shutdown-debate-damages-gop-f8C11374626.

82 Jeanne Sahadi, "Deficit Continues to Drop Sharply—CBO," CNN, February 4, 2014, http://money.cnn.com/2014/02/04/news/economy /budget-outlook-deficits-cbo/.

83 "Press Briefing by Press Secretary Jason Carney," White House, February 2, 2014, https://www.whitehouse.gov/the-press-office/2014/02/04/press -briefing-press-secretary-jay-carney-242014.

84 Ryan Grim and Emily Swanson, "New poll shows political futility of defi-cit reduction," *Huffington Post,* February 4, 2014, http://www.huffington post.com/2014/02/04/deficit-poll_n_4724877.html.

85 Ted Kaufman, "Three years later, Dodd-Frank is a failure," *USA Today,* July 22, 2013, http://www.usatoday.com/story/opinion/2013/07/22/dodd -frank-wall-street-reform-economy-column/2572929/.

86 Ibid.

87 "Press Briefing by Press Secretary Josh Earnest," White House, October 6, 2014, https://www.whitehouse.gov/the-press-office/2014/10/06/press-briefing-press-secretary-josh-earnest-1062014.

88 Michael McAuliffe, "Elizabeth Warren's New Book Skewers the White House Boy's Club," *Huffington Post*, April 18, 2014, http://www.huffingtonpost.com/2014/04/17/elizabeth-warren-book_n_5170018.html.

89 Ben Protess, "Wall Street Seeks to Tuck Dodd-Frank Changes in Budget Bill," *New York Times*, December 8, 2014, http://dealbook.nytimes.com/2014/12/09/wall-street-seeks-to-tuck-dodd-frank-changes-in-budget-bill/.

90 Seung Min Kim, "Warren to Dems: Kill the Bill," *Politico*, December 10, 2014, http://www.politico.com/story/2014/12/elizabeth-warren-budget-bill-opposition-113470.

91 Steven Mufson and Tom Hamburger, "Jamie Dimon himself called to urge support for the derivatives rule in the spending bill," *Washington Post*, December 11, 2014, http://www.washingtonpost.com/news/wonkblog/wp/2014/12/11/the-item-that-is-blowing-up-the-budget-deal/.

92 Gretchen Morgenson and Louise Story, "In Financial Crisis, No Prosecutions of Top Figures," *New York Times*, April 14, 2011, http://www.nytimes.com/2011/04/14/business/14prosecute.html.

93 James O'Toole, "Still No Charges for Wall Street Execs, Five Years After Crash," CNN, September 15, 2013, http://money.cnn.com/2013/09/15/news/economy/financial-crisis-cases/.

94 Alan Pyke, "Legal Costs for Biggest Banks Pale In Comparison To Profits, Harm of Crisis," *ThinkProgress*, August 23, 2013, http://thinkprogress.org/economy/2013/08/23/2519281/legal-costs-biggest-banks-pale-comparison-profits-harm-crisis/.

95 Morgenson and Story, "No Prosecutions of Top Figures." Julia La Roche, "These 22 Wall Street Titans Have Visited President Obama's White House," *Business Insider*, January 19, 2012, http://www.businessinsider.com/wall-street-titans-visited-president-barack-obamas-white-house-2012-1.

96 Ben White and Darren Samuelsohn, "Obama's Dimon in the Rough," *Politico*, March 15, 2012, http://www.politico.com/story/2012/05/the-dimon-obama-saga-076304.

97 O'Toole, "Still No Charges for Wall Street Execs, Five Years After Crash."

98 Danny Vinik, "Eric Holder's Biggest Failure," *New Republic*, September 25, 2014, http://www.newrepublic.com/article/119586/eric-holders-legacy-weak-record-prosecuting-wall-street.

99 David Dayen, "The Government Program that Failed Homeowners," *The Guardian*, March 30, 2014, http://www.theguardian.com/money/2014/mar/30/government-program-save-homes-mortgages-failure-banks.

100 Ibid.

101 Ibid. David Dayen, "Obama's housing programs still more hype than help," *Fiscal Times*, January 9, 2015, http://www.thefiscaltimes.com/Columns/2015/01/09/Obama-s-Housing-Programs-Still-More-Hype-Help.

102 Neil Barofsky, *Bailout: How Washington Abandoned Main Street While Rescuing Wall Street* (New York: Free Press, 2012), 156–58.

103 David Dayen, "Portrait of HAMP Failure: It Makes Your Financial Situation Worse," *Firedoglake*, August 23, 2010, http://shadowproof.com/2010/08/23/portrait-of-hamp-failure-it-makes-your-financial-situation-worse/. Robert Kuttner, *Debtor's Prison: The Politics of Austerity vs. Possibility* (New York: Alfred A. Knopf, 2013), 225–26.

104 "66 Straight Months of Private Sector Job Growth," DPCC, September 4, 2015, http://www.dpcc.senate.gov/?p=blog&id=462. "The Employment Situation—August 2015," Bureau of Labor Statistics, September 4, 2015, http://www.bls.gov/news.release/pdf/empsit.pdf.

105 Steve Liesman, "Confidence in Obama on economy sinks to new low," CNBC, October 6, 2014, http://www.cnbc.com/2014/10/06/roving-obama-not-so-much-survey.html.

106 Timothy Noah, "Has Income Inequality Lessened Under Obama?," MSNBC, August 5, 2014, http://www.msnbc.com/msnbc/how-inequality-has-changed-under-obama.

107 Ibid.

108 Janet Yellen, "Perspectives on Inequality and Opportunity from the Survey of Consumer Finances," October 17, 2014, http://www.federalreserve.gov/newsevents/speech/yellen20141017a.htm.

109 Ibid.

110 Hennenberger, "Poverty is finally having its day."

111 Michiko Kakutani, "A Memoir from the Eye of a Financial Storm," *New York Times*, May 11, 2014, http://www.nytimes.com/2014/05/12/books/in-stress-test-timothy-f-geithner-recalls-crisis-days.html.

Chapter Two: Health Care

1 "Remarks by the President and Vice President at the signing of the health insurance reform bill," White House, March 23, 2010, https://www.whitehouse.gov/the-press-office/remarks-president-and-vice-president-signing-health-insurance-reform-bill.

2 Ibid.

3 Reena Flores, "Report: America's Uninsured Rate Falls Below 10%," *CBS News*, August 12, 2015, http://www.cbsnews.com/news/report-americas-uninsured-rate-falls-below-10/.

4 Angie Drobnic Holan, "Obama's Views on Single-Payer Have Changed a Bit," *Politifact*, July 16, 2009, http://www.politifact.com/truth-o-meter/statements/2009/jul/16/barack-obama/obama-statements-single-payer-have-changed-bit/.

5 Ibid.

6 Ibid.

7 Ibid.

8 Froma Hallop, "Single-payer is not dead," Physicians for a National Health Program, January 14, 2014, http://www.pnhp.org/news/2014/january/single-payer-health-plan-is-not-dead.

9 Reid Wilson, "Vermont ends push for single-payer health care," *Washington Post*, December 18, 2014, http://www.washingtonpost.com/blogs/govbeat/wp/2014/12/18/vermont-ends-push-for-single-payer-health-care/.

10 Avik Roy, "How the Heritage Foundation, a conservative think tank, invented the individual mandate," *Forbes*, October 20, 2011, http://www.forbes.com/sites/theapothecary/2011/10/20/how-a-conservative-think-tank-invented-the-individual-mandate/.

11 Michael Tanner, "Lessons from the Fall of Romneycare," Cato Institute, January/February 2008, http://www.cato.org/policy-report/januaryfebruary-2008/lessons-fall-romneycare.

12 Mark Schmitt, "The History of the Public Option," *American Prospect*, August 18, 2009, http://prospect.org/article/history-public-option. Jonathan Cohn, "How they did it," *New Republic*, May 21, 2010, http://www.newrepublic.com/article/75077/how-they-did-it.

13 Marjorie Connelly, "Polls and the Public Option," *New York Times*, October 28, 2009, http://prescriptions.blogs.nytimes.com/2009/10/28/polls-and-the-public-option/. Miles Mogulescu, "NY Times reports confirms Obama made deal to kill public option," *Huffington Post*, May 16, 2010, http://www.huffingtonpost.com/miles-mogulescu/ny-times-reporter-confirm_b_500999.html.

14 Max Fisher, "Why Obama Dropped the Public Option," *Atlantic Wire*, February 24, 2010, http://www.thewire.com/politics/2010/02/why-obama-dropped-the-public-option/25408/.

15 Ezra Klein, "A Failure of White House Leadership," *Washington Post*,

February 23, 2010, http://voices.washingtonpost.com/ezra-klein/2010/02/a_failure_of_white_house_leade.html.

16 Igor Volsky, "Daschle: Public Option 'Taken Off the Table' in July Due to 'Understanding People Had With Hospitals,'" *ThinkProgress*, October 5, 2010, http://thinkprogress.org/health/2010/10/05/171689/daschle-interview/. Glenn Greenwald, "Truth about the public option momentarily emerges, quickly scampers back into hiding," *Salon*, October 5, 2010, http://www.salon.com/2010/10/05/public_option_24/.

17 Ibid.

18 Ibid.

19 Alexander Bolton, "Lieberman expresses regret to colleagues over healthcare tension," *The Hill*, December 15, 2009, http://thehill.com/homenews/senate/72375-lieberman-expresses-regret-to-colleagues-over-healthcare-tension. Glenn Greenwald, "White House as helpless victims on health care," *Salon*, December 16, 2009, http://www.salon.com/2009/12/16/white_house_5/.

20 "Healthcare Flashbacks," *Huffington Post*, August 9, 2009, http://www.huffingtonpost.com/2009/08/09/flashback-obama-promises_n_254833.html.

21 Ibid.

22 Ibid.

23 Ibid.

24 Ibid.

25 Ibid.

26 David Kilpatrick, "White House Affirms Drug Deal," *New York Times*, August 6, 2009, http://www.nytimes.com/2009/08/06/health/policy/06insure.html. Cohn, "How They Did It."

27 Glenn Greenwald, "Obamacare architect leaves White House for pharmaceutical industry job," December 2012, http://www.theguardian.com/commentisfree/2012/dec/05/obamacare-fowler-lobbyist-industry1.

28 Ibid.

29 Ibid.

30 Cohn, "How They Did It."

31 Ibid.

32 Ibid. Paul Kane, "Pelosi makes history, and enemies, as an effective House speaker," *Washington Post*, May 2, 2010, http://www.washingtonpost.com/wp-dyn/content/article/2010/05/02/AR2010050202769.html.

33 Rosa DeLauro, "Remarks at the Americans United For Change/Protect Your Care ACA Benefits Press," Washington D.C., September 10, 2013.

34 David Blumenthal, "Testimony Before the Senate: The Affordable Care Act at Five Years," Washington, D.C., March 19, 2005, http://www.commonwealthfund.org/~/media/files/publications/testimony/2015/mar/1807_blumenthal_aca_at_five_years_senate_finance_comm_testimony_03_19_2015.pdf.

35 Ibid.

36 "Where the States Stand on Medicaid Expansion," The Advisory Board, September 1, 2015, https://www.advisory.com/daily-briefing/resources/primers/medicaidmap.

37 Rachel Garfield and Katherine Young, "Adults who remained uninsured at the end of 2014," Kaiser Family Foundation, January 29, 2015, http://kff.org/report-section/adults-who-remained-uninsured-at-the-end-of-2014-issue-brief/.

38 Michael Moore, "The Obamacare We Deserve," New York Times, January 1, 2014, http://www.nytimes.com/2014/01/01/opinion/moore-the-obamacare-we-deserve.html.

39 Steven Brill, "Obama's Trauma Team," Time, February 27, 2014, http://time.com/10228/obamas-trauma-team/.

40 Ibid.

41 "Press Briefing by Press Secretary Jay Carney," White House, October 23, 2013, https://www.whitehouse.gov/the-press-office/2013/10/23/press-briefing-press-secretary-jay-carney-10232013. "Press briefing by Press Secretary Jay Carney," White House, October 24, 2013, https://www.whitehouse.gov/the-press-office/2013/10/25/press-briefing-press-secretary-jay-carney-10242013. Brill, "Obama's Trauma Team."

42 Brill, "Obama's Trauma Team."

43 "Remarks by the President on the Affordable Care Act," White House, October 21, 2013, https://www.whitehouse.gov/the-press-office/2013/10/21/remarks-president-affordable-care-act.

44 Brill, "Obama's Trauma Team."

45 Ricardo Alonso-Zaldivar, "Probe finds reasons for Obamacare website failure," Associated Press, July 31, 2014, http://www.inc.com/associated-press/management-failure-results-in-healthcare.gov-woes.html.

46 Ibid.

47 "If you like your health-care plan, you'll get to keep your health care plan," Politifact, November 4, 2013, http://www.politifact.com/obama-like-health-care-keep/.

48 Ibid.

49 Ibid.

50 Ibid.

51 Ibid.

52 Ibid. Louise Jacobson, "Barack Obama says what he'd said was you can keep your plan 'if it hasn't changed since the law passed,'" *Politifact*, November 6, 2013. http://www.politifact.com/truth-o-meter/statements /2013/nov/06/barack-obama/barack-obama-says-what-hed-said-was -you-could-keep/.

53 Angie Drobnic Holan, "Lie of the Year: 'If you like your health care plan, you can keep it,'" *Politifact*, December 12, 2013, http://www.politi fact.com/truth-o-meter/article/2013/dec/12/lie-year-if-you-like-your -health-care-plan-keep-it/.

54 Juliet Eilperin and Amy Goldstein, "White House delays health insurance mandate for medium-sized employers until 2016," *Washington Post*, February 20, 2014, https://www.washingtonpost.com/national /health-science/white-house-delays-health-insurance-mandate-for -medium-sized-employers-until-2016/2014/02/10/ade6b344-9279 -11e3-84e1-27626c5ef5fb_story.html.

55 "Nationwide nearly 11.7 million consumers are enrolled in 2015 Health Insurance Marketplace coverage," HHS.Gov, March 10, 2015, http:// www.hhs.gov/news/press/2015pres/03/20150310a.html. Douglas Elmendorf, "CBO's Analysis of the Major Health Care Legislation Enacted in March 2010," Congressional Budget Office, March 30, 2011, http:// www.cbo.gov/sites/default/files/03-30-healthcarelegislation.pdf.

56 Ed O'Keefe, "The House has voted 54 times in four years on Obamacare—here's the full list," *Washington Post*, March 21, 2014, http://www.washingtonpost.com/news/the-fix/wp/2014/03/21/the -house-has-voted-54-times-in-four-years-on-obamacare-heres-the -full-list/.

57 Troy Griggs, Haeyoun Park, Alicia Parlapiano, Sona Patel, Karl Russell, and R. Smith, "Is the Affordable Care Act Working?" *New York Times*, October 26, 2014, http://www.nytimes.com/interactive/2014/10/27/us /is-the-affordable-care-act-working.html/.

58 Adam Liftak, "Supreme Court Upholds Health Care Law, 5-4, in Victory for Obama," *New York Times*, June 28, 2012, http://www.nytimes.com /2012/06/29/us/supreme-court-lets-health-law-largely-stand.html.

59 Kimberly Leonard, "Supreme Court upholds Obamacare subsidies in King v. Burwell," *U.S. News & World Report*, June 25, 2015, http:// www.usnews.com/news/articles/2015/06/25/supreme-court-upholds -obamacare-subsidies-in-king-v-burwell. "Remarks by the President on

the Supreme Court's ruling on the Affordable Care Act," White House, June 25, 2015, https://www.whitehouse.gov/the-press-office/2015/06/25 /remarks-president-supreme-courts-ruling-affordable-care-act.

Chapter Three: National Security

1 Dahlia Lithwick, "See No Evil: Why is the Obama administration clinging to an indefensible state-secrets doctrine?," *Slate*, February 10, 2009, http://www.slate.com/articles/news_and_politics/jurisprudence/2009 /02/see_no_evil.single.html.

2 Ibid.

3 Ibid. Jamie Doward, "Torture claims by British resident are given credence by American judge," *The Observer*, December 20, 2009, http://www.theguardian.com/world/2009/dec/20/torture-claims-binyam -mohamed.

4 Lithwick, "See No Evil."

5 "Obama's Speech at Woodrow Wilson Center," Council on Foreign Relations, August 1, 2007, http://www.cfr.org/elections/obamas-speech -woodrow-wilson-center/p13974.

6 Dan Froomkin, "Obama Makes Bushism the New Normal," *The Intercept*, September 3, 2014, https://firstlook.org/theintercept/2014/09/03 /froomkin-blogs-again/.

7 Glenn Greenwald, "Obama's justice department grants final immunity to Bush's CIA torturers," *The Guardian*, August 31, 2012, http://www.theguardian.com/commentisfree/2012/aug/31/obama-justice -department-immunity-bush-cia-torturer.

8 "Obama names intel picks, vows no torture," Associated Press, January 9, 2009, http://www.nbcnews.com/id/28574408/ns/politics-white _house/t/obama-names-intel-picks-vows-no-torture/.

9 Scott Shane, Mark Mazetti, and Helene Cooper, "Obama Reverses Key Bush Security Policies," *New York Times*, January 22, 2009, http://www .nytimes.com/2009/01/23/us/politics/23obama.html.

10 Lithwick, "See No Evil." Philip Rucker, "Leahy proposes panel to investigate Bush era," *Washington Post*, February 9, 2009, http://www.washing tonpost.com/wp-dyn/content/article/2009/02/09/AR2009020903221 .html.

11 Lithwick, "See No Evil."

12 Greenwald, "Obama's justice department grants final immunity."

13 Ibid.

14 Ibid.

15 Ibid.

16 Andrew Sullivan, "Much Worse than Nothing," *Daily Dish,* August 9, 2009, http://www.theatlantic.com/daily-dish/archive/2009/08/much-worse-than-nothing/197750/.

17 Greenwald, "Obama's justice department grants final immunity." Josh Meyer and Greg Miller, "Holder opens investigations into CIA interrogations," *Los Angeles Times,* August 25, 2009, http://articles.latimes.com/2009/aug/25/nation/na-interrogate-prosecutor25. Ken Dilanian, "Most CIA interrogations won't be pursued," *Los Angeles Times,* June, 30, 2011, http://articles.latimes.com/2011/jun/30/nation/la-na-cia-interrogations-20110701.

18 Scott Shane, "Holder Rules Out Prosecutions in CIA Interrogations," *New York Times,* August 31, 2012, http://www.nytimes.com/2012/08/31/us/holder-rules-out-prosecutions-in-cia-interrogations.html. Greenwald, "Obama's justice department grants final immunity."

19 Greenwald, "Obama's justice department grants final immunity."

20 Ibid.

21 Ibid.

22 Greg Miller, Adam Goldman, and Julie Tate, "Senate report on CIA program details brutality, dishonesty," *Washington Post,* December 9, 2014, http://www.washingtonpost.com/world/national-security/senate-report-on-cia-program-details-brutality-dishonesty/2014/12/09/1075c726-7f0e-11e4-9f38-95a187e4c1f7_story.html. Dylan Matthews, "16 absolutely outrageous abuses detailed in the CIA torture report," *Vox,* December 9, 2014, http://www.vox.com/2014/12/9/7360823/cia-torture-roundup.

23 Greenwald, "Obama's justice department grants final immunity."

24 Dahlia Lithwick, "Nowhere to Hide: Ignoring Maher Arar won't make his torture claims go away," *Slate,* June 16, 2010, http://www.slate.com/articles/news_and_politics/jurisprudence/2010/06/nowhere_to_hide.html. Glenn Greenwald, "The U.S. wins the right to abduct innocent people with impunity," June 14, 2010, http://www.salon.com/2010/06/14/arar_3/.

25 Ibid.

26 Richard Norton-Taylor, "Guantanamo is 'Gulag of our Times,' says Amnesty," *The Guardian,* May 26, 2005, http://www.theguardian.com/world/2005/may/26/usa.guantanamo.

27 Paul Koring, "Tough question for US candidates: What to do with

Guantanamo," *Globe and Mail,* June 18, 2007, http://www.theglobeand
mail.com/news/world/tough-question-for-us-candidates-what-to-do
-with-guantanamo/article687910/.

28 "The Democratic Debate," *New York Times,* November 15, 2007, http://
www.nytimes.com/2007/11/15/us/politics/15debate-transcript.html.

29 Erica Landau, "Barack Obama on 60 Minutes: No More Gitmo, Torture," November 17, 2008, https://www.thenation.com/article/barack
-obama-60-minutes-no-more-gitmo-torture/.

30 David M. Herszenhorn, "Funds to Close Guantanamo Denied," *New
York Times,* May 20, 2009, http://www.nytimes.com/2009/05/21/us
/politics/21detain.html.

31 Peter Finn, "Obama now endorses indefinite detention without trial for
some at Guantanamo," *Washington Post,* May 21, 2009, http://www.wash
ingtonpost.com/wp-dyn/content/article/2009/05/21/AR2009052104045
.html.

32 Ibid.

33 Max Fisher, "Why hasn't Obama closed Guantanamo Bay," *Washington
Post,* April 30, 2013, http://www.washingtonpost.com/blogs/worldviews
/wp/2013/04/30/obama-just-gave-a-powerful-speech-about-the-need
-to-close-gitmo-so-why-hasnt-he/.

34 Charlie Savage, "Uruguay Accepts 6 Detainees Held at Guantanamo,"
New York Times, December 8, 2014, http://www.nytimes.com/2014/12
/08/world/americas/us-transfers-6-guantanamo-detainees-to-uruguay
.html.

35 Eric Posner, "President Obama can shut Guantanamo whenever he
wants to," *Slate,* May 2, 2013, http://www.slate.com/articles/news_and
_politics/view_from_chicago/2013/05/president_obama_can_shut
_guantanamo_whenever_he_wants_to.html. Fisher, "Why hasn't Obama
closed Guantanamo Bay."

36 Mark Mazzetti, *The Way of the Knife: The CIA, a Secret Army, and a War
at the Ends of the Earth* (New York: Penguin, 2013), 220. Jim Acosta,
"Obama to make new push to shift control of drones from CIA to Pentagon," CNN, April 27, 2015, http://www.cnn.com/2015/04/27/politics
/drones-cia-pentagon-white-house//.

37 Micah Zenko, "Reforming US Drone Strike Policies," Council on Foreign Relations, February 2013, http://www.cfr.org/wars-and-warfare
/reforming-us-drone-strike-policies/p29736. Bruce Ramsay, "On drones,
Obama is Bush," *Seattle Times,* February 12, 2013, http://www.seattle
times.com/opinion/on-drones-obama-is-bush/.

38 Ibid.

39 Michelle Nichols, "Pakistan tells U.N. at least 400 civilians killed by drone strikes," Reuters, October 18, 2013, http://www.reuters.com/article/2013 /10/18/us-un-drones-idUSBRE99H16Z20131018. Jack Serle, "More than 2400 dead as Obama's drone campaign marks five years," *Bureau of Investigative Journalism,* January 23, 2014, https://www.thebureau investigates.com/2014/01/23/more-than-2400-dead-as-obamas-drone -campaign-marks-five-years/. "Will I Be Next? Drone Strikes in Pakistan," Amnesty International, October 22, 2013, http://www.amnestyusa .org/research/reports/will-i-be-next-us-drone-strikes-in-pakistan.

40 Jeremy Scahill, "The Assassination Complex: The Drone Papers," *The Intercept,* October 15, 2015, https://theintercept.com/drone-papers/the -assassination-complex/.

41 Spencer Ackerman, "US drone strikes more deadly to Afghan civilians than manned aircraft—adviser," *The Guardian,* July 2, 2013, http://www .theguardian.com/world/2013/jul/02/us-drone-strikes-afghan-civilians. Tim Craig, "Karzai says U.S. drone strike killed child, won't sign security deal if similar attacks continue," *Washington Post,* November 29, 2013, https://www.washingtonpost.com/world/karzai-says-us-drone-strike -killed-child-refuses-to-sign-security-deal-if-attacks-continue/2013/11 /28/0b19b6aa-586a-11e3-ba82-16ed03681809_story.html.

42 Karen McVeigh, "Drone strikes: tears in Congress as Pakistani family tells of mother's death," *The Guardian,* October 29, 2013, http://www .theguardian.com/world/2013/oct/29/pakistan-family-drone-victim -testimony-congress.

43 Ibid.

44 Ibid.

45 Ibid.

46 Ibid.

47 Jo Becker and Scott Shane, "Secret 'Kill List' Proves a Test of Obama's Principles and Will," *New York Times,* May 29, 2012, http://www.nytimes .com/2012/05/29/world/obamas-leadership-in-war-on-al-qaeda.html.

48 Jake Tapper, "How Does the President Have the Right to Target for Killing a U.S. Citizen?" *ABC News,* September 30, 2011, http://abcnews.go .com/blogs/politics/2011/09/how-does-the-president-have-the-right -to-target-for-killing-a-us-citizen/. Glenn Greenwald, "Chilling legal memo from Obama DOJ justifies assassination of U.S. citizens," *The Guardian,* February 5, 2013, http://www.theguardian.com/commentisfree /2013/feb/05/obama-kill-list-doj-memo.

49 "Remarks by the President at the National Defense University," White House, May 23, 2013, https://www.whitehouse.gov/the-press-office /2013/05/23/remarks-president-national-defense-university.

50 Ibid.

51 "US mulls drone strike on American Al-Qaeda suspect in Pakistan," CBS News, February 11, 2014, http://www.cbsnews.com/news/us-mulls -drone-strike-on-america-al-qaeda-suspect-in-pakistan/.

52 Paul Lewis, Spencer Ackerman, and Jon Boone, "Obama regrets drone strike that killed hostages but hails US for transparency," The Guardian, April 23, 2015, http://www.theguardian.com/world/2015/apr/23/us -drone-strike-killed-american-italian-al-qaida. Adam Taylor, "The U.S. keeps killing Americans in drone strikes, mostly by accident," Washington Post, April 23, 2015, https://www.washingtonpost.com/news /worldviews/wp/2015/04/23/the-u-s-keeps-killing-americans-in-drone -strikes-mostly-by-accident/.

53 Ibid. Spencer Ackerman, Sabrina Siddiqui, and Paul Lewis, "White House admits: we didn't know who drone strike was aiming to kill," The Guardian, April 23, 2015, http://www.theguardian.com/world/2015/apr /23/drone-strike-al-qaida-targets-white-house.

54 Ibid.

55 Becker and Shane, "Secret kill list." Greenwald, "Chilling legal memo from Obama."

56 Greenwald, "Chilling legal memo from Obama."

57 Becker and Shane, "Secret kill list." Spencer Ackerman, "41 men targeted but 1,147 people killed: US drone strikes—the facts on the ground," The Guardian, November 24, 2014, http://www.theguardian.com/us-news /2014/nov/24/-sp-us-drone-strikes-kill-1147.

58 Becker and Shane, "Secret kill list."

59 Ibid.

60 Steve Coll, "Remote Control," New Yorker, May 6, 2013, http://www .newyorker.com/magazine/2013/05/06/remote-control.

61 Glenn Greenwald, "NSA collecting phone records of millions of Verizon customers daily," The Guardian, June 6, 2013, http://www.theguardian .com/world/2013/jun/06/nsa-phone-records-verizon-court-order.

62 Dustin Volz, "Everything we learned from Edward Snowden in 2013," National Journal, December 31, 2013, http://www.nationaljournal .com/defense/everything-we-learned-from-edward-snowden-in-2013 -20131231.

63 "Transcript: What Obama said on NSA controversy," Wall Street Jour-

nal, June 7, 2013, http://blogs.wsj.com/washwire/2013/06/07/transcript
-what-obama-said-on-nsa-controversy/.

64 Ibid.

65 Alex Seitz-Wald, "Despite Obama's claim, FISA court rarely much of
a check," June 7, 2013, http://www.salon.com/2013/06/07/despite
_obamas_claim_fisa_court_rarely_much_of_a_check/. Spencer Ackerman, "FISA chief judge defends integrity of court over Verizon records
collection," *The Guardian,* June 6, 2013, http://www.theguardian.com
/world/2013/jun/06/fisa-court-judge-verizon-records-surveillance.

66 "Transcript: What Obama said on NSA controversy," June 6, 2013.

67 Matthew Feeney, "On NSA spying, Senator Obama would've disagreed
with President Obama," *Reason,* June 7, 2013, http://reason.com/blog
/2013/06/07/on-nsa-spying-sen-obama-wouldve-disagree.

68 Ibid.

69 David Jackson, "White House: No Amnesty for Snowden," *USA Today,*
December 16, 2013, http://www.usatoday.com/story/theoval/2013/12
/16/obama-snowden-nsa-nsc-caitlin-hayden/4038753/.

70 "The ten biggest revelations from the Edward Snowden leaks," *Mash-
able,* June 5, 2014, http://mashable.com/2014/06/05/edward-snowden
-revelations/.

71 Tom McCarthy, "NSA review panel recommends dozens of new restrictions on surveillance—live," *The Guardian,* December 18, 2013, http://
www.theguardian.com/world/2013/dec/18/nsa-review-panel-release
-findings-live.

72 Ellen Nakashima, "Independent review board says NSA phone data
program is illegal and should end," *Washington Post,* January 23, 2014,
https://www.washingtonpost.com/world/national-security/independent
-review-board-says-nsa-phone-data-program-is-illegal-and-should
-end/2014/01/22/4cebd470-83dd-11e3-bbe5-6a2a3141e3a9_story
.html.

73 Ibid.

74 Josh Gerstein, "President Obama hits Edward Snowden over NSA
Leaks," *Politico,* January 17, 2014, http://dyn.politico.com/printstory.cfm
?uuid=685B8CBA-37F4-4027-B69B-3097A75CAB95. Andrea Peterson,
"Snowden: I raised NSA concerns internally over 10 times before going
rogue," *Washington Post,* March 7, 2014, https://www.washingtonpost
.com/news/the-switch/wp/2014/03/07/snowden-i-raised-nsa-concerns
-internally-over-10-times-before-going-rogue/. Kevin Gozstola, "NBC
News confirms attempt by Edward Snowden to go through channels

at NSA," *Firedoglake*, May 29, 2014, http://shadowproof.com/2014/05
/29/nbc-news-confirms-attempt-by-edward-snowden-to-go-through
-channels-at-nsa/.

75 Michael Isikoff, "Eric Holder: The Justice Department could strike
deal with Edward Snowden," *Yahoo News*, July 6, 2015, https://www
.yahoo.com/politics/eric-holder-the-justice-department-could-strike
-123393663066.html. Michael Isikoff, "FBI head Comey: No deal with
Snowden," *Yahoo News*, July 9, 2015, http://news.yahoo.com/fbi-head
-comey--no-deal-with-snowden-201533169.html.

76 Alec Luhn, Miriam Elder, and Paul Lewis, "Edward Snowden accuses
US of illegal, aggressive campaign," *The Guardian*, July 12, 2013, http://
www.theguardian.com/world/2013/jul/12/edward-snowden-accuses
-us-illegal-campaign.

77 Timm, "Petraeus won't serve a day in jail for his leaks. Edward
Snowden shouldn't either," *The Guardian*, March 5, 2015, http://www
.theguardian.com/commentisfree/2015/mar/05/petraeus-jail-leaks
-edward-snowden. Jesselyn Radack, "Petraeus, Snowden, and the
Department of Two-Tiered Justice," *Foreign Policy*, March 4, 2015,
http://foreignpolicy.com/2015/03/04/petraeus-snowden-and-the
-department-of-two-tiered-justice/.

78 Timm, "Petraeus won't serve a day in jail."

79 *Citizenfour*, directed by Laura Poitras (New York: Radius-TWC, 2014).

80 Ryan Lizza, "State of Deception," *New Yorker*, December 16, 2013,
http://www.newyorker.com/magazine/2013/12/16/state-of-deception.
Glenn Kessler, "James Clapper's least untruthful statement to the Senate," *Washington Post*, June 12, 2013, http://www.washingtonpost.com
/blogs/fact-checker/post/james-clappers-least-untruthful-statement-to
-the-senate/2013/06/11/e50677a8-d2d8-11e2-a73e-826d299ff459_blog
.html.

81 Ibid. Justin Sink, "Obama: Clapper 'should have been more careful' in
congressional testimony," *The Hill*, January 31, 2014, http://thehill.com
/policy/technology/197060-obama-clapper-should-have-been-more
-careful-in-congressional.

82 Lizza, "State of Deception."

83 Ibid.

84 Dustin Volz, "Federal Appeals Court Rules NSA Spying Illegal," *National Journal*, May 7, 2015, http://www.nationaljournal.com/tech/2015
/05/07/Federal-Appeals-Court-Rules-NSA-Spying-Illegal.

85 Jennifer Steinhauer and Jonathan Weisman, "U.S. Surveillance in Place

Since 9/11 Is Sharply Limited," *New York Times*, June 3, 2015, http://www.nytimes.com/2015/06/03/us/politics/senate-surveillance-bill-passes-hurdle-but-showdown-looms.html.

86 Glenn Greenwald, "Liberal icon Frank Church on the NSA," *The Guardian*, June 25, 2013, http://www.theguardian.com/commentisfree/2013/jun/25/frank-church-liberal-icon.

87 Connie Lawn, "White House Correspondents' Association Honors Reporters and Seeks Access," *Huffington Post*, October 26, 2014, http://www.huffingtonpost.com/connie-lawn/white-house-correspondent_3_b_6050168.html.

88 Dylan Byers, "Jill Abramson: This is the most secretive White House I have ever dealt with," *Politico*, January 23, 2014, http://www.politico.com/blogs/media/2014/01/jill-abramson-this-is-the-most-secretive-white-house-i-have-ever-dealt-with-181742. Leonard Downie, "In Obama's war on leaks, reporters fight back," *Washington Post*, October 4, 2013, https://www.washingtonpost.com/opinions/in-obamas-war-on-leaks-reporters-fight-back/2013/10/04/70231e1c-2aeb-11e3-b139029811dbb57f_story.html.

89 Leonard Downie, "The Obama Administration and the Press," Committee to Protect Journalists, October 10, 2014, https://cpj.org/reports/2013/10/obama-and-the-press-us-leaks-surveillance-post-911.php. Downie, "In Obama's war on leaks, reporters fight back." Hadas Gold, "James Risen: Obama hates the press," *Politico*, October 6, 2014, http://www.politico.com/blogs/media/2014/10/james-risen-obama-hates-the-press-196641.

90 Erik Wemple, "USA Today's Susan Page: Obama administration most dangerous to media in history," *Washington Post*, October 27, 2014, https://www.washingtonpost.com/blogs/erik-wemple/wp/2014/10/27/usa-todays-susan-page-obama-administration-most-dangerous-to-media-in-history/.

91 Downie, "The Obama Administration and the Press."

92 Carrie Johnson, "Justice Department secretly obtains AP phone records," NPR, May 14, 2013, http://www.npr.org/2013/05/14/183810320/justice-department-secretly-obtains-ap-phone-records.

93 Ibid.

94 Brian Stelter and Michael D. Shear, "White House Defends Tracking Fox Reporter Over Leak," *New York Times*, May 21, 2013, http://www.nytimes.com/2013/05/21/us/politics/white-house-defends-tracking-fox-reporter.html. Ann Marimow, "Justice Department's scrutiny of Fox

News reporter James Rosen in leak case draws fire," *Washington Post*, May 20, 2013, https://www.washingtonpost.com/local/justice-departments -scrutiny-of-fox-news-reporter-james-rosen-in-leak-case-draws-fire /2013/05/20/c6289eba-c162-11e2-8bd8-2788030e6b44_story.html.

95 Ryan Reilly, "Eric Holder: Media Probe got 'a little out of whack,'" *Huffington Post*, June 5, 2013, http://www.huffingtonpost.com/2013/06/05/eric -holder-media-probe_n_3393072.html.

96 Ibid.

97 Charlie Savage, "Under Fire, White House Pushes to Revive Media Shield Bill," *New York Times*, May 16, 2013, http://www.nytimes.com/2013/05 /16/us/politics/under-fire-white-house-pushes-to-revive-media-shield -bill.html.

98 Carol Cratty, "Holder runs into roadblocks on off-the-record meetings on leaks," CNN, May 29, 2013, http://politicalticker.blogs.cnn.com /2013/05/29/holder-runs-into-roadblocks-on-off-the-record-meetings -on-leaks/.

99 John Hudson, "Obama's war on whistleblowers," *Atlantic Wire*, May 24, 2011, http://www.thewire.com/politics/2011/05/obamas-war-whistle -blowers/38106/. "Former CIA man Jeffrey Sterling gets 42 months in prison over Iran leaks," Associated Press, May 11, 2015, http://www .theguardian.com/us-news/2015/may/11/former-cia-man-jeffrey -sterling-42-months-prison-iran-leaks.

100 Adam Liptak, "Supreme Court Rejects Appeal From Times Reporter Over Refusal to Identify Source," *New York Times*, June 3, 2014, http:// www.nytimes.com/2014/06/03/us/james-risen-faces-jail-time-for -refusing-to-identify-a-confidential-source.html. Matt Apuzzo, "Times Reporter James Risen Will Not Be Called to Testify in Leak Case, Lawyers Say," *New York Times*, January 13, 2015, http://www.nytimes.com/2015 /01/13/us/times-reporter-james-risen-will-not-be-called-to-testify-in -leak-case-lawyers-say.html.

Chapter Four: Foreign Policy

1 Angie Drobnic Holan, "Mitt Romney said Barack Obama began his presidency with an apology tour," *Politifact*, August 31, 2012, http:// www.politifact.com/truth-o-meter/statements/2012/aug/31/mitt -romney/mitt-romney-said-barack-obama-began-his-presidency/.

2 David Remnick, "World-Weary," *New Yorker*, September 15, 2014, http://www.newyorker.com/magazine/2014/09/15/world-weary.

3 Jeffrey Goldberg, "Hillary Clinton: Failure to help Syrian rebels led to rise of ISIS," *The Atlantic,* August 10, 2014, http://www.theatlantic.com /international/archive/2014/08/hillary-clinton-failure-to-help-syrian -rebels-led-to-the-rise-of-isis/375832/. Remnick, "World-Weary."

4 Juliet Eilperin, "Obama lays out his foreign policy doctrine: Singles, doubles and the occasional home run," *Washington Post,* April 29, 2014, https://www.washingtonpost.com/world/obama-lays-out-his-foreign -policy-doctrine-singles-doubles-and-the-occasional-home-run/2014 /04/28/e34ec058-ceb5-11e3-937f-d3026234b51c_story.html.

5 "Transcript: Obama's speech against the war, October 2, 2002," NPR, January 20, 2009, http://www.npr.org/templates/story/story.php?storyId= 99591469. Karen DeYoung, "Obama Sets Timetable for Iraq Withdrawal, Calling It Part of Broader Middle East Strategy," *Washington Post,* February 28, 2009, http://www.washingtonpost.com/wp-dyn/content/article /2009/02/27/AR2009022700566.html.

6 Alissa Rubin, "Iraq Marks Withdrawal of US Troops from Cities," *New York Times,* June 30, 2009, http://www.nytimes.com/2009/07/01/world /middleeast/01iraq.html. Greg Jaffe, "War in Iraq will be called 'Operation New Dawn' to reflect reduced U.S. role," *Washington Post,* February 18, 2010, http://www.washingtonpost.com/wp-dyn/content/article /2010/02/18/AR2010021805888.html. Richard Engel, Charlene Gubash, and Alex Johnson, "Last full U.S. combat brigade leaves Iraq," *NBC News,* August 19, 2010, http://www.nbcnews.com/id/38744453 /ns/world_news-mideast_n_africa/t/last-full-us-combat-brigade -leaves-iraq/.

7 Lara Jakes and Rebecca Santana, "Iraq PM: Immunity Issue Scuttled Troop Deal," Associated Press, October 22, 2011, http://www.nbc news.com/id/44998833/ns/world_news-mideast_n_africa/t/iraq-pm -immunity-issue-scuttled-us-troop-deal/.

8 J. Freedom du Lac, "In Iraq, the last to fall: David Hickman, the 4,474th U.S. service member killed," *Washington Post,* December 17, 2011, https://www.washingtonpost.com/world/middle_east/in-iraq-the-last -to-fall-david-hickman-the-4474th-us-service-member-killed/2011 /12/15/gIQAgwl00O_story.html. Joseph Logan, "Last U.S. troops leave Iraq, ending war," Reuters, December 18, 2011, http://www.reuters.com /article/2011/12/18/us-iraq-withdrawal-idUSTRE7BH03320111218.

9 Martin Chulov, "ISIS insurgents seize control of Iraqi city of Mosul," *The Guardian,* June 10, 2014, http://www.theguardian.com/world/2014 /jun/10/iraq-sunni-insurgents-islamic-militants-seize-control-mosul.

Dan Roberts and Spencer Ackerman, "US begins air strikes against Isis targets in Iraq, Pentagon says," *The Guardian*, August 8, 2014, http://www .theguardian.com/world/2014/aug/08/us-begins-air-strikes-iraq-isis. Jim Sciutto, Mariano Castillo, and Holly Yan, "U.S. airstrikes hit ISIS inside Syria for first time," CNN, September 23, 2014, http://www.cnn.com /2014/09/22/world/meast/u-s-airstrikes-isis-syria/. Phil Stewart and Roberta Rampton, "Obama to send 1,500 more troops to Iraq as campaign expands," Reuters, November 8, 2014, http://www.reuters.com/article /2014/11/08/us-mideast-crisis-usa-iraq-idUSKBN0IR22I20141108.

10 Peter Baker and Thom Shanker, "Obama Sets New Afghan Srategy," *New York Times*, March 27, 2009, http://www.nytimes.com/2009/03/27 /washington/27prexy.html.

11 "McChrystal wanted 50,000 troops," Associated Press, October 7, 2009, http://www.cbsnews.com/news/mcchrystal-wanted-50000-troops/. Rosa Brooks, "Obama vs. the Generals," *Politico*, November 2013, http:// www.politico.com/magazine/story/2013/11/obama-vs-the-generals -99379_Page2.html.

12 Jonathan S. Landay, Dion Nissenbaum, and John Walcott, "Another Afghan war: Media leaks spark administration fight," *McClatchy*, November 12, 2009, http://www.mcclatchydc.com/news/nation-world/world /middle-east/article24563713.html.

13 Byron Tau, "Obama calls Afghan surge his most difficult decision," *Politico*, August 29, 2012, http://www.politico.com/blogs/politico44/2012/08 /obama-calls-afghan-surge-his-most-difficult-decision-133727. Sheryl Gay Stolberg and Helene Cooper, "Obama Adds Troops, but Maps Exit Plan," *New York Times*, December 1, 2009, http://www.nytimes.com /2009/12/02/world/asia/02prexy.html.

14 "Final US 'surge' troops withdraw from Afghanistan," Associated Press, September 21, 2012, http://www.theguardian.com/world/2012/sep/21 /us-surge-troops-withdraw-afghanistan.

15 "Poll: Confidence in Iraq War down sharply," CNN, March 18, 2007, http://www.cnn.com/2007/POLITICS/03/18/poll.wars/. "CNN Poll: Afghanistan war most unpopular in U.S. history," CNN, December 30, 2013, http://politicalticker.blogs.cnn.com/2013/12/30/cnn-poll-afghanistan -war-most-unpopular-in-u-s-history/.

16 Mark Landler, "U.S. troops to leave Afghanistan by 2016," *New York Times*, May 28, 2014, http://www.nytimes.com/2014/05/28/world/asia /us-to-complete-afghan-pullout-by-end-of-2016-obama-to-say.html.

17 Kay Johnson, "U.S.-led mission in Afghanistan ends combat role;

thousands of foreign troops remain," Reuters, December 28, 2014, http://www.reuters.com/article/2014/12/28/us-afghanistan-war -idUSKBN0K60FB20141228.

18 "'Humbled' Obama awarded Nobel peace prize," Associated Press, October 9, 2009, http://www.independent.co.uk/news/world/americas /humbled-obama-awarded-nobel-peace-prize-1800112.html.

19 "Barack Obama aide condemned Norway for 'fawning' over president by awarding him Nobel Prize," Associated Press, May 15, 2014, http:// www.telegraph.co.uk/news/worldnews/barackobama/10834779/Barack -Obama-aide-condemned-Norway-for-fawning-over-president-by -awarding-him-Nobel-Prize.html.

20 "Remarks by the President on winning the Nobel Peace Prize," White House, October 9, 2009, https://www.whitehouse.gov/the-press-office /remarks-president-winning-nobel-peace-prize.

21 "Remarks by the President at the Acceptance of the Nobel Peace Prize," White House, December 10, 2009, https://www.whitehouse.gov/the -press-office/remarks-president-acceptance-nobel-peace-prize.

22 Martin Luther King, Jr., "Acceptance Speech," December 10, 1964, http://www.nobelprize.org/nobel_prizes/peace/laureates/1964/king -acceptance_en.html.

23 "Arab Spring activists win Sakharov prize," *The Telegraph*, October 27, 2011, http://www.telegraph.co.uk/news/worldnews/africaandindian ocean/tunisia/8852987/Arab-Spring-activists-win-Sakharov-prize .html.

24 Bob Simon, "How a slap sparked Tunisia's revolution", *CBS News*, February 22, 2011, http://www.cbsnews.com/news/how-a-slap-sparked-tunisias -revolution-22-02-2011/.

25 Ibid. Gregory White, "This is the Wikileak that spawned the Tunisian crisis," *Business Insider*, January 14, 2011, http://www.businessinsider .com/tunisia-wikileaks-2011-1.

26 Garry Blight, Sheila Pulham, and Paul Torpey, "Arab Spring: An interactive timeline of Middle East protests," *The Guardian*, January 5, 2012, http:// www.theguardian.com/world/interactive/2011/mar/22/middle-east -protest-interactive-timeline. "The Arab Spring: One year later," NPR, January 2, 2012, http://www.npr.org/series/144636890/the-arab-spring-one -year-later. Kelley McEvers, "Bahrain: The Revolution that Wasn't," NPR, January 5, 2012, http://www.npr.org/2012/01/05/144637499/bahrain-the -revolution-that-wasnt.

27 Helene Cooper and Steven Lee Myers, "U.S. Tactics in Libya May Be a

Model for Other Efforts," *New York Times,* August 29, 2011, http://www
.nytimes.com/2011/08/29/world/africa/29diplo.html.

28 Conor Friedensdorf, "How Obama ignored Congress and misled America on war in Libya," *The Atlantic,* September 13, 2012, http://www.the
atlantic.com/politics/archive/2012/09/how-obama-ignored-congress
-and-misled-america-on-war-in-libya/262299/. Bill Press, "On Libya,
it depends on how you define war," June 17, 2011, http://billpressshow
.com/on-libya-it-depends-on-how-you-define-war/.

29 Press, "On Libya, it depends on how you define war."

30 Ibid. Charlie Savage, "Barack Obama's Q&A," *Boston Globe,* December
20, 2007, http://www.boston.com/news/politics/2008/specials/Candidate
QA/ObamaQA/.

31 Alan J. Kuperman, "Obama's Libya Debacle," *Foreign Affairs,* March
/April 2015, https://www.foreignaffairs.com/articles/libya/2015-02-16
/obamas-libya-debacle. "UN says Libya 'at the limit,' risks becoming a
failed state," AFP, June 3, 2015, http://news.yahoo.com/un-says-libya
-limit-risks-becoming-failed-state-155442844.html.

32 David Rohde and Warren Strobel, "How Syria policy stalled under
the 'analyst in chief,'" Reuters, October 28, 2014, http://www.reuters
.com/article/2014/10/28/us-usa-diplomacy-obama-specialreport
-idUSKBN0IH28L20141028. Matthew Lee and Julie Pace, "Obama Authorizes Sending Weapons to Syrian Rebels," Associated Press, June 13,
2013, http://www.huffingtonpost.com/2013/06/13/obama-syrian-rebels
_n_3438625.html. Adam Entous, "Legal Fears slowed U.S. aid to Syria,"
Wall Street Journal, July 14, 2013, http://www.wsj.com/articles/SB10001
424127887323848804578606100558048708. Jessica Shulberg, "Obama's
Going to Arm the Syrian Rebels? He's Already Been Doing It Covertly
for Over a Year," *New Republic,* September 11, 2014, http://www.new
republic.com/article/119418/arming-syrias-rebels-obamas-been-doing
-it-covertly-2013.

33 Rohde and Strobel, "How Syria policy stalled." Glenn Kessler, "President Obama and the 'red line' on Syria's chemical weapons," *Washington
Post,* September 6, 2013, http://www.washingtonpost.com/blogs/fact
-checker/wp/2013/09/06/president-obama-and-the-red-line-on-syrias
-chemical-weapons/.

34 Kessler, "President Obama and the 'red line.'"

35 Thomas Gibbons-Neff, "Declared Syrian chemical weapons stockpile
now completely destroyed," *Washington Post,* August 28, 2014, https://
www.washingtonpost.com/news/checkpoint/wp/2014/08/18/declared

-syrian-chemical-weapon-stockpile-now-completely-destroyed/. Anne Barnard and Somini Sengupta, "Syria Is Using Chemical Weapons Again, Rescue Workers Say," *New York Times*, May 6, 2015, http://www.nytimes.com/2015/05/07/world/middleeast/syria-chemical-weapons.html. Theodore Schleifer, "Kerry: Syrian regime 'absolutely' used chlorine in attacks," CNN, June 17, 2015, http://www.cnn.com/2015/06/16/politics/john-kerry-syrian-chemical-weapons-chlorine/.

36 Joe Klein, "Obama and Syria—Stumbling toward Damascus," September 11, 2013, http://swampland.time.com/2013/09/11/obama-and-syria-stumbling-toward-damascus/.

37 Stephen Erlanger, "Saudi Prince Accuses Obama of Indecision on Middle East," *New York Times*, December 16, 2013, http://www.nytimes.com/2013/12/16/world/middleeast/saudi-prince-accuses-obama-of-indecision-on-middle-east.html. Michael Weiss, "The Unraveling: How Obama's Syria Policy Fell Apart," *Politico*, January 2, 2014, http://www.politico.com/magazine/story/2014/01/how-obamas-syria-policy-fell-apart-101704.

38 Karen Yourish, K. K. Rebecca Lai, and Derek Watkins, "Death in Syria," *New York Times*, September 14, 2015, http://www.nytimes.com/interactive/2015/09/14/world/middleeast/syria-war-deaths.html.

39 Alan Yuhas, "Ukraine crisis: an essential guide to everything that's happened so far," *The Guardian*, April 11, 2014, http://www.theguardian.com/world/2014/apr/11/ukraine-russia-crimea-sanctions-us-eu-guide-explainer. Leila Hudson, "How Putin Outmaneuvered Obama in Syria and Ukraine," *Huffington Post*, April 25, 2014, http://www.huffingtonpost.com/leila-hudson/how-putin-outmaneuvered-o_b_5210426.html.

40 Ibid.

41 Ibid. Ilya Somin, "The dubious Crimean referendum on annexation by Russia," *Washington Post*, March 17, 2014, https://www.washingtonpost.com/news/volokh-conspiracy/wp/2014/03/17/the-dubious-crimean-referendum-on-annexation-by-russia/.

42 "Transcript: President Obama gives speech addressing Europe, Russia on March 26, *Washington Post*, March 26, 2014, https://www.washingtonpost.com/world/transcript-president-obama-gives-speech-addressing-europe-russia-on-march-26/2014/03/26/07ae80ae-b503-11e3-b899-20667de76985_story.html.

43 Serge Schmemann, "Putin Rushes In, Pretending Not to; Obama Stands Back," *New York Times*, August 29, 2014, http://www.nytimes.com/2014/08/31/opinion/sunday/putin-rushes-in-pretending-not-to

-obama-stands-back.html. "Significant escalation: Russian tanks enter Ukraine," *CBS News,* August 28, 2014, http://www.cbsnews.com/news /significant-escalation-russian-tanks-enter-ukraine/.

44 Ibid.

45 Tim Bowler, "Falling oil prices: Who are the winners and losers?" *BBC News,* January 19, 2015, http://www.bbc.com/news/business-29643612. Myles Udland, "Crude oil prices fall another 10% after another massive inventory build," *Business Insider,* September 1, 2015, http://www.business insider.com/crude-oil-price-september-1-2015-9. "Russia braces for longest recession in decades with oil near 50," *Bloomberg,* July 22, 2015, http:// www.bloomberg.com/news/articles/2015-07-22/russia-braces-for-longest -recession-in-decades-with-oil-near-50.

46 "Remarks by the President in State of the Union Address," White House, January 20, 2015, https://www.whitehouse.gov/the-press-office/2015/01 /20/remarks-president-state-union-address-january-20-2015.

47 Marvin Kalb, "Putin Won His War in Ukraine," *Washington Post,* September 7, 2015, https://www.washingtonpost.com/opinions/putin-won -in-ukraine/2015/09/07/02a0283c-5341-11e5-933e-7d06c647a395 _story.html.

48 Chulov, "ISIS insurgents seize control of Iraqi city of Mosul."

49 "ISIS Fast Facts," CNN, September 17, 2015, http://www.cnn.com/2014 /08/08/world/isis-fast-facts/.

50 David Remnick, "Going the Distance: On and Off the Road with Barack Obama," *New Yorker,* January 27, 2014, http://www.newyorker .com/magazine/2014/01/27/going-the-distance-david-remnick.

51 Josh Hicks, "Obama foreign policy sparks bipartisan criticism," *Washington Post,* August 31, 2014, http://www.washingtonpost.com/news /post-politics/wp/2014/08/31/obama-foreign-policy-sparks-bipartisan -criticism/. Michael Hirsh, "Team of Bumblers? Are Susan Rice and Chuck Hagel Up to Today's New National Security Challenges," *Politico,* October 2014, http://www.politico.com/magazine/story/2014/10/susan -rice-chuck-hagel-team-of-bumblers-112208_full.html.

52 Hirsch, "Team of Bumblers." Stewart and Rampton, "Obama to send 1500 more troops to Iraq as campaign expands."

53 Chelsea J. Carter, Catherine E. Shoichet, and Hamdi Alkhshali, "Obama on ISIS in Syria: 'We don't have a strategy yet,'" *CNN,* September 4, 2014, http://www.cnn.com/2014/08/28/world/meast/isis-iraq-syria/.

54 David Hudson, "President Obama: "We Will Degrade and Ultimately Destroy ISIL," White House, September 20, 2014, https://www.white

house.gov/blog/2014/09/10/president-obama-we-will-degrade-and
-ultimately-destroy-isil.

55 Leon Panetta, *Worthy Fights: A Memoir of Leadership in War and Peace*
    (New York: Penguin, 2014), 387.

56 Ibid. Bill Press, "Panetta bites hand that fed him," *Chicago Tribune*, Oc-
    tober 9, 2014, http://www.chicagotribune.com/news/columnists/sns
    -201410091730--tms--bpresstt--m-a20141009-20141009-column.html.
    Ben Armbruster, "Panetta lectures McCain on Iraq withdrawal: 'This is
    about negotiating with a sovereign country,'" *ThinkProgress*, November
    15, 2011, http://thinkprogress.org/security/2011/11/15/368840/panetta
    -lectures-mccain-on-iraq-withdrawal-this-is-about-negotiating-with-a
    -sovereign-country/.

57 Bruce Ackerman, "Obama's Betrayal of the Constitution," *New York Times*,
    September 12, 2014, http://www.nytimes.com/2014/09/12/opinion/obamas
    -betrayal-of-the-constitution.html.

58 Ibid. Josh Keating, "Obama's post-congressional foreign policy," *Slate*,
    October 20, 2014, http://www.slate.com/blogs/the_world_/2014/10/20
    /when_it_comes_to_foreign_policy_president_obama_is_acting_like
    _congress.html.

59 Peter Kornbluh and William M. LeoGrande, *Back Channel to Cuba:
    The Hidden History of Negotiations between Washington and Havana*
    (Chapel Hill: University of North Carolina Press, 2014). Peter Kornbluh
    and William M. LeoGrande, "Cuba Confidential: Inside the crazy back
    -channel negotiations that revolutionized our relationship with Cuba,"
    Mother Jones, September/October 2015, http://www.motherjones.com
    /politics/2015/07/secret-negotiations-gross-hernandez-kerry-pope
    -obama-castro-cuba.

60 Azam Ahmed and Julie Hirschfeld David, "U.S. and Cuba Reopen Long
    -Closed Embassies," *New York Times*, July 20, 2015, http://www.ny
    times.com/2015/07/21/world/americas/cuba-us-embassy-diplomatic
    -relations.html. Nancy Trejos, "Jetblue expands service to Cuba," *USA
    Today*, July 3, 2015, http://www.usatoday.com/story/todayinthesky/2015
    /07/03/jetblue-flights-havana-cuba/29625009/. David Taintor, "US com-
    panies react to Cuba deal," MSNBC, December 18, 2014, http://www
    .msnbc.com/msnbc/us-companies-react-cuba-deal.

61 John Cassidy, "The Iran Deal Is a Victory for Reason and Economic Sanc-
    tions," *New Yorker*, September 3, 2015, http://www.newyorker.com
    /news/john-cassidy/the-iran-deal-is-a-victory-for-reason-and-economic
    -sanctions. Max Fisher, "9 questions about Iran's nuclear program you were

too embarrassed to ask," *Washington Post*, November 25, 2013, https://www.washingtonpost.com/news/worldviews/wp/2013/11/25/9-questions-about-irans-nuclear-program-you-were-too-embarrassed-to-ask/.

62 Cassidy, "The Iran deal is a victory." Michael R. Gordon and David E. Sanger, "Iran Agrees to Detailed Nuclear Outline, First Step Toward a Wider Deal," *New York Times*, April 2, 2015, http://www.nytimes.com/2015/04/03/world/middleeast/iran-nuclear-talks.html.

63 Michael R. Gordon and David E. Sanger, "Deal Reached on Iran Nuclear Program; Limits on Fuel Would Lessen with Time," *New York Times*, July 14, 2015, http://www.nytimes.com/2015/07/15/world/middleeast/iran-nuclear-deal-is-reached-after-long-negotiations.html. "Press conference by the President," White House, July 15, 2015, https://www.whitehouse.gov/the-press-office/2015/07/15/press-conference-president.

64 Peter Baker, "Seeking to Ease Worries, Obama Says the World Has Always Been 'Messy,'" *New York Times*, August 29, 2014, http://www.nytimes.com/2014/08/30/us/politics/obama-decides-to-cut-short-trip-to-new-york-area.html. "President Obama and the World," *New York Times*, May 4, 2014, http://www.nytimes.com/2014/05/04/opinion/sunday/president-obama-and-the-world.html.

Chapter Five: Immigration Reform

1 Michael Von Sickler, "Yep, Reagan did the A-Word," *Politifact*, January 6, 2008, http://www.politifact.com/truth-o-meter/statements/2008/jan/06/rudy-giuliani/yep-reagan-did-the-a-word/.

2 Aaron Blake, "Make no mistake: Immigration reform hurt Eric Cantor," *Washington Post*, June 11, 2014, http://www.washingtonpost.com/news/the-fix/wp/2014/06/11/yes-immigration-reform-hurt-eric-cantor/.

3 "Trump's immigrant-bashing rhetoric breeds violence," *Washington Post*, August 21, 2015, https://www.washingtonpost.com/opinions/mr-trumps-politics-of-incitement/2015/08/21/c33d0f2e-483d-11e5-8ab4-c73967a143d3_story.html. Anna Brand, "Donald Trump: I would force Mexico to build a border wall," MSNBC, June 28, 2015, http://www.msnbc.com/msnbc/donald-trump-i-would-force-mexico-build-border-wall.

4 Jens Manuel Krogstad and Jeffrey S. Passel, "5 facts about illegal immigration in the U.S.," Pew Research Center, July 24, 2015, http://www.pewresearch.org/fact-tank/2015/07/24/5-facts-about-illegal-immigration-in-the-u-s/.

5 Robert Pear and Carl Hulse, "Immigration Bill Fails to Survive Senate Vote," *New York Times,* June 28, 2007, http://www.nytimes.com/2007 /06/28/washington/28cnd-immig.html. Rachel Weiner, "How immigration reform failed, over and over," *Washington Post,* January 30, 2013, http://www.washingtonpost.com/news/the-fix/wp/2013/01/30/how -immigration-reform-failed-over-and-over/.

6 Molly Ball, "Obama's long immigration betrayal, *The Atlantic,* September 9, 2014, http://www.theatlantic.com/politics/archive/2014/09/obamas -long-immigration-betrayal/379839/.

7 Ibid.

8 Ibid.

9 Josh Hicks, "Obama's failed promise of a first year immigration overhaul," *Washington Post,* September 25, 2012, http://www.washington post.com/blogs/fact-checker/post/obamas-failed-promise-of-a-first -year-immigration-overhaul/2012/09/25/06997958-0721-11e2-a10c -fa5a255a9258_blog.html.

10 Ibid.

11 Ibid.

12 Ibid.

13 Ibid. Ginger Thompson and David M. Herszenhorn, "Obama Set for First Step on Immigration Reform," *New York Times,* June 24, 2009, http://www.nytimes.com/2009/06/25/us/politics/25immig.html.

14 Thompson and Herszenhorn, "Obama set for first step on immigration reform."

15 Ibid.

16 Hicks, "Obama's failed promise."

17 Ibid. Scott Wong and Shira Toeplitz, "DREAM Act dies in Senate," *Politico,* December 18, 2010, http://www.politico.com/story/2010/12/dream -act-dies-in-senate-046573.

18 Wong and Toeplitz, "DREAM Act dies in Senate." Michael O'Donnell, "How LBJ saved the Civil Rights Act," *The Atlantic,* April 2014, http:// www.theatlantic.com/magazine/archive/2014/04/what-the-hells-the -presidency-for/358630/.

19 Louis Jacobson, "Barack Obama touts record high border agents, lowest immigration from Mexico in 40 years," *Politifact,* October 17, 2012, http://www.politifact.com/truth-o-meter/statements/2012/oct /17/barack-obama/barack-obama-touts-record-high-border-agents -lowes/. William Booth, "National Guard deployment on US-Mexico border has mixed results," *Washington Post,* November 21, 2011, https://

www.washingtonpost.com/world/national-security/national-guard
-deployment-on-us-mexico-border-has-mixed-results/2011/11/21
/gIQAly6qXO_story.html.

20 Amy Sherman, "Barack Obama says illegal border crossings lowest
   it has been since the 1970's," *Politifact*, November 25, 2014, http://
   www.politifact.com/florida/statements/2014/nov/25/barack-obama
   /obama-says-illegal-border-crossings-lowest-it-has-/. Jeffrey S. Passel, D'Vera Cohn, Jens Manuel Krogstad, and Ana Gonzalez-Barrera,
   "As growth stalls, unauthorized immigrant population becomes more
   settled," Pew Research Center, September 3, 2014, http://www.pew
   hispanic.org/2014/09/03/as-growth-stalls-unauthorized-immigrant
   -population-becomes-more-settled/. Jerry Markon, "Fewer immigrants are entering the U.S. illegally, and that's changed the border
   security debate," *Washington Post*, May 27, 2015, http://www.wash
   ingtonpost.com/politics/flow-of-illegal-immigration-slows-as-us
   -mexico-border-dynamics-evolve/2015/05/27/c5caf02c-006b-11e5
   -833c-a2de05b6b2a4_story.html. "The Great Expulsion," *The Economist*, February 8, 2014, http://www.economist.com/news/briefing
   /21595892-barack-obama-has-presided-over-one-largest-peacetime
   -outflows-people-americas.

21 Molly O'Toole, "Analysis: Obama deportations raise immigration policy questions," Reuters, September 20, 2011, http://www.reuters.com
   /article/2011/09/20/us-obama-immigration-idUSTRE78J05720110920.
   Ana Gonzalez-Barrera and Jens Manuel Krogstad, "U.S. deportations
   of immigrants reach record high in 2013," Pew Research Center, October 2, 2014, http://www.pewresearch.org/fact-tank/2014/10/02/u-s
   -deportations-of-immigrants-reach-record-high-in-2013/.

22 David Rutz, "Watch Obama make the case against his executive amnesty," *Washington Free Beacon*, November 13, 2014. http://freebea
   con.com/issues/watch-obama-make-the-case-against-his-executive
   -amnesty/.

23 Ibid.

24 Ibid.

25 Ball, "Obama's long immigration betrayal."

26 "Remarks by the President on Immigration," White House, June 15,
   2012, https://www.whitehouse.gov/the-press-office/2012/06/15/remarks
   -president-immigration.

27 Ibid.

28 Lucy Madison, "Romney on Immigration: I'm for 'Self-Deportation,'"

CBS News, January 24, 2012, http://www.cbsnews.com/news/romney
-on-immigration-im-for-self-deportation/.

29 Mark Hugo Lopez and Paul Taylor, "Latino voters in the 2012 election,"
Pew Research Center, November 7, 2012, http://www.pewhispanic.org
/2012/11/07/latino-voters-in-the-2012-election/. Ashley Parker, "Romney Blames Loss on Obama's Gifts to Minorities and Young Voters,"
New York Times, November 14, 2012, http://thecaucus.blogs.nytimes
.com/2012/11/14/romney-blames-loss-on-obamas-gifts-to-minorities
-and-young-voters/.

30 Rosalind S. Helderman and Jon Cohen, "As Republican convention em-
phasizes diversity, racial incidents intrude," *Washington Post*, August 29,
2012, http://www.washingtonpost.com/politics/2012/08/29/b9023a52
-f1ec-11e1-892d-bc92fee603a7_story.html.

31 Igor Volsky, "Lindsey Graham warns GOP: 'It doesn't matter who we run
in 2016 if immigration reform fails,'" *ThinkProgress*, June 16, 2013, http://
thinkprogress.org/immigration/2013/06/16/2165161/lindsey-graham
-warns-gop-it-doesnt-matter-who-we-run-in-2016-if-immigration
-reform-fails/.

32 RNC Growth and Opportunity Project, http://goproject.gop.com/.
Martin Longman, "For RNC, how'd it go so wrong?" *Washington
Monthly*, August 25, 2015, http://www.washingtonmonthly.com/ten
-miles-square/2015/08/for_rnc_howd_it_go_so_wrong057296.php.

33 Ezra Klein, "President Obama lays out his second term," *Washington
Post*, October 24, 2012, http://www.washingtonpost.com/news/wonk
blog/wp/2012/10/24/president-obama-lays-out-his-second-term/. Rick
Green, "Register editor: Obama off the record comments deserve to be
shared with voters," *Des Moines Register*, October 23, 2012, http://blogs
.desmoinesregister.com/dmr/index.php/2012/10/23/register-editor
-obama-off-the-record-comments-deserve-to-be-shared-with-voters.

34 "Inaugural Address of President Barack Obama," White House, January 21, 2013, https://www.whitehouse.gov/the-press-office/2013/01/21
/inaugural-address-president-barack-obama.

35 "Remarks by the President in the State of the Union address," White
House, February 12, 2013, https://www.whitehouse.gov/the-press-office
/2013/02/12/remarks-president-state-union-address.

36 Ibid.

37 Ball, "Obama's long immigration betrayal." David Nakamura and Ed
O'Keefe, "Boehner: Immigration reform stalls because GOP has 'widespread doubt' about Obama," *Washington Post*, February 6, 2014, http://

www.washingtonpost.com/politics/boehner-immigration-reform
-stalls-because-gop-has-widespread-doubt-about-obama/2014/02/06
/233b497a-8f55-11e3-b46a-5a3d0d2130da_story.html. Lindsey Boerma,
"House will do our own thing on immigration, McCaul says," CBS News,
July 7, 2013, http://www.cbsnews.com/news/house-will-do-our-own
-thing-on-immigration-mccaul-says/.

38 Gonzalez-Barrera and Krogstad, "U.S. deportations of immigrants
reach record high."

39 Julia Preston, "Amid Steady Deportation, Fear and Worry Multiply Among
Immigrants," New York Times, December 23, 2013, http://www.nytimes
.com/2013/12/23/us/fears-multiply-amid-a-surge-in-deportation.html.

40 Seung Min Kim, "Obama pressed to stop deportations," Politico, February 4, 2014, http://www.politico.com/story/2014/02/obama-deportation
-immigration-executive-power-103096. Erica Pearson, "Petition asks
Obama to halt millions of deportations," New York Daily News, February 5, 2014, http://www.nydailynews.com/news/national/petition-asks
-obama-halt-millions-deportations-article-1.1603384.

41 Pearson, "Petition asks Obama to halt millions of deportations."

42 "'Obama Is Trying to Vanish Us': Immigrants Fight Record Deportations
with Protests, Hunger Strikes," Democracy Now, March 13, 2014, http://
www.democracynow.org/2014/3/13/obama_is_trying_to_vanish_us.

43 Mary Bruce, "Obama engages heckler on immigration reform," ABC
News, November 25, 2013, http://abcnews.go.com/blogs/politics/2013
/11/obama-engages-heckler-on-immigration-reform/.

44 Ball, "Obama's long immigration betrayal." Erica Werner, "Immigration activists urge Obama to act boldly," Associated Press, April 15,
2014, http://bigstory.ap.org/article/immigration-activists-urge-obama
-act-boldly. Reid J. Epstein, "National Council of La Raza president
calls Obama 'deporter-in-chief,'" Politico, March 4, 2014, http://dyn
.politico.com/printstory.cfm?uuid=19CBD3B8-3409-4954-AA1F
-C1E8AD794473.

45 Werner, "Immigration activists urge Obama to act boldly."

46 Ball, "Obama's long immigration betrayal."

47 Rebecca Bratek, "57,000 migrant children picked up at U.S. border since
Oct. 1," Los Angeles Times, July 9, 2014, http://www.latimes.com/nation
/nationnow/la-na-nn-senate-immigration-hearing-20140709-story.
html. Haeyoun Park, "Children at the Border," New York Times, October
21, 2014, http://www.nytimes.com/interactive/2014/07/15/us/questions
-about-the-border-kids.html.

48 Ibid. Sonia Nazario, "Children of the Drug Wars," *New York Times,* July 13, 2014, http://www.nytimes.com/2014/07/13/opinion/sunday/a -refugee-crisis-not-an-immigration-crisis.html. Anna Altman, "Obama's Humanitarian Immigration Crisis," *New York Times,* July 11, 2014, http://op-talk.blogs.nytimes.com/2014/07/11/obamas-humanitarian -immigration-crisis/.

49 "Remarks by the President on border security and immigration reform," White House, June 30, 2014, https://www.whitehouse.gov/the-press -office/2014/06/30/remarks-president-border-security-and-immigration -reform. Serena Marshall and Jon Garcia, "Obama announces unilateral action on immigration," *ABC News,* June 30, 2014, http://abcnews.go.com /Politics/president-obama-announces-unilateral-action-immigration /story?id=24368748.

50 Ibid. Ball, "Obama's long immigration betrayal."

51 Ibid.

52 Edward-Isaac Dovere, "Obama disappoints, again," *Politico,* September 6, 2014, http://www.politico.com/story/2014/09/barack-obama-immigration -executive-order-delay-110670.html.

53 Laura Barron-Lopez, "Immigration activists rip Obama," *The Hill,* September 6, 2014, http://thehill.com/blogs/blog-briefing-room/news /216855-latino-community-outraged-by-Obamas-immigration-delay. Ball, "Obama's long immigration betrayal."

54 Ibid.

55 Ibid.

56 Dovere, "Obama disappoints, again."

57 Ibid. Kendall Breitman, "Sanchez: 'Disappointed in Obama,'" *Politico,* September 8, 2014, http://www.politico.com/story/2014/09/loretta-sanchez -obama-immigration-delay-110700.html.

58 Ed O'Keefe, "Growing evidence that Obama's decision to wait on immi- gration is hurting Democrats," *Washington Post,* October 2, 2014, http:// www.washingtonpost.com/politics/growing-evidence-that-obamas -decision-to-wait-on-immigration-is-hurting-democrats/2014/10/01 /8ed108c8-4981-11e4-b72e-d60a9229cc10_story.html.

59 Dovere, "Obama disappoints, again."

60 Ed O'Keefe, "Growing evidence that Obama's decision to wait on im- migration is hurting Democrats." Alexandra Jaffe, "As Dems lose Lati- nos, Senate could follow," *The Hill,* October 30, 2014, http://thehill.com /blogs/ballot-box/senate-races/222298-latinos-fall-out-of-love-with -democrats.

61 Roque Planas, "Latino activists angry, but vindicated, after Democrats lose Senate," *Huffington Post,* November 5, 2014, http://www.huffing tonpost.com/2014/11/05/latino-activists-midterms_n_6108254.html. Adrian Carrasquillo, "Colorado Democrat didn't embrace immigration and that's why he lost, advocates and pollster day," *BuzzFeed,* November 5, 2014, http://www.buzzfeed.com/adriancarrasquillo/colorado -democrat-didnt-embrace-immigration-and-thats-why-he.

62 "Remarks by the President in an address to the nation on immigration," White House, November 20, 2014, https://www.whitehouse .gov/the-press-office/2014/11/20/remarks-president-address-nation -immigration. Jamie Fuller, "Why the major networks didn't give President Obama primetime real estate for his immigration speech," *Washington Post,* November 21, 2014, http://www.washingtonpost .com/news/the-fix/wp/2014/11/20/why-the-networks-arent-giving -president-obama-primetime-real-estate-for-his-immigration -speech/.

63 "Remarks by the President in an address to the nation on immigration."

64 Ibid.

65 Steve Holland and Roberta Rampton, "Obama unveils U.S. immigration reform, setting up fight with Republicans," Reuters, November 21, 2014, http://www.reuters.com/article/2014/11/21/us-usa-immigration -obama-idUSKCN0J420W20141121.

66 Lesley Clark, "Obama signs DHS funding bill after Republicans cave," *McClatchy,* March 4, 2015, http://www.mcclatchydc.com/news/nation -world/national/article24780997.html.

67 Gonzalez-Barrera and Krogstad, "U.S. deportations of immigrants reach record high." William Finnegan, "The Deportation Machine," *New Yorker,* April 29, 2013, http://www.newyorker.com/magazine/2013 /04/29/the-deportation-MAChine.

68 Lauren Walker, "Promise fulfilled? Activists respond differently to Obama's executive order," *Newsweek,* November 21, 2014, http://www .newsweek.com/promise-fulfilled-activists-respond-differently-obamas -executive-order-286214.

69 Ibid.

Chapter Six: Guns

1 "Fact-Check: Does Obama want to ban guns and rifles?", CNN, September 23, 2008, http://politicalticker.blogs.cnn.com/2008/09/23/fact-check

-does-obama-want-to-ban-guns-and-rifles/. Robert Farley, "Did Obama flip-flop on gun control?", Factcheck.org, February 5, 2013, http://www .factcheck.org/2013/02/did-obama-flip-flop-on-gun-control/.

2 Farley, "Did Obama flip-flop on gun control?"

3 Ali Frick, "Is the Obama administration walking back its commitment to reinstating the assault weapons ban?", *ThinkProgress,* April 9, 2009, http://thinkprogress.org/security/2009/04/09/37434/obama-assault -weapons/. Pete Williams, "First 100 Days; Assault Weapons Ban," *NBC News,* April 24, 2009, http://www.nbcnews.com/id/30389664/ns /politics-white_house/t/first-days-assault-weapons-ban/.

4 Mark Lacey and David M. Herszenhorn, "In Attack's Wake, Political Repercussions," *New York Times,* January 8, 2011, http://www.nytimes .com/2011/01/09/us/politics/09giffords.html.

5 "Remarks by the President at a memorial service for the victims of the shooting in Tucson, Arizona," White House, January 11, 2011, https:// www.whitehouse.gov/the-press-office/2011/01/12/remarks-president -barack-obama-memorial-service-victims-shooting-tucson.

6 "Obama delivers 'intensely personal' Tucson speech," *PBS Newshour,* January 12, 2011, http://www.pbs.org/newshour/bb/politics-jan-june11 -historical9_01-12/. Garry Wills, "Obama's finest hour," *New York Review of Books,* January 13, 2011, http://www.nybooks.com/blogs/nyrblog /2011/jan/13/obamas-finest-hour/. Howard Kurtz, "Obama's next im- possible speech," *Daily Beast,* January 13, 2011, http://news.yahoo.com /obamas-next-impossible-speech-20110113-193944-536.html.

7 "Remarks by the President at the Sandy Hook interfaith vigil," White House, December 16, 2012, https://www.whitehouse.gov/the-press -office/2012/12/16/remarks-president-sandy-hook-interfaith-prayer -vigil. Reid J. Epstein and Jennifer Epstein, "Obama: 'These tragedies must end,' " *Politico,* December 16, 2012, http://www.politico.com/story /2012/12/obama-to-speak-at-newtown-vigil-085155.

8 Ibid.

9 Peter Baker and Michael D. Shear, "Obama to Put 'Everything I've Got' Into Gun Control," *New York Times,* January 16, 2013, http://www.ny times.com/2013/01/17/us/politics/obama-to-ask-congress-to-toughen -gun-laws.html.

10 Ibid. "What's in Obama's Gun Control Proposal," *New York Times,* Janu- ary 16, 2013, http://www.nytimes.com/interactive/2013/01/16/us/obama -gun-control-proposal.html.

11 Scott Clement, "90 percent of Americans want expanded background

checks on guns: Why isn't this a political slam dunk?" *Washington Post*, April 3, 2013, http://www.washingtonpost.com/news/the-fix/wp/2013 /04/03/90-percent-of-americans-want-expanded-background-checks -on-guns-why-isnt-this-a-political-slam-dunk/. Aaron Blake, "Man-chin-Toomey gun amendment fails," *Washington Post*, April 17, 2013, http://www.washingtonpost.com/news/post-politics/wp/2013/04/17 /manchin-toomey-gun-amendment-fails/.

12 Dana Ford, "4 dead, including shooter, at Fort Hood," CNN, April 3, 2014, http://www.cnn.com/2014/04/02/us/fort-hood-shooting/. Ashley Cusick, Sarah Kaplan, and Elahe Izadi, "'Slow and methodical': Officials describe deadly La. theater shooting," *Washington Post*, July 24, 2015, http://www.washingtonpost.com/news/morning-mix/wp/2015/07 /23/gunman-opens-fire-on-la-movie-theater-injuring-several-before -killing-himself/. Ana Cabrera, Greg Botelho, and Dana Ford, "James Holmes found guilty of murder in Colorado theater shooting," CNN, July 16, 2015, http://www.cnn.com/2015/07/16/us/james-holmes-trial -colorado-movie-theater-shooting-verdict/. Dylan Stableford, "WDBJ journalists Alison Parker, Adam Ward shot and killed in live broad-cast, suspect dead from self-inflicted gunshot wound," *Yahoo News*, Au-gust 26, 2015, http://news.yahoo.com/cbs-journalists-shot-killed-live -broadcast-130723506.html.

13 German Lopez and Soo Oh, "Mass shootings since Sandy Hook, in one map," *Vox*, September 21, 2015, http://www.vox.com/a/mass-shootings -sandy-hook. Nick Kristof, "Lessons from the Virginia Shooting," *New York Times*, August 27, 2015, http://www.nytimes.com/2015/08/27 /opinion/lessons-from-the-murders-of-tv-journalists-in-the-virginia -shooting.html.

14 Sophia Rosenbaum, David K. Li, and Bob Fredericks, "'I have to do it': Suspect in killing of 9 at historic black church captured," *New York Post*, June 18, 2015, http://nypost.com/2015/06/18/suspect-captured-in-killing -of-9-at-historic-black-church/. Ed Kilgore, "'You rape our women and you're taking over our country . . . you have to go,'" *Washington Monthly*, June 18, 2015, http://www.washingtonmonthly.com/political-animal-a /2015_06/you_rape_our_women_and_youre_t056156.php.

15 Erin Dooley, "Looking Back at the 'Too Many Times' Obama Has Re-sponded to a Mass Shooting," *ABC News*, June 18, 2015, http://abc news.go.com/Politics/back-times-president-obama-responded-mass -shooting/story?id=31868547. "Statement by the President on the Shoot-ing in Charleston, South Carolina," White House, June 18, 2015, https://

www.whitehouse.gov/the-press-office/2015/06/18/statement-president
-shooting-charleston-south-carolina. Chris Cillizza, "President Obama
waves the white flag on gun control," *Washington Post,* June 18, 2015,
http://www.washingtonpost.com/news/the-fix/wp/2015/06/18/president
-obama-waves-the-white-flag-on-gun-control/.

16 Cillizza, "President Obama waves the white flag on gun control."

17 Ibid.

18 Colby Itkowitz, "Manchin, Toomey both interested in reviving gun
control push, *Washington Post,* June 23, 2015, http://www.washington
post.com/news/powerpost/wp/2015/06/23/manchin-toomey-both
-interested-in-reviving-gun-control-push/.

19 "U.S. Attorney General Eric Holder sits down with CNN's Evan Perez,"
CNN, October 20, 2014, http://cnnpressroom.blogs.cnn.com/2014/10
/20/us-attorney-general-eric-holder-sits-down-with-cnns-evan-perez/.
Benjamin Goad, "Holder: Gun control among biggest failures," *The Hill,*
October 21, 2014, http://thehill.com/regulation/administration/221326
-holder-lists-thwarted-gun-control-push-among-biggest-failures.

20 Anne Applebaum, "No Nukes? No thanks," *Slate,* April 6, 2009, http://
www.slate.com/articles/news_and_politics/foreigners/2009/04/no
_nukes_no_thanks.html.

21 "Remarks by the President in Prague, as delivered," White House,
April 5, 2009, https://www.whitehouse.gov/the-press-office/remarks
-president-barack-obama-prague-delivered. "Obama promotes nuclear
-free world," BBC, April 5, 2009, http://news.bbc.co.uk/2/hi/7983963
.stm. William Broad, "Which President Cut the Most Nukes?", *New York
Times,* November 2, 2014, http://www.nytimes.com/2014/11/02/sunday
-review/which-president-cut-the-most-nukes.html.

22 Broad, "Which President cut the most nukes?" "The Nobel Peace Prize
for 2009," Nobel Committee, October 9, 2009, http://www.nobelprize
.org/nobel_prizes/peace/laureates/2009/press.html.

23 Broad, "Which president cut the most nukes?"

24 Ibid. Hans M. Kristensen, "How presidents arm and disarm," Federation
of American Scientists, October 15, 2014, http://fas.org/blogs/security
/2014/10/stockpilereductions/.

25 Ibid.

26 Theodore A. Postol, "How the Obama Administration Learned to Stop
Worrying and Love the Bomb," *The Nation,* December 29, 2014, http://
www.thenation.com/article/how-obama-administration-learned-stop
-worrying-and-love-bomb/.

27 Ibid. William J. Broad and David Sanger, "U.S. Ramping Up Major Renewal in Nuclear Arms," *New York Times,* September 22, 2014, http://www.nytimes.com/2014/09/22/us/us-ramping-up-major-renewal-in-nuclear-arms.html.

28 Ibid.

29 Ibid.

30 Broad, "Which president cut the most nukes?" "U.S. modernization funding threatens disarmament efforts," Alliance for Nuclear Accountability, September 24, 2015, http://www.ananuclear.org/the-nuclear-free-frontpage/2014/9/23/modernization-threatens-disarmament-efforts. Joe Cirincione, "How big an arsenal do we really need?" *Los Angeles Times,* October 22, 2014, http://www.latimes.com/opinion/op-ed/la-oe-cirincione-nuclear-weapons-20141022-story.html.

31 Postol, "How the Obama Administration Learned to Stop Worrying."

32 Ibid.

33 Ibid.

34 Broad and Sanger, "U.S. Ramping Up Major Renewal in Nuclear Arms."

Chapter Seven: Climate Change

1 "Obama's nomination victory speech in St. Paul," *Huffington Post,* June 3, 2008, http://www.huffingtonpost.com/2008/06/03/obamas-nomination-victory_n_105028.html.

2 "Inaugural Address of President Barack Obama," White House, January 21, 2013, https://www.whitehouse.gov/the-press-office/2013/01/21/inaugural-address-president-barack-obama. "Remarks by the President on climate change," White House, June 25, 2013, https://www.whitehouse.gov/the-press-office/2013/06/25/remarks-president-climate-change. Juliet Eilperin, "Obama unveils ambitious agenda to combat climate change, bypassing Congress," *Washington Post,* June 25, 2013, http://www.washingtonpost.com/politics/obama-climate-strategy-represents-piecemeal-approach/2013/06/25/7bd9f20a-dd0a-11e2-bd83-e99e43c336ed_story.html.

3 Ibid.

4 "American Recovery and Reinvestment Act: Overview of Funding," Recovery.gov, http://www.recovery.gov/arra/Transparency/fundingoverview/Pages/contractsgrantsloans-details.aspx#EnergyEnvironment. Steve Hargreaves, "What we got for $50 billion in green stimulus," CNN,

October 3, 2012, http://money.cnn.com/2012/10/03/news/economy /green-stimulus/.

5 "Obama administration finalizes historic 54.5 MPG fuel efficiency standards," White House, August 28, 2012, https://www.whitehouse.gov/the
   -press-office/2012/08/28/obama-administration-finalizes-historic-545
   -mpg-fuel-efficiency-standard. Bill Vlasic, "U.S. Sets Much Higher Fuel
   Efficiency Standards," *New York Times,* August 28, 2012, http://www.ny
   times.com/2012/08/29/business/energy-environment/obama-unveils
   -tighter-fuel-efficiency-standards.html.

6 David Corn and Kate Sheppard, "Obama's Copenhagen Deal," *The
   Nation,* December 2009, http://www.motherjones.com/environment
   /2009/12/obamas-copenhagen-deal. Mark Hertsgaard, "The Ugly
   Truth about Obama's Copenhagen accord," *Vanity Fair,* December
   21, 2009, http://www.vanityfair.com/news/2009/12/the-ugly-truth
   -about-obamas-copenhagen-accord. Juliet Eilperin and Anthony
   Faiola, "Climate deal falls short of key goals," *Washington Post,* December 18, 2009, http://www.washingtonpost.com/wp-dyn/content
   /article/2009/12/18/AR2009121800637.html. Juliet Eilperin, "U.S.
   pledges 17% emissions reduction by 2020," *Washington Post,* January 28, 2010, http://www.washingtonpost.com/wp-dyn/content
   /article/2010/01/28/AR2010012803632.html.

7 Joanna M. Foster, "EPA Publishes First Rule Limiting Carbon Pollution
   From New Power Plants," *ThinkProgress,* January 9, 2014, http://think
   progress.org/climate/2014/01/09/3139921/epa-carbon-rule-power
   -plants/. Tim McDonald, "The first lawsuit against EPA's new coal regs
   just got filed," *Mother Jones,* January 14, 2014, http://www.motherjones
   .com/blue-marble/2014/01/first-lawsuit-against-epas-new-coal-regs
   -just-got-filed.

8 Coral Davenport, "Obama to Take Action to Slash Coal Pollution,"
   New York Times, June 2, 2014, http://www.nytimes.com/2014/06/02
   /us/politics/epa-to-seek-30-percent-cut-in-carbon-emissions.html.
   Adam Liptak and Coral Davenport, "Supreme Court Blocks Obama's
   Limits on Power Plants," *New York Times,* June 30, 2015, http://www
   .nytimes.com/2015/06/30/us/supreme-court-blocks-obamas-limits
   -on-power-plants.html. Chris Mooney, "What you need to know about
   Obama's biggest global warming move yet: the clean power plan,"
   Washington Post, August 1, 2015, http://www.washingtonpost.com
   /news/energy-environment/wp/2015/08/01/what-you-need-to-know
   -about-obamas-biggest-global-warming-move-yet-the-clean-power

-plan/. Adam Vaughn, "Obama's clean power plan hailed as strongest ever climate action by a US president," *The Guardian,* August 3, 2015, http://www.theguardian.com/environment/2015/aug/03/obamas -clean-power-plan-hailed-as-strongest-ever-climate-action-by-a-us -president.

9 Mark Landler, "U.S. and China Reach Climate Deal After Months of Talks," *New York Times,* November 12, 2014, http://www.nytimes.com /2014/11/12/world/asia/china-us-xi-obama-apec.html.

10 Coral Davenport and Mark Landler, "U.S. to Give $3 Billion to Climate Fund to Help Poor Nations, and Spur Rich Ones," *New York Times,* November 15, 2014, http://www.nytimes.com/2014/11/15/us/politics/obama -climate-change-fund-3-billion-announcement.html.

11 Julian Brookes, "Al Gore Calls Out Obama, News Media on Climate Change," *Rolling Stone,* June 22, 2011, http://www.rollingstone.com /politics/news/al-gore-calls-out-obama-news-media-on-climate-change -20110622. John M. Broder, "Gore Criticizes Obama for Record on Climate," *New York Times,* June 23, 2011, http://www.nytimes.com/2011/06 /23/science/earth/23gore.html.

12 Will Oremus, "Obama makes it clear he isn't willing to fight for action on climate change," *Slate,* November 14, 2012, http://www.slate.com /blogs/future_tense/2012/11/14/obama_on_climate_change_carbon _tax_isn_t_going_to_happen.html.

13 Ibid.

14 Ibid.

15 Coral Davenport, "U.S. Will Allow Drilling in Arctic Ocean," *New York Times,* May 11, 2015, http://www.nytimes.com/2015/05/12/us /white-house-gives-conditional-approval-for-shell-to-drill-in-arctic .html. Eric Holthaus, "Obama is a climate hypocrite—his trip to Alaska proves it," *Mother Jones,* September 1, 2015, http://www.motherjones .com/environment/2015/09/obama-climate-hypocrite-alaska. Elizabeth Kolbert, "The Obama Administration's Self-Sabotaging Coal Leases," *New Yorker,* June 4, 2015, http://www.newyorker.com/news/daily -comment/obama-powder-river-basin-coal-leases. Juliet Eilperin and Steven Mufson, "White House lifts ban on deepwater drilling," *Washington Post,* October 12, 2010, http://www.washingtonpost.com/wp-dyn /content/article/2010/10/12/AR2010101202326.html.

16 Bill McKibben, "Obama and Climate Change: The Real Story," *Rolling Stone,* December 17, 2013, http://www.rollingstone.com/politics/news /obama-and-climate-change-the-real-story-20131217.

17 Ibid.

18 Ibid.

19 Jim Snyder, "Even Keystone XL foes are sick of waiting for Obama to decide pipeline's fate," *Bloomberg News*, May 7, 2015, http://business.financialpost .com/news/energy/even-keystone-xl-foes-are-sick-of-waiting-for-obama -to-decide-pipelines-fate?__lsa=d115-5bf9. Coral Davenport, "U.S. Senate Fails to Override Obama's Keystone Pipeline Veto," *New York Times*, March 4, 2015, http://www.nytimes.com/2015/03/05/us/senate-fails-to-override -obamas-keystone-pipeline-veto.html.

20 Brad Plumer, "9 Questions about the Keystone Pipeline you were probably too embarrassed to ask," *Vox*, September 21, 2015, http://www .vox.com/2014/11/14/7216751/keystone-pipeline-facts-controversy. Zoe Schlanger, "State Department: Keystone XL would only create 35 permanent jobs," *Newsweek*, February 12, 2014, http://www.newsweek .com/state-department-keystone-xl-pipeline-would-only-create-35 -permanent-jobs-228898.

21 Kolbert, "The Obama administration's self-sabotaging coal leases." Holthaus, "Obama is a climate hypocrite." Bill McKibben, "Obama's Catastrophic Climate Change Denial," *New York Times*, May 13, 2015, http://www.nytimes.com/2015/05/13/opinion/obamas-catastrophic -climate-change-denial.html.

22 McKibben, "Obama and Climate Change: The Real Story."

Chapter Eight: Race Relations

1 Barack Obama, *Dreams from My Father: A Story of Race and Inheritance* (New York: Random House, 1995). Martin Luther King, Jr., "I Have a Dream," Washington, D.C., August 28, 1963, http://www.americanrhet oric.com/speeches/mlkihaveadream.htm.

2 Brian Ross and Rehab El-Buri, "Obama's pastor: God damn America, U.S. to blame for 9/11," *ABC News*, March 3, 2008, http://abcnews.go .com/Blotter/DemocraticDebate/story?id=4443788.

3 "Barack Obama's Speech on Race," *New York Times*, March 18, 2008, http://www.nytimes.com/2008/03/18/us/politics/18text-obama.html.

4 Ibid.

5 "Obama and Wright controversy dominate news cycle," Pew Research Center, March 27, 2008, http://www.people-press.org/2008 /03/27/obama-and-wright-controversy-dominate-news-cycle/. Jeff Zeleney and Adam Nagourney, "An Angry Obama Renounces Ties

to His Ex-Pastor," *New York Times*, April 30, 2008, http://www.ny times.com/2008/04/30/us/politics/30obama.html.

6 "Transcript: Illinois Senator Barack Obama," *Washington Post*, July 7, 2004, http://www.washingtonpost.com/wp-dyn/articles/A19751 -2004Jul27.html. Paul Butler, "Why don't black leaders demand more of the president?" *Daily Beast*, September 24, 2012, http://www.thedaily beast.com/articles/2012/09/24/why-don-t-black-leaders-demand-more -of-the-president.html. Sheryl Gay Stolberg, "For Obama, Nuance on Race Invites Questions," *New York Times*, February 9, 2010, http://www .nytimes.com/2010/02/09/us/politics/09race.html. Randall Kennedy, "Did Obama fail black America?" *Politico*, July/August 2014, http:// www.politico.com/magazine/story/2014/06/black-president-black -attorney-general-so-what-108017_full.html.

7 "Remarks by the President at the NAACP Centennial Convention," White House, July 16, 2009, https://www.whitehouse.gov/the-press-office /remarks-president-naacp-centennial-convention-07162009.

8 Maeve Reston and Steven Collinson, "Obama's balancing act on race," CNN, November 25, 2014, http://www.cnn.com/2014/11/25/politics /obama-race-ferguson/.

9 Abby Goodnough, "Harvard Professor Jailed; Officer Is Accused of Bias," *New York Times*, July 21, 2009, http://www.nytimes.com/2009 /07/21/us/21gates.html. "Obama: Police who arrested professor 'acted stupidly,'" CNN, July 22, 2009, http://www.cnn.com/2009/US/07/22 /harvard.gates.interview/.

10 Adam Weinstein, "The Trayvon Martin killing, explained," *Mother Jones*, March 18, 2012, http://www.motherjones.com/politics/2012/03 /what-happened-trayvon-martin-explained. Krissah Thompson and Scott Wilson, "Obama on Trayvon Martin: If I had a son, he'd look like Trayvon," *Washington Post*, March 23, 2012, http://www.washington post.com/politics/obama-if-i-had-a-son-hed-look-like-trayvon/2012 /03/23/gIQApKPpVS_story.html.

11 "Remarks by the President on Trayvon Martin," White House, July 19, 2013, https://www.whitehouse.gov/the-press-office/2013/07/19/remarks -president-trayvon-martin. Paul Lewis, "'Trayvon Martin could have been me 35 years ago,' Obama says," *The Guardian*, July 19, 2013, http:// www.theguardian.com/world/2013/jul/19/trayvon-martin-obama -white-house.

12 Ibid.

13 Ibid.

14 Edward Isaac-Dovere, "Obama keeps quiet on race—again," *Politico*, July 16, 2013, http://www.politico.com/story/2013/07/obama-keeps-quiet-on-race-again-094250.

15 Jonathan Capeheart, "From Trayvon Martin to Black Lives Matter," *Washington Post*, February 27, 2015, http://www.washingtonpost.com/blogs/post-partisan/wp/2015/02/27/from-trayvon-martin-to-black-lives-matter/. Larry Buchanan, Ford Fessenden, K. K. Rebecca Lai, Haeyoun Park, Alicia Parlapiano, Archie Tse, Tim Wallace, Derek Watkins, and Karen Yourish, "What Happened in Ferguson?" *New York Times*, August 13 2014, http://www.nytimes.com/interactive/2014/08/13/us/ferguson-missouri-town-under-siege-after-police-shooting.html. J. David Goodman and Al Baker., "Wave of Protests After Grand Jury Doesn't Indict Officer in Eric Garner Chokehold Case," *New York Times*, December 3, 2014, http://www.nytimes.com/2014/12/04/nyregion/grand-jury-said-to-bring-no-charges-in-staten-island-chokehold-death-of-eric-garner.html.

16 Ibid. Shaila DeWan and Richard Oppel, Jr., "In Tamir Rice Case, Many Errors by Cleveland Police, Then a Fatal One," *New York Times*, January 22, 2015, http://www.nytimes.com/2015/01/23/us/in-tamir-rice-shooting-in-cleveland-many-errors-by-police-then-a-fatal-one.html. Laura Gambino, "Tamir Rice shooting: Cleveland police handcuffed sister as 12-year-old lay dying," *The Guardian*, January 8, 2015, http://www.theguardian.com/us-news/2015/jan/08/cleveland-police-handcuffed-sister-tamir-rice-lay-dying-video.

17 Nia-Malika Henderson, "White House officials to attend Michael Brown's funeral," *Washington Post*, August 23, 2014, https://www.washingtonpost.com/news/post-nation/wp/2014/08/23/white-house-officials-to-attend-michael-browns-funeral/. Amie Parnes, "Obama sends Holder to Ferguson, *The Hill*, August 18, 2014, http://thehill.com/homenews/administration/215435-holder-going-to-ferguson. Wesley Lowery and Kimberly Kindy, "2nd NYPD officer honored at funeral; many again turn backs on de Blasio," *Washington Post*, January 4, 2015, http://www.washingtonpost.com/politics/2015/01/04/9b11964a-92c7-11e4-a900-9960214d4cd7_story.html.

18 George Condon, "Obama exhibits trademark caution wrestling with race," *National Journal*, December 1, 2014, http://www.nationaljournal.com/white-house/2014/12/01/obama-exhibits-trademark-caution-wrestling-with-race.

19 Ibid.

20 Ibid. Trymaine Lee, "Obama declares personal investment in change after Ferguson," MSNBC, December 1, 2014, http://www.msnbc.com /msnbc/obama-declares-personal-investment-change-after-ferguson.

21 Tanya Somanader, "President Obama Delivers a Statement on the Grand Jury Decision in the Death of Eric Garner," White House, December 3, 2014, https://www.whitehouse.gov/blog/2014/12/03/president-obama -delivers-statement-grand-jury-decision-death-eric-garner.

22 Julie Hirschfeld Davis and Michael D. Shear, "Unrest Over Race Is Testing Obama's Legacy," *New York Times*, December 9, 2014, http://www.ny times.com/2014/12/09/us/politics/unrest-over-race-is-testing-obamas -legacy-.html. Robert Samuels, "Disillusioned black voters ask: Is voting even worth it?" June 9, 2015, https://www.washingtonpost.com/local /disappointment-in-obama-leads-some-blacks-to-ask-is-voting-even -worth-it/2015/06/09/5922363c-052b-11e5-bc72-f3e16bf50bb6_story .html.

23 Condon, "Obama exhibits trademark caution wrestling with race."

24 Hirschfeld Davis and Shear, "Unrest Over Race Is Testing Obama's Legacy."

25 "Timeline: Freddie Gray's arrest, death and the aftermath" *Baltimore Sun*, April 19, 2015, http://data.baltimoresun.com/news/freddie-gray/.

26 Ibid.

27 "Remarks by President Obama and Prime Minister Abe of Japan in Joint Press Conference," White House, April 28, 2015, https://www.white house.gov/the-press-office/2015/04/28/remarks-president-obama-and -prime-minister-abe-japan-joint-press-confere. Eric Bradner, "Obama: No excuse for violence in Baltimore," CNN, April 28, 2015, http://www .cnn.com/2015/04/28/politics/obama-baltimore-violent-protests/.

28 Dalia Sussman, "Negative view of US race relations grows, poll finds," *New York Times*, May 4, 2015, http://www.nytimes.com/2015/05/05/us /negative-view-of-us-race-relations-grows-poll-finds.html.

29 "Remarks by the President in eulogy for the Reverend Clementa Pinckney," White House, June 26, 2015, https://www.whitehouse.gov /the-press-office/2015/06/26/remarks-president-eulogy-honorable -reverend-clementa-pinckney.

30 Ibid.

31 "The Fair Sentencing Act corrects a long-time wrong in cocaine sentencing cases," *Washington Post*, August 3, 2010, http://www.washing tonpost.com/wp-dyn/content/article/2010/08/02/AR2010080204360 .html.

32 "My Brother's Keeper," White House.Gov, https://www.whitehouse.gov
    /my-brothers-keeper. "Fact Sheet: White House launches My Broth-
    er's Keeper Community Challenge," White House, September 30, 2014,
    https://www.whitehouse.gov/the-press-office/2014/09/30/fact-sheet
    -white-house-launches-my-brother-s-keeper-community-challenge.

33 Kennedy, "Did Obama fail black America?"

34 Ibid.

Chapter Nine: Labor and Trade

1 Lori Wallach, "NAFTA at 20: One million U.S. jobs lost; Higher income
   inequality," *Huffington Post,* January 6, 2014, http://www.huffingtonpost
   .com/lori-wallach/nafta-at-20-one-million-u_b_4550207.html.

2 Matt Stoller, "The TransPacific Partnership, the biggest deal you've
   never heard of," *Salon,* October 23, 2012, http://www.salon.com/2012
   /10/23/everything_you_wanted_to_know_about_the_trans_pacific
   _partnership/.

3 George Miller, Rosa DeLauro, and Louise Slaughter, "Free trade on steroids: the threat of the Trans-Pacific Partnership," *Los Angeles Times,*
   April 21, 2014, http://www.latimes.com/opinion/op-ed/la-oe-miller
   -trans-pacific-trade-pact-20140421-story.html. Lori Wallach, "NAFTA
   on Steroids," *The Nation,* June 27, 2012, http://www.thenation.com
   /article/nafta-steroids/. Jaime Fuller, "Why everyone hates the trade
   deal Obama's negotiating in Japan," *Washington Post,* April 23, 2014,
   http://www.washingtonpost.com/news/the-fix/wp/2014/04/23/why
   -almost-everyone-hates-the-trade-deal-obamas-negotiating-in-japan/.

4 Ibid.

5 Julie Hirschfield Davis, "Democrats Step Up Efforts to Block Obama on
   Trade Authority," *New York Times,* January 9, 2015, http://www.nytimes
   .com/2015/01/09/business/democrats-step-up-efforts-to-block-obama
   -on-trade-promotion-authority.html.

6 Ibid.

7 Ibid.

8 Mike Masnick, "Obama Complains That TPP Critics Are 'Conspiracy
   Theorists' Who 'Lack Knowledge' About Negotiations," *Techdirt,* May
   1, 2014, https://www.techdirt.com/articles/20140429/14333827067
   /obama-complains-that-tpp-critics-are-conspiracy-theorists-who-lack
   -knowledge-about-negotiations.shtml.

9 Eric Bradner and Deirdre Walsh, "Democrats reject Obama on trade,"

CNN, June 12, 2015, http://www.cnn.com/2015/06/12/politics/white
-house-tpp-trade-deal-congress/. Alexander Bolton, "Senate advances
fast-track trade bill for Obama," *The Hill*, June 23, 2015, http://thehill
.com/policy/finance/245827-senate-advances-fast-track-trade-bill-for
-obama. David Nakamura, "Obama scores a major trade win, burnish-
ing his foreign policy legacy" *Washington Post*, June 24, 2015, http://
www.washingtonpost.com/politics/obama-poised-for-a-major-trade
-win-burnishing-his-foreign-policy-legacy/2015/06/24/e940c6fa-1a77
-11e5-93b7-5eddc056ad8a_story.html.

10 Jason Margolis, "As NAFTA memories linger, unions hold fast against
new trade deal," NPR, June 16, 2015, http://www.npr.org/sections/itsall
politics/2015/06/16/414893279/as-nafta-memories-linger-unions-hold
-fast-against-new-trade-deal.

11 Mike Lillis, "Obama's trust-me approach falls flat with Dems," *The Hill*,
June 3, 2015, http://thehill.com/policy/finance/243969-obamas-trust
-me-approach-fall-flat-with-dems.

12 Steve Greenhouse, "After Push for Obama, Unions Seek New Rules,"
New York Times, November 9, 2008, http://www.nytimes.com/2008/11
/09/us/politics/09labor.html.

13 Ibid.

14 George Miller, "Introduction of the H.R. 800: The Employee Free
Choice Act," February 5, 2007, Congressional Record, V. 153, PT. 3.
Steven L. Goldstein, "Employee Free Choice Act should be law," *Florida Sun-Sentinel*, September 28, 2008, http://www.sun-sentinel.com/sfl
-duelersstephen091208-story.html. "Pro-Union organizing bill coming
in U.S. House," Reuters, March 9, 2009, http://www.reuters.com/article
/2009/03/09/labor-congress-idUSN0947517020090309.

15 Ken Silverstein, "Labor's Last Stand: The corporate campaign to kill
the Employee Free Choice Act," *Harper's*, July 2009, http://harpers.org
/archive/2009/07/labors-last-stand/. Manu Raju, "Specter says he will oppose labor bill," *Politico*, March 29, 2009, http://www.politico.com/story
/2009/03/specter-says-he-will-oppose-labor-bill-020425. Jane Hamsher,
"What happened to the Employee Free Choice Act?", *Firedoglake*, April
13, 2010, http://shadowproof.com/2010/04/13/what-happened-to-the
-employee-free-choice-act/.

16 Hamsher, "What happened to the Employee Free Choice Act?"

17 Josh Eidelson, "Obama to unions: see you later," *Salon*, February 15,
2012, http://www.salon.com/2012/02/15/obama_to_unions_see_you
_next_year/. Josh Eidelson, "Attacks on Labor Put Unions on Defensive

in Election 2012," *The Nation*, November 2, 2012, http://www.thenation
.com/article/170980/attacks-labor-put-unions-defensive-election-2012.

18 Ibid.

19 Ibid.

20 Ibid.

21 Ibid.

22 Steven Mufson and Tom Hamburger, "Labor union officials say Obama
betrayed them in health care rollout," *Washington Post,* January 31,
2014, http://www.washingtonpost.com/business/economy/labor-union
-officials-say-obama-betrayed-them-in-health-care-rollout/2014/01/31
/2cda6afc-8789-11e3-833c-33098f9e5267_story.html.

23 Ibid. Ezra Klein, "Obama administration denies labor's request for health
care waiver," *Washington Post,* September 13, 2013, http://www.washing
tonpost.com/news/wonkblog/wp/2013/09/13/obama-administration
-denies-labors-request-for-health-care-waiver/.

24 Klein, "Obama administration denies labor's request."

25 Eidelson, "Attacks on Labor Put Unions on Defensive."

26 Ibid.

27 Ibid.

28 Lori Montgomery, "Congress approves minimum-wage hike," *Washington Post,* May 24, 2007, http://www.washingtonpost.com/wp-dyn
/content/article/2007/05/24/AR2007052402241.html.

29 "Remarks by the President on the State of the Union," White House,
February 12, 2013, https://www.whitehouse.gov/the-press-office/2013
/02/12/remarks-president-state-union-address.

30 Daniel Strauss, "Liberals call for $10.10 minimum wage—more than
Obama requested," *The Hill,* February 28, 2013, http://thehill.com
/homenews/house/285413-liberals-press-for-1010-minimum-wage
-more-than-obama-requested.

31 "President Barack Obama's State of the Union address," White House,
January 28, 2014, https://www.whitehouse.gov/the-press-office/2014/01
/28/president-barack-obamas-state-union-address.

32 Ibid. Jason Furman and Betsey Stevenson, "The economic case for raising the minimum wage," White House, February 12, 2014, https://www
.whitehouse.gov/blog/2014/02/12/economic-case-raising-minimum
-wage.

33 Noam Scheiber, "Obama Making Millions More Americans Eligible for Overtime," *New York Times,* June 30, 2015, http://www.nytimes
.com/2015/06/30/business/obama-plan-would-make-more-americans

-eligible-for-overtime.html. Marianna Levine, "Obama raising 5 million workers' pay? Not so fast," *Politico*, 2015, July 2, 2015, http://www.politico .com/story/2015/07/barack-obama-raising-5-million-workers-pay-not -so-fast-119695.

34 Noam Scheiber, "Democrats Rallying Around $12 an Hour Minimum Wage," *New York Times*, April 22, 2015, http://www.nytimes.com/2015 /04/23/business/economy/democrats-are-rallying-around-12-wage -floor.html.

35 "What's the minimum wage in your state?" Raise the Minimum Wage, http://www.raisetheminimumwage.com/pages/minimum-wage-state. Lisa Baertlein, "McDonald's raising average worker wage to about $10 an hour," Reuters, April 2, 2015, http://www.reuters.com/article/2015 /04/02/us-mcdonalds-minimumwage-idUSKBN0MS5A220150402.

36 Dean Baker and Will Kimball, "The Minimum Wage and Economic Growth," Center for Economic and Policy Research, February 12, 2013, http://www.cepr.net/blogs/cepr-blog/the-minimum-wage-and-economic -growth.

Chapter Ten: The Democrat in Chief

1 Shane Harris, "Who's counting at the White House? Mark Knoller is," *Washingtonian*, January 8, 2013, http://www.washingtonian.com /articles/people/whos-counting-at-the-white-house-mark-knoller-is/.

2 Paul Blumenthal, "Obama's fundraising best in history," *Huffington Post*, December 7, 2012, http://www.huffingtonpost.com/2012/12/07/obama -fundraising-campaign_n_2257283.html.

3 David McCabe, "Obama has lost nearly 70 house seats since taking office," *The Hill*, November 5, 2014, http://thehill.com/blogs/ballot-box/house -races/223047-obama-has-lost-nearly-70-house-seats-since-taking-office.

4 Philip Rucker and Robert Costa, "Battle for the Senate: How the Republicans did it," *Washington Post*, November 5, 2014, http://www.washing tonpost.com/politics/battle-for-the-senate-how-the-gop-did-it/2014 /11/04/a8df6f7a-62c7-11e4-bb14-4cfea1e742d5_story.html.

5 Ibid.

6 McCabe, "Obama has lost nearly 70 house seats since taking office."

7 Katie Sanders, "Have Democrats lost 900 seats in state legislatures since Obama has been president?" *Politifact*, January 25, 2015, http://www .politifact.com/punditfact/statements/2015/jan/25/cokie-roberts/have -democrats-lost-900-seats-state-legislatures-o/.

8 Ibid. McCabe, "Obama has lost nearly 70 house seats since taking office."
    David Sirota, "Republicans Crush Democrats At State Level, Control
    Two-Thirds Of Legislatures Now," *International Business Times,* No-
    vember 5, 2014, http://www.ibtimes.com/republicans-crush-democrats
    -state-level-control-two-thirds-legislatures-now-1719717.

Conclusion

1 "President Barack Obama's State of the Union address," White House,
    January 28, 2015, https://www.whitehouse.gov/the-press-office/2014/01
    /28/president-barack-obamas-state-union-address.
2 Michael A. Memoli, "Obama's message to supporters who want more
    from him: I'm making progress," *Los Angeles Times,* June 22, 2015, http://
    www.latimes.com/nation/la-na-obama-maron-podcast-20150622
    -story.html.
3 Ibid.
4 Ibid.
5 Michael O'Donnell, "How LBJ saved the Civil Rights Act," *The Atlantic,*
    April 2014, http://www.theatlantic.com/magazine/archive/2014/04/what
    -the-hells-the-presidency-for/358630/.